# POST-FORDIST CINEMA

FILM AND CULTURE

# FILM AND CULTURE

## A series of Columbia University Press

*Edited by John Belton*

*For the list of titles in this series, see pages 261–262.*

# POST-FORDIST CINEMA

## Hollywood Auteurs and the Corporate Counterculture

### JEFF MENNE

Columbia University Press
*New York*

Columbia University Press
*Publishers Since 1893*
New York   Chichester, West Sussex
cup.columbia.edu
Copyright © 2019 Columbia University Press

Library of Congress Cataloging-in-Publication Data
Names: Menne, Jeff, 1974– author.
Title: Post-Fordist cinema : Hollywood auteurs and the corporate
    counterculture / Jeff Menne.
Description: New York, NY: Columbia University Press, [2019] |
    Series: Film and culture | Includes bibliographical references and index.
Identifiers: LCCN 2018025467 | ISBN 9780231183703 (cloth : alk. paper) |
    ISBN 9780231183710 (pbk. : alk. paper)
Subjects: LCSH: Auteur theory (Motion pictures) | Motion picture producers
    and directors—United States—History—20th century. | Motion picture
    industry—United States—History—20th century.
Classification: LCC PN1995.9.A837 M46 2019 | DDC 791.4302/3301—dc23
LC record available at https://lccn.loc.gov/2018025467

Cover design: Lisa Hamm

Cover image: *Dennis Hopper* copyright © 2018 the Andy Warhol Foundation for
the Visual Arts, Inc. / Licensed by Artists Rights Society (ARS), New York

Photo credit: HIP/Art Resource, NY

# CONTENTS

Acknowledgments   vii

INTRODUCTION: THE BUSINESS OF AUTEUR THEORY   1

1. POST (HENRY AND JOHN) FORDISM: KIRK DOUGLAS
   AND GUERRILLA ECONOMY   33

2. THE CINEMA OF DEFECTION: THE CORPORATE
   COUNTERCULTURE AND ROBERT ALTMAN'S LION'S GATE   75

3. TELEVISION TOTALITIES: ZANUCK-BROWN AND
   THE PRIVATELY HELD COMPANY   125

4. THE ETHOS OF INCORPORATION: BBS AND THE LAW
   OF UNNATURAL PERSONS   169

AFTERWORD: AUTEURS, AMATEURS, ANIMATORS   209

Notes   223
Index   255

# ACKNOWLEDGMENTS

I t is perhaps cliché to say that scholarly books are the product of a community, even if they are attributed to a single individual. But it is true, and here is my chance to affirm it by acknowledging how much the argument of this book and the insights in support of it were derived from conversations with friends and colleagues, engagements with other scholarly work, and the encouragement of mentors. I thank the first set of interlocutors, my dissertation committee—Paul Young, Jay Clayton, Gregg Horowitz, and Deak Nabers—who helped give the project the definition it needed. Their fingerprints are all over this. Their support got me going, and it has kept me going.

This project became the book that it is thanks to the support of the Department of English at Oklahoma State University. There, I have been lucky to have supportive department heads and research grants, particularly from the Oklahoma Humanities Council, to get me from one archive to the next. I thank the archivists at the Margaret Herrick Library, the Wisconsin Center for Film and Theater Research, the American Heritage Center at the University of Wyoming, and the Hatcher Graduate Library at University of Michigan. I am grateful, too, to have had amazing librarians at the Edmon Low Library at my home institution, where I have surely tested the patience of the interlibrary loan office. But they are unflappable. In particular, I want to express my deep gratitude to the late David Oberhelman, who was a fellow scholar and a more dogged researcher than I will ever be. He is profoundly missed.

I was able to get the research on the page, however, thanks to my writing group, which has rotated out members such as Toby Beauchamp and Seth Perlow, but has kept the hard core of Kate Hallemeier, Lisa Hollenbach, and Graig Uhlin. They are brilliant, patient readers. I must single out Graig Uhlin, whose brilliance and patience I have called on so many times. He has read draft upon draft, and whatever lucidity the argument has attained is thanks to his insight; whatever opacity remains is my own fault. I have been helped along as well by research assistance from Andrew Davis and Jacob Floyd. Thanks, too, to Caetlin Benson-Allott, J. D. Connor, Jennifer Fay, Alla Gadassik, Jane Gaines, Josh Glick, Peter Labuza, Jon Lewis, Christian Long, James Morrison, the New England Americanist Collective, Justus Nieland, Derek Nystrom, Ben Rogerson, and Lawrence Webb. I have to give Brian Jacobson his own line, because his friendship and support have made this academic life all the better.

I thank the editorial team at Columbia University Press for making this an enjoyable process. Philip Leventhal is perfect to work with, both attentive and energizing. I thank Miriam Grossman, Susan Pensak, and Abby Graves for their help in different phases, and I thank the anonymous readers for the depth of their insights. A version of chapter 2 appeared in *Representations* 114 (Spring 2011) as "The Cinema of Defection: Auteur Theory and Institutional Life."

Finally, I want to thank my family—my parents, Gary and Kathy Menne, whose support has made things like graduate school and academic aspirations possible (when I am not sure they would have been otherwise). But in the end, this book would not have happened without Anne Kuhbander and our sons, Owen and Max. They have lived with it so long, and I am sure they are happy that I can come out of the office now. Let's do something else for a change.

# POST-FORDIST CINEMA

# INTRODUCTION

## The Business of Auteur Theory

*There is Professionalism above all. For example, the Old concept of
selling out, which used to drive good men crazy, causing them to cry
in their beer and bemoan their wasted talent (writing ad copy, for
instance), has disappeared. Now we glory in what pros we are, and
a man loves himself for writing the best jingle on the market.*

David Newman and Robert Benton, "The New Sentimentality"

The Directors Company is a rather literal name. Established
in the early 1970s, it signaled—Jon Lewis has suggested—the
acceptance and instrumentalization of the auteur theory
within the Hollywood studios. In broad lines, the auteur theory holds
that film is art to the extent that directors are free to express their vision
by way of it. When Paramount's Frank Yablans created the Directors
Company with Francis Ford Coppola, Peter Bogdanovich, and William
Friedkin, he was ostensibly granting power, in some degree, to three
directors who had recent commercial successes with, respectively, *The
Godfather* (Paramount, 1972), *The Last Picture Show* (Columbia, 1971),
and *The French Connection* (20th Century Fox, 1971). If we are cynical,
we might suppose that their artistic success was only incidental. Yablans

claimed, after all, that they had outgrown "their esoteric tastes" and that Coppola, for instance, was not "interested in filming a pomegranate growing in the desert." Their interests, he implied, were in line with Paramount's.[1] It was, however, a failed venture. Peter Bart, Paramount's production vice-president at the time, said that it did not work because "it was never really a company." Yablans tried to create the look of a company by yoking together three important directors with the promise of "complete creative control."[2] But in substance, as Jon Lewis remarks, the deal Yablans struck with these directors was just an updated version of "the old Hollywood practice of contracting talent."[3] Indeed, Peter Bart said, "The corporate suits in New York were suspicious of the mandate of creative freedom."[4] So Coppola, Bogdanovich, and Friedkin were merely famous and well-treated employees. What gave Yablans the idea to throw up a shingle for them, as *Variety* might say, was that two of them (Coppola and Bogdanovich) had worked in small, independent companies (American Zoetrope and BBS) where they had won for themselves a kind of autonomy that studios were known to deny.[5] Why would they want to work as subordinates in a studio after that? How, as head of Paramount, was Yablans to attract the best talent to a large, conglomerated corporation that was short on personality and long on hierarchy? He had the right idea but was in the wrong place to enact it: it was a bottom-up model—the small, independent company—designed in opposition to the type of organization that Yablans managed, yet he was trying to implement it in a top-down system that was certain to deform it.

We can imagine, then, that the Directors Company was too literal an understanding of the auteur theory. It is not that the emancipated director was so galvanizing a figure; rather, the emancipated workplace was. The appeal that the auteur theory had for the baby-boom generation, I will argue, was of a general kind: because directors were figures of creative labor entirely dependent on capital, they became emblems for a segment of the workforce that rose to dominance in a postindustrial economy—the college graduates; the knowledge workers, as management theorist Peter Drucker would call them; what, down the road, would be called the "creative class."[6] The lot of this class would be to depend on capital, as directors do, but to insist all the while on their own authority by way of their claims to expertise.[7] Film directors became emblems because this generation lifted the cinema from its low regard and made it their preferred art form. Film critic Andrew Sarris would say in retrospect that in his generation, there was a "perception that a great many things that were considered disreputable, grubby, cheap, vulgar, were really much more interesting than that."[8] Cinephilia was a version of seeing through cultural codes that kept things in their rightful place (cinema below, say, and the novel above), which students took up in another form in their confrontations with university administrations that characterized the New Left and the other movements.[9] Both cinephiles and university students—and they were often coarticulated—liked to imagine themselves in resistance to programming from above. During the Berkeley protests, for instance, Hal Draper said that at Cal a student was "nothing but a cog going through pre-programmed motions—the IBM syndrome." Fred Turner says that for these students, their "assigned organizational roles" in the university were a "mirror" of the rote activity forthcoming in the corporate world.[10] They had scaled their protest against that world on the horizon—the corporate workplace—in their experience as an administered mass in the university, demanding self-determination and participation in one setting as a rehearsal for claiming it in the next. "The college graduate," as Student Nonviolent Coordinating Committee (SNCC) member Ivanhoe Donaldson explained, "can't figure out how he fits in, how he gives meaning to the job that he does."[11]

For social critic Paul Goodman, what marked the loss of meaning was that students no longer believed in "the professions in general." He and his generation were suspicious of large corporations, no doubt, but for them the professions remained the preserve of autonomy. While teaching a graduate seminar at the New School in 1967, though, Goodman realized that his class did not accept his article of faith; they believed instead that "every professional was co-opted and corrupted by the System, all decisions were made top-down by the power structure and bureaucracy, professional peer-groups were conspiracies to make more money," and so on.[12] This had been the message of C. Wright Mills's sociology, in particular his 1951 study, *White Collar*, and his impress on the student Left was great. Daniel Bell would note that when Tom Hayden, a main force in Students for a Democratic Society (SDS), paid him a visit at the turn of the 1960s, "he was sort of caught between Wright Mills and myself," and "clearly, he chose Mills."[13] For Mills, the scientific management of factory labor had been extended into white-collar labor, and hence the professions had been "standardized and fitted into new hierarchical organizations of educated skill and service," and "narrow specialization ha[d] replaced self-cultivation and wide knowledge." If, historically, the professions were both the basis for intellectual life and the public for the intellectual's activity, then the tug of this class into "the technical machinery" might be understood as the "ascendancy of the technician over the intellectual."[14] Indeed, Gore Vidal understood the Hollywood director in just these terms. Directors, he said, were, "at best, bright technicians." Opposing the auteur theory, Vidal claimed that directors "spent too much time with cameras and machines" to relate intelligently to "that living world without whose presence there is no art."[15] Andrew Sarris acknowledged, of course, that directors had to show "technical competence," but a main point of the auteur theory was that they could not be reducible to it.[16]

In fact, one of the few movies the Directors Company made, *The Conversation* (Coppola, Paramount, 1974), is a meditation on this problem. Harry Caul (Gene Hackman) is a surveillance specialist who claims early on to only want a "nice, fat recording" on a job. He is a technician par excellence, ignoring the content of his work to better execute its form. But as he immerses himself in the particulars of his assignment, it "makes [him] feel ... something." He refuses to turn the tapes over, per contractual agreement, and instead wants to control the effects of his work. He is fending off his status as a technician ("It's a job," he is told. "You're not supposed to feel anything about it, you're just supposed to do it.") and choosing to define the value of his work. His formal technique gives him authority, it makes him "preeminent in the field," as he is billed in the trade journal, *Security World*, but controlling the content involves him in his skill.

Much of the postwar management literature, indeed, called for employee "involvement" in "managerial planning." Douglas McGregor, most notably, insisted that a "subordinate" be "encouraged to take

**FIGURE 0.1** Francis Ford Coppola's image of autonomy.

responsibility for his own performance."[17] Consider, in this light, what I take to be an essential image in *The Conversation*: when Harry returns home, he unlocks several locks on his apartment door, which is forti-fied as though many valuables lie within (see fig. 0.1). Inside, however, we see rather bare walls and largely empty rooms. He tells his landlady, who has left a gift inside despite the many locks, that he does not care whether his "personal things burn up in a fire," because he has "nothing of value, nothing personal except my keys, which I really would like to have the only copy of." It is an odd confession, which amounts, I think, to a credo: he has installed these many locks not to protect what is inside but rather so that he can hold the key. The only thing to guard, this implies, is the power to say what is of value.

And the only thing we see him do in his apartment is play his saxo-phone. Insofar as the movie is about the self-definition of creative labor, it is a movie about the state of management, which, defined heretofore by the "Taylorist separation between design and execution," has been thrown into crisis in an economy that was now configured around a class whose professional prowess backed up its claim to self-manage.[18] This will be Peter Drucker's ultimate verdict on knowledge workers: that "they cannot, in effect, be supervised."[19] In their labor, design and execution must be joined. In part, New Hollywood is product of a broader managerial revolution. Coppola seemed to understand it this way. To him, it was a problem of "creative management."[20] The "film business," he said, "should be providing not only a product, something it can sell, but a hospitable place for creative people to work." Instead, "there are fine writers and all kinds of talented people, but it's a sad, pent-up place."[21] Steven Spielberg appraised it in the same terms, recognizing on one hand that, in the studio system, "the crafts people and the creative people" had outgrown its supervision and "wanted to make their own decisions," but on the other hand that, in the poststudio era, there were "talented, creative people who aren't organized"—"loads of talent," he said, "but they are not part of a system."[22]

This book assesses the industrial shakeup that led to New Hollywood by disclosing the crucial part that a radicalized management theory played in both its formation and stabilization. The auteur theory functioned as a kind of management theory for a cohort of filmmakers who were made cine-literate through university education (the film schools of USC, UCLA, NYU, and AFI) in the same moment that management theory was gaining a foothold in the university by way of proliferating MBA programs.[23] Both auteur theory and business management theory, I argue, had the same object in their sights: the large corporation, which was made sclerotic by a combination of its hypertrophy and its centralized command structure. In its place would emerge a smaller-scale, more flexible system of labor. This system would still deploy the legal agency of the corporation, but the tight bond between workers and firms that had obtained in the Fordist-Keynesian era would be severed. Such a bond was essential in Hollywood and beyond, and hence the auteur theory reimagined it. In what follows, I explain that New Hollywood looks different once inserted into the long march of economic history, and in this perspective, the film directors who previously looked like Hollywood outsiders assume a privileged role in the corporation's renegotiation of its inside and outside.

## YEAR ONE: 1962

The problem one gleans in instances here, there, and everywhere in the postwar landscape is that the arrangements of capitalism seemed too organized to permit the flexible regroupings that both capital and labor required in different measures. In the early '60s, the avatars of a systematized economy were the Keynesians in the Kennedy administration who believed, on the evidence of current trends, that fiscal policy could strike the right balance between employment rates and inflation in perpetuity.[24] This was the moment of the technocrats, the "best and brightest," as David Halberstam calls them; faith in expertise carried the day.[25] An early and important dissenting voice on the side of capital was Milton Friedman, whose 1962 collection *Capitalism and Freedom* and 1963 coauthored study *A Monetarist History of the United States, 1867–1960* would furnish an infrastructure of ideas for the undoing of the welfare state and the freeing of capital. On the side of labor, though, the reasons for dissent were less obvious given that organized labor had helped generalize middle-class living standards. But in the 1962 SDS manifesto, "The Port Huron Statement" (PHS), even this standard ("the majority of Americans are living in relative comfort") came in for critique. In part, the object of this critique was the fact that "hardcore poverty exist[ed] just beyond the neon lights of affluence," but the gains in living standard had nonetheless "instilled quiescence in liberal hearts." Yet part of the critique was addressed to organized labor, which had "succumbed to institutionalization, its social idealism waning under the tendencies of bureaucracy."[26] Their critique of labor anticipated what the critic (and later screenwriter) Jacob Brackman would say of Benjamin Braddock (Dustin Hoffman), protagonist of *The Graduate* (Nichols, Embassy, 1967), namely that one generation's success would steal the upcoming generation's motivation to succeed. "A son can pursue ambitions that his parents cherished and failed to fulfill," Brackman argued, "but not ambitions that they fulfilled and then found wanting."[27] Likewise, in the PHS assessment, labor's very successes had put a brake on its "zeal for change."[28] What was found wanting in each situation—with

Benjamin Braddock and with organized labor—was the Fordist work-place wherein "the individual is regulated as part of the system." The PHS envisioned a form of labor, by contrast, in which "self-direction, self-understanding, and creativity" could be realized. "Work should involve incentives worthier than money," it argued. "It should be educa-tive, not stultifying; creative, not mechanical; self-directed, not mani-pulated."[29] The PHS's authors surely did not know it, but they were sounding the themes of contemporary management theory.

In the same year that the PHS set forth its generalized critiques, Andrew Sarris published his "Notes on the Auteur Theory in 1962," a document that is given over to specialized interests, it seems, until one brushes against its grain and reveals a red thread connecting it to the PHS. In it, Sarris imagined that good work in Hollywood has to be "miraculously extracted" from a "money-oriented environment."[30] Money is not only a weak incentive, in his reckoning, but an impediment. When he elaborates the three concentric rings through which an auteur must pass—technique, personal style, and interior meaning—the last of them, the source of cinema's "ultimate glory . . . as an art," is something like workplace frustration. Sarris says that "interior meaning is extrapo-lated from the tension between a director's personality and his mate-rial."[31] Rival film critic Pauline Kael ridiculed this, suggesting that Sarris was simply putting a happy spin on "what has generally been considered the frustrations of a man working against the given material." Such criti-cism, she said, idealizes "the man who signs a long-term contract, directs any script that's handed to him, and expresses himself by shoving bits of style up the crevasses of the plots."[32] Kael is right, but because she ratio-nally engages Sarris's polemic, she misses its point. The object of Sarris's criticism, I believe, is something he cannot name. There is an aporia in Sarris's logic; hence we need to read him symptomatically.[33] What he is attacking, just as the PHS does, is work that is "stultifying," "mechani-cal," and "manipulated." The "given material" is not a bad screenplay, or not only that, because improving the screenplay would not materially change the structure of this labor.

The "given material" is, in fact, the Fordist corporation in which work is rationalized and mechanized. Kael senses as much. In one rather-extraordinary passage she says, "This is curiously reminiscent of a view common enough in the business world, that it's better not to get too involved, too personally interested in business problems, or they take over your life."[34] Again, Kael is highly perceptive. Sarris wants proof that personality can still subsist within the business world, that is, within Hollywood's commercial system, because from that proof, a system of another kind altogether can be extrapolated. Kael errs, then, when she opposes a business world sensibility to Sarris's auteur. "This is the *opposite* of how an artist works," she objects.[35] Yet, for Sarris, the artist is over-involved, not in spite of but due to the business imperative. "The auteur theory values the personality of a director precisely because of the barriers to its expression," he specifies, praising the "few brave spirits" who have "managed to overcome the gravitational pull" of the system. Sarris might be accused of trying to square a circle ("Circles and Squares" is the title of Kael's rebuttal) but it is clear elsewhere that he found the "personal cinema" that Jonas Mekas promoted all but meaningless, the "individuals singing their song" within a local community—New York City in the '60s, say, at the Film-Makers' Cinematheque or the Bleecker Street Cinema. Instead, he wanted a mass public of a kind that corporations were designed to service. "I think you have to reach someone, there has to be an audience there," he says, and hence movies were keyed to popular "mythologies," as he calls them, which are "things that people believe. . . . They serve some social function. There is a market."[36] Sarris tries to square a circle, then, by bringing an "anti-establishment ferment" within the fold of a commercial industry. François Truffaut, he says, did this by "ascribing authorship to Hollywood directors hitherto tagged with the deadly epithets of commercialism."[37] To imagine that commerce, particularly in the form of the capital structure of the corporation, was a condition of this art, and that the barriers it threw up—in the form of a division of labor or the monetization of a market—gave measure of a spirit's braveness and indeed helped disclose an "*élan* of the soul" was to imagine that business stopped feeling "grubby" or "vulgar" to its practitioners when conceived in artistic terms. The difference between Kael and Sarris, put simply, is that Kael holds the stock belief that artists are interested in the means (the work itself) while business people are interested in the ends (the profit gained from work). But Sarris hopes that by some alchemy, the means and ends can be fused: following one's passion and committing oneself to the work and not to the money it might earn can ipso facto be good for business.

Reading Sarris in this way helps to iron out what Kael thinks are contradictions. They are real, these contradictions—Sarris was hard-pressed to defend them, indeed, and harbored lifelong bitterness against Kael for ridiculing them—but they were contradictions in the workplace itself, and Sarris was trying to solve them in roughly the same way as management theorists.[38] Peter Drucker, in fact, believed that only the corporation could solve the contradictions inherent in industrial society, which he took to be genetic, not accidental, to this form of social organization. Nils Gilman says, "Drucker accepted the left's argument that the fundamental source of the existential and political crisis of modernity stemmed from problems at the core of the economic system."[39] Alienation was a problem, Drucker thought, because the "divorce of the worker from product and means of production is essential and absolute." The worker was not "even capable of defining his own contribution to the productive organization and to the product" and often could not "even point to a part of the process and say: this is *my* work."[40] Because he addressed the problem by way of Søren Kierkegaard, Friedrich Stahl, and Ferdinand Tönnies, Drucker gave an intellectual background to a field that he was forming—management studies (latter-day guru Tom Peters would say, "no true discipline of management" existed before Drucker)—even as he was pushing forward two preexisting schools of thought: one stressing the social responsibility of the corporation, which is an offshoot of New Deal thinking, and another advocating humanistic management rather than scientific management, which is a tradition including Elton Mayo, Mary Parker Follett, and in a more contemporary parallel with Drucker's work, Elliott Jacques and the postwar attention to human relations at England's Tavistock Institute. Drucker's series of books— *The Future of Industrial Man* (1942), *Concept of the Corporation* (1946), and *The New Society* (1950)—combine the themes of social responsibility and humanistic management, positing that the legitimacy of industrial society will spring from them. His chief argument is that because the "representative institution" in postwar America is the corporation, there can be no essential disharmony between "the interest of the corporation and the interest of society." But neither is such harmony established "automatically" "in nature"; it is, rather, "the final end and the finest fruit of statesmanship."[41]

On this point, Andrew Sarris has nothing to say. One can presume that he considered its "money-orientation" endemic to the corporation. He did not seem to have a historical analysis of capitalism, really, unlike a critic such as Dwight Macdonald, who coordinated his analyses of cinema and capitalism in a historical perspective.[42] But on the point of humanistic management, Sarris was in line with Drucker. Sarris's obsession "with the wholeness of art and the artist," and with a "director as a whole," seems a counterpoint to the scientific manager's obsession with disaggregating workers into a set of functions in order to reconfigure them for efficiency. At no point does Sarris grant the "so-called system" determinant power (even if Hollywood studios were clearly organized as a system); he is always swinging determinacy back to the individual. In this he is in step with William H. Whyte's critique of the "organization man," which urges individualism "precisely because it *is* an age of organization," and hence "it is the other side of the coin that needs emphasis."[43] Indeed, in the same period, Drucker was in the process of converting this into a management doctrine, which, Nils Gilman says, "insisted that men be considered and treated as integrated wholes."[44] Imagining workers as parts that are consecrated in use to the organization is not only bad for morale, Drucker argues, but is actually less efficient than was claimed by scientific management. "It is very dubious whether the unimaginative and unthinking application of machine tool principles to man does not: (a) fail to utilize man's real efficiency; and (b) lead to real and tangible inefficiency in the form of fatigue, stresses and strains." He marshals an example from World War II, a time when, because "it was not possible to set up the traditional assembly-line-in-space," labor was done by "what might be called assembly-line-in-concept," which meant that workers did a series of "operations instead of just one." Engineers were surprised, he says, that it led to an "increase in efficiency and production instead of a drop." Not only did productivity change, so too did "the atmosphere." The "rhythm" of production remained "even and strong," and it made "the people friendly and easygoing."[45]

This would also be the insight of Douglas McGregor's famous book *The Human Side of Enterprise* (1960), which alongside Drucker's *The Practice of Management* (1954) was the foundation of Management Studies in its institutionalized form. To get the fullness of a worker's potential most readily, McGregor argues, a manager needs to conceive human nature in terms of its wholeness. A main influence on McGregor's theory was Abraham Maslow, whose ideas about human potentiality made him, according to his biographer, Edward Hoffman, "an uneasy hero of the counterculture" as it emerged in the '60s.[46] McGregor transposed Maslow's 1943 paper "A Theory of Human Motivation" into his management studies in the mid-fifties. McGregor was sure that if labor were considered a human rather than a capital asset, "unimagined resources of creative energy could become available within the organizational setting." He believed that human nature, as understood by scientific management, was simply a construction built from management assumptions. What he calls Theory X (i.e., Taylorism) holds that "the average man is indolent," "works as little as possible," "lacks ambition, dislikes responsibility," and therefore must be "rewarded, punished, controlled," if management is to discharge its function "of getting things done through other people." McGregor believes instead in the need "for realizing one's own potentialities, for continued self-development, for being creative in the broadest sense of that term."[47] McGregor's Theory Y gave traction to the idea that value lies not in what people produce in the moment—as single-tooling is keyed to—but what they are capable of imagining as the products of the future, and this leads down the road to what Jeff Mauzy and Richard Harriman call "systemic creativity."[48] Much of management theory in the '60s and beyond, Thomas Frank says, would be a "string of corollaries" to McGregor, including Robert Townsend's *Up the Organization* (1970), Rosabeth Moss Kanter's *The Change Masters* (1983), and Tom Peters's *Liberation Management* (1992).[49]

Sarris's redescription of erstwhile technicians as artists is a local instance of McGregor's theory. Because Sarris was a film critic, not a management theorist, he would not have thought that the transformation of the corporation was in his bailiwick. But if studio directors such as John Ford and Howard Hawks identified "as technical workers more than as artists," Shyon Baumann argues, it was because there was no "institutional support" for self-regard of the latter kind.[50] In lending such institutional support, Sarris helped catalyze a change in Hollywood corporate structure by swapping out one form of motivation for another: remuneration for autonomy. Drucker's most striking claim, indeed, is that "profitability is not the purpose of business enterprise" and that the "so-called 'profit motive'" likely does not exist.[51] Money could *become* a problem, McGregor notes: "People *will* make insistent demands for more money" if management thinks the "physiological needs" of its employees are the only needs to satisfy. Money can become "the focus of interest if it is the *only* means available."[52] But it became axiomatic in New Hollywood that people would take less money to work on a project that they believed in and that gave them scope to self-realize. Coppola's American Zoetrope was organized around this principle. It caused a problem, Carol Ballard admits, because "the conditions under which Francis wanted everyone to work were more than Spartan—they were practically non-earning." Yet this separated Zoetrope enough from Warner Bros. (its financing source) to grant everyone their autonomy. Coppola's credo, Peter Cowie reports, was that "all talent consists of being comfortable with your instincts, and being able to act on them," and this belief, that one should control the sphere of one's instinctive action, "explains the unusual measure of autonomy given" to Coppola's collaborators such as "Vittorio Storaro, [Dean] Tavoularis, [Walter] Murch, and Richard Beggs."[53]

Sarris's auteur theory, as film criticism, was descriptive. It pointed its light on the past in an effort to find artists there. But its influence on the emergent talent in New Hollywood was prescriptive insofar as those who encountered it in film school and film culture generally came to think they ought to call themselves auteurs and behave accordingly. In its industrial application, however, it led not only to the redoubled power of the director but also to the emancipation of film talent in all spheres of operation—that is, the auteur theory spread to cinematographers, production designers, sound designers, and beyond. All were urged to conceive of themselves as artists. This is the ultimate claim that Pauline Kael makes for *Citizen Kane* (Welles, RKO, 1941); in effect, it proves that the "director should be in control not because he is the sole creative intelligence but because only if he is in control can he liberate and utilize the talents of his co-workers, who languish (as directors do) in studio-factory productions."[54] In short, it distributes authority downward, relocating decision making and risk taking from the executive layer (the production chiefs, studio heads, et al.) to the various craft positions. On *Citizen Kane*, Kael says, "technicians and designers came forth with ideas they'd been bottling up for years; they were all in on the creative process" thanks to the "atmosphere of freedom" that Welles established.[55] This is the model, in fact, that Peter Drucker endorsed when he made a study of General Motors in *Concept of the Corporation* and credited its success to the practice of "establishing high-level goals while devolving authority for executing" them to self-governing units. He called GM *"an essay in federalism"* for its combination of "the greatest corporate unity with the greatest divisional autonomy and responsibility."[56] This recommendation, perhaps more than any other, marked the transformation of the corporation in the coming years. "By the 1980s," John Micklethwait and Adrian Wooldridge note, Drucker was credited with "moving 75%–80% of the Fortune 500 to radical decentralization."[57] The point was to effect the look of the small firm in a time when corporations were metastasizing, often by way of conglomeration. "In a small firm or shop," Drucker explains, "even the apprentice was forced by his contacts with his fellow employees and their work to see the business as a whole and to understand the points of view and the problems of other departments."[58]

I mark 1962 as an epochal year, not simply for what Sarris's and SDS's documents attest but for material changes within Hollywood. In that year, MCA completed its acquisition of Universal Pictures, the first salvo in Hollywood's conglomeration. MCA, a talent agency run by founder Jules Stein and president Lew Wasserman, had begun in music but grew with television, by way of its Revue Productions, to dominate the entertainment industry. Wasserman bought Universal in two stages, first acquiring the studio's land and property and then buying its corporate brand. The deal was remarkable because it suggested that Universal, the corporation, was not the same thing as its land and holdings; in its purest form, it was a structure of capital. Other studios came to the same understanding. At 20th Century Fox, president Spyros Skouras had parceled and sold studio backlots to finance its troubled balance sheet.[59] But Wasserman was the first to conceive of a studio in terms of "federalist" organization. Whereas 20th Century Fox tried to recover in 1962 by reconsolidating under the authority of central producer Darryl Zanuck, this was a superannuated model because, by then, Aubrey Solomon explains, "most major actors and directors had formed their own corporations," and this led to what Janet Staiger would call the "package-unit system."[60] Because, by trade, Wasserman was an agent, though, he was already in the habit of laterally connecting a series of corporations in one package. Once he sat atop a conglomerate, he knew how to engineer decentralized power. Thomas Schatz notes that Universal, with "its long-standing dual agenda of low-cost formula pictures and A-class productions via outside independents," was structured better than other studios for "TV and the New Hollywood." "Telefilm series production," Schatz says, was a way to keep the studio's "production facilities" in operation, and the predictability of profit derived from it could "offset the rising costs of feature filmmaking."[61] The filmmaking, then, was farmed out to small production companies—sometimes housed in bungalows on the studio lot, sometimes located off-site—and in them, the auteur theory was like a management doctrine that helped to structure the small firm, insulate its labor from the executive layer, and generally lend its workplace the look of a maverick redoubt despite its dependency on the larger conglomerate enfolding it.

I have placed special emphasis on Universal and 20th Century Fox, juxtaposing their divergent paths as Universal courted small companies such as Kirk Douglas's Bryna Productions while 20th Century Fox tried grooming a next-generation mogul in Darryl Zanuck's son, Richard, a project that flamed out spectacularly at the end of the '60s and left the Zanuck father-son relationship in ruins. When Richard Zanuck eventually formed a small production company with his close associate David

Brown, it was Universal that brought the Zanuck-Brown Company into its decentralized structure. In cases such as Bryna and Zanuck-Brown, we can profile the corporation at its different scales, letting us see at once the arena of self-realization within the small company and also, through the prism of the small company, the forms assumed in the historical emergence of media conglomerates.

## NEW HOLLYWOOD AND THE AUTUMN OF INDUSTRY

In many critical accounts, the year 1967 is thought to have inaugurated New Hollywood, with *The Graduate* and *Bonnie and Clyde* (Penn, Warner Bros.) being received *as new movies*. They were, in short, events. But as Mark Harris makes clear, "They had all been imagined for the first time many years earlier."[62] Their arrival was the formal declaration of a substantive change that had been in the making for some years. The case of 20th Century Fox selling their backlot shows that they were caught in the process yet unable (or perhaps did not wish) to give it textual form in the movies they were making. The movies, after all, were only epiphenomenal. The phenomenon was economic, and it was greater in scope than any given industry. Stephanie Frank has situated Fox's real estate liquidation in relation to the "restructuration" of both the economy and the urban space of Los Angeles, which made the city, in the words of Edward Soja, "one of the world's prototypical post-Fordist industrial metropolises." From the '60s on, its Fordist industries were "dismantled," Frank says, in "a smaller-scale version of the Rust Belt while the regional space economy (successor of the aircraft industry) and small craft-based industrial firms, such as those in the film industry, have risen as flexibly specialized."[63] One might suggest that Skouras had foreseen the obsolescence of Fordist production, but Darryl Zanuck and his deputies had not, in turn, flexibly specialized but instead chased the model of yesteryear in producing a rigid blockbuster roadshow throughout the '60s that yielded the boom-and-bust cycle of *Cleopatra* (Mankiewicz, 1963), *The*

*Sound of Music* (Wise, 1965), *Doctor Dolittle* (Fleischer, 1967), and *Star!* (Wise, 1968).[64]

An alternative way to trace New Hollywood's emergence, then, is in the coordination of the product with the transformed site of production. For instance, Lawrence Webb's study *The Cinema of Urban Crisis* offers a reading of Hollywood cinema and beyond in terms of the coarticulation of film textuality and the post-Fordist redesign of urban space.[65] The studios changed in relative status throughout the '60s and into the '70s (MGM, for instance, was gutted for its brand after Kirk Kerkorian acquired it in 1969 and would never regain its status afterward) based on how cannily they equilibrated their aesthetic products and their production models.[66] This is all to say that 1967 is a significant year because in *The Graduate* and *Bonnie and Clyde*, a new balance had been recognizably struck at the level of film form in the contending influences of location shooting, lightweight camera technology and its attendant lighting procedures, labor force self-understanding, and Off Broadway performance idioms.[67] But the rejiggering had been on view in such movies as *Shadows* (Cassavetes, British Lion, 1959), *David and Lisa* (Perry, Continental Distributing, 1962), *Tom Jones* (Richardson, United Artists, 1963), *Dr. Strangelove* (Kubrick, Columbia, 1964), *Mickey One* (Penn, Columbia, 1965), *A Thousand Clowns* (Coe, United Artists, 1965), and so on. All this was happening alongside or in conjunction with the Living Theatre and Off Broadway, the directors of British Free Cinema and Woodfall Productions, Richard Lester and Swinging London, and the postwar cinemas of Italy and France and of Europe in general. The year 1967 theatricalized the standoff between Old and New Hollywood personnel (the "dragons" and the "dragonflies" among the Oscar nominees, as the *Los Angeles Times* put it) more than it inaugurated a mode of production.[68]

Thus, in this book, I put some pressure on the periodizing assumptions of New Hollywood historiography. The years 1967–1975 have been viewed as the "Hollywood Renaissance," in which, for a brief period, a vacuum of power was filled by Hollywood auteurs, whose range of motion was then tightly circumscribed when *Jaws* (Spielberg, Universal, 1975) minted the formula for the blockbuster. This line of thinking has led critics to posit two discontinuous periods, which Derek Nystrom summarizes as New Hollywood I and New Hollywood II.[69] The warrant for this history issues from the movies' reception: *The Graduate* and *Bonnie and Clyde* disclosed one kind of market; *Jaws* disclosed another.[70] However, telling it this way does not account for the fact that their industrial arrangements and personnel fall well outside this reception window.[71] My own periodizing of New Hollywood is informed by Denise Mann, who narrates the industry's reconfiguration at the hands of the talent agencies and the self-incorporation of talent that flowed from it and rolls back New Hollywood to include the 1950s. She notes an inversion of the "Big Five" studios (Paramount, MGM, 20th Century Fox, Warner Bros., and RKO) that led in the era of the studio system and the "Little Three" studios (Universal, Columbia, and United Artists) that, she argues, were better geared to lead in the poststudio era because they were "more streamlined, flexible operations" with "less burdensome overhead costs." They were ready to outsource production to independent companies, and their "familiarity with lower-budget, factory-like B pictures" was easily adapted to "telefilm production starting in the mid-1950s."[72] My point is that when we bring to bear larger historical forces on New Hollywood, the significant moments start to look different. By setting Hollywood change within the emergent regime of post-Fordism, in particular, it becomes consistent with postwar change on a greater scale.

The deep perspective of economic history, as Giovanni Arrighi constructs it in *The Long Twentieth Century*, for instance, allows us to assess the breakdown in the Hollywood production model as the outcome of both the local factor of the 1948 Paramount decree and the general factor of systemic exhaustion. Though capitalism has periods of "specialization," as Arrighi says, such as industrialization, it has always been in capitalists' interests not to specialize, to be mobile and unconstrained. Arrighi explains this in terms of Karl Marx's general formula of M-C-M', denoting money capital (M), commodity capital (C), and then an expanded form of money capital (M'), which is also known in the *longue durée* studies of Fernand Braudel as "financial expansion." Arrighi explains that "capitalist agencies do not invest money in particular input-output combinations, with all the attendant loss of flexibility and freedom of choice, as an end in itself" but rather "as a *means* toward the end of securing an even greater flexibility and freedom of choice at some future point." So the manufacturing plant is not an end in itself, despite what might be thought by a community that has grown up around it or employees that have made their careers within it. It is a sign of its mature development—indeed, "a sign of autumn," as Braudel says—that capital divests from it and takes flight to other regions, sometimes other sectors.[73] The twin expressions of this in Hollywood were "runaway production" (to other regions) and "conglomeration" (to other sectors). "Runaway production" describes a trend in the immediate postwar years to finance productions abroad with only above-the-line talent from studios (directors and stars, say) but crews from foreign industries. "Conglomeration," on the other hand, refers to a trend in capital organization wherein businesses in various sectors were banded together under one corporate umbrella. The studios could remain in Hollywood but act as financial centers while production was reconstituted on different geopolitical foundations (the depredated European industries, emergent Canadian industries, the U.S. "Sun Belt," etc.). Many factors played into this industrial reconstruction, such as World War II and the laws that kept Hollywood studios from repatriating profits made abroad, which led to the establishment of international branches and productions, the tax laws that incentivized actors to make their money outside the country, and the unionization of Hollywood labor that multiplied the average budget of a production.[74] What these shifts signal is the exhaustion of a cycle, an alternation from "material expansion" to "financial expansion" across U.S. industries that, regarded abstractly, has been called the post-Fordist economy and, regarded concretely, we should designate as New Hollywood.

In this book I draw variously from the post-Fordist tradition. Though David Harvey does not call it by this name (and instead calls it "flexible accumulation"), he describes the same formation. The period from 1965 to 1973, Harvey says, "was one in which the inability of Fordism and Keynesianism to contain the inherent contradictions of capitalism became more and more apparent," and the symptom of this failing was "rigidity." Because "fixed capital investments in mass-production systems" stunted the impulse to innovate, the regime that would emerge in place of Fordism would be built around the flexibility of production models and labor markets. Within production, "the organizational form and managerial technique appropriate to high volume, standardized mass production" resisted conversion to the "highly specialized responses" and the "adaptability of skills to special purposes," which were required for flexible accumulation. Hence, a turn to "small business sub-contracting" helped "buffer" large corporations "from the cost of market fluctuations." The growth of subcontracting permitted "activities formerly internalized within manufacturing firms (legal, marketing, advertising, typing, etc.) to be hived off to separate enterprises." What this meant for labor markets was a downtick in "regular employment" and an "increasing reliance upon part-time, temporary, or sub-contracted work arrangements."[75] The culture of the temporary contract emerges in this context. But it also "opens up opportunities for small business formation, and in some instances permits" a revival of "older systems of domestic, artisanal, familial" labor. Attending this is the development of "'black,' 'informal,' or 'underground' economies." Thus, for Harvey, the large corporation is not decentered; rather, the contract connects "small firms to large-scale, often multinational, operations."[76]

The stress placed here on small firms (and the artisanal or craft production they can insulate) is at the heart of Michael Piore and Charles Sabel's study *The Second Industrial Divide* in which they suggest that the nineteenth-century "collision" between craft and mass production might be harmonized in the "industrial dualism" of a post-Fordist economy. Their analysis depends on a number of theories, but the most basic for my purposes is the idea that an investment in "mass-production equipment" required the stabilization of markets. This result was the upshot of two historical contingencies: first, the evolution of the large corporation from the latter nineteenth century through the 1920s and, second, the emergence of a Keynesian fiscal policy in response to the Depression in the 1930s.[77] What that yielded, in turn, was the Fordist-Keynesian détente, which presided over the unusually robust prosperity of the postwar years. The conditions it held in place did not occur naturally, however, and the so-called liberal consensus (another name for

Fordism-Keynesianism) fell apart once systemic exhaustion began to show. The one-size-fits-all character of production could not shift as demand did, and from their secondary position, the flexibly specialized firms emerged to supply the markets that mass production could not. The same trajectory is evident in the motion picture industry, where the Hollywood studios were established as vertically integrated manufacturing plants (coupled to the banks) throughout the '20s, after which the unions and guilds established a Keynesian accord between labor and capital throughout the '30s.[78] A decline in the absolute size of the audience after 1946 (a 40 percent fall in box-office receipts between 1945 and 1955) volatilized the production process and labor relations.[79] Throughout the late '50s and into the '60s, the industry tried to find its equilibrium by resting more power on the talent agencies, which freed studios to become centers for the subcontracting of production. If the studios had always been a mix of mass-production technique and batch-production scale, as Allen Scott has argued, and if they had always "sustained many elements of a craft community" within their industrial system, as Susan Christopherson and Michael Storper have argued, then the ratio flipped at the turn of the '60s, and an industrial dualism favoring small firms in a "specialized complex" began to characterize Hollywood's mode of production.[80]

I posit the small firm—the small production company in particular—as the unit of analysis for New Hollywood. It was the framework for reckoning what the collapsing studio system had thrown into confusion. It constructed a zone for renegotiating labor relations, one in which the collectivized identity of labor (i.e., union solidarity) was scaled down to an individualist self-understanding. Because these small firms were often started by actors or directors, individually or severally, it was more straightforward for them to project their personhood (i.e., star power) onto the firms' corporate agencies, and in turn for the firms' personhood to reflect on the stars. This practical exercise in corporate personhood, as I demonstrate in a set of case studies, constitutes a main line of inquiry in my argument. Such immediate identification happened more regularly in the post-Fordist era, in part because only "core" labor was secured within the corporation while "peripheral" labor was ejected from it and casualized.[81] This, Christopher Newfield argues, informs the corporate experience in general going forward because, as "jobs outside the corporate world seem more difficult, scarce, and despotic, jobs on the inside are said to be ever more liberating and democratic."[82] These corporate spaces were hedonized in the '60s, in part as a sop to the counterculture taking shape outside them and in part as a repudiation of the scientific management that was long considered orthodox inside them. If Fordism had shrunk the "time and energy required for the day's work" in order to give more scope to the "real life" lived off the time clock, then its repudiation would entail mending the "big split," as C. Wright Mills calls it, so that work was not merely a sacrifice for the "holiday" beyond it but was itself nourishing and enlivening and what made a person whole rather than divided.[83]

In film companies such as Robert Altman's Lion's Gate, for instance, the line between daytime work and nighttime parties was impossible to draw. But such a fusion required that the "holiday" be redefined as a special case of productivity because the pleasure it induced limbered up one's laboring energies, and this, in turn, required a model for the discharge of such energies in work, which was available in the arts. In Thomas Frank's study of '60s business culture *The Conquest of Cool*, he shows that the artist became the ego ideal in various industries. The "defining characteristic of post-Organization white-collar workers," he says, "is a powerful artistic impulse."[84] This was the case in small Hollywood firms such as Kirk Douglas's Bryna Productions, Robert Altman's Lion's Gate, the Zanuck-Brown Company, and BBS Productions. In these firms, the auteur theory was deployed as a license to reorganize the corporation in favor of the artist—no more were these "creatives" to be treated as contract employees or as technicians at the behest of the studio; they were now claiming prerogatives of their own. Lew Wasserman turned to these, the self-described artists who were willing to assume a measure of risk in return for professional autonomy, as he was restructuring Universal in 1962. In this respect, he did what United Artists had been doing in running a streamlined operation that subcontracted with independent producers, but Wasserman's strategy was novel because he raised these flexibly specialized units on the back of the routinized, Fordist production of television series.[85] New Hollywood, in other words, is a dualistic industry, and the side of it that is most mistaken for the whole has been called, among other things, the "Hollywood Renaissance."[86] It is often imagined that, on this side, the auteur theory separated the director from the industry—that these directors were "mavericks," liberated from business imperatives—but my point is that they were more intimately joined in the corporate reconstitution of Hollywood by virtue of the new production models they established in small firms.

New Hollywood arrived with the regime of the small production company, and in these companies, the auteur theory functioned as something like an organizational chart, always pressing authority downward to the artists in the ranks—because, as Douglas McGregor says, organizational "dependence downward [had become] too great to permit [a] unilateral means of control."[87] My focus was anticipated by Thomas Elsaesser, who tried to find continuity between what he calls "New Hollywood" and "New New Hollywood," which, I note earlier, had otherwise been seen as the discontinuous periods of New Hollywood I and New Hollywood II. Elsaesser suggests in passing that the two might not be distinct phases but rather sectors nested within a single formation. The "canonical story" of the end of New Hollywood, he says, had imagined that the "nimble, small-is-beautiful, artisanal mode of American independent film production" was displaced by the blockbuster packages. However, the small-is-beautiful units should instead be seen as "pilot fish," which attracted "risk capital and creative talent" to the "old studios," which were now reconfigured as "corporate conglomerates" that had decentralized management in response to the "nature of conglomerate ownership."[88]

In what follows I demonstrate that the emblematic blockbuster *Jaws* was made, in fact, by the small, nimble Zanuck-Brown Company, which had a short-term contract with Universal's Lew Wasserman. What counts for some as a break, therefore, is but a continuation. Just before this, Spielberg had made *The Sugarland Express* (Universal, 1974) with Zanuck-Brown, a movie that falls within what I call the "defection genre." In chapter 2, I describe the defection genre as a main locus of auteurist filmmaking, joining together such movies as *The Graduate, Bonnie and Clyde*, and *Five Easy Pieces* (Rafelson, Columbia, 1970) by way of appeals to social defection. In them, defection from society is a narrative trope that New Hollywood auteurs deployed to mediate the New Left debates at the heart of counterculture politics. If Spielberg's first uptake of the genre in *The Sugarland Express* was unsuccessful, in *Jaws* he called on it again, combining it with the disaster genre to a much greater effect. However possible it is to separate *The Sugarland Express* from *Jaws* in aesthetic terms, it is impossible to assign them to different modes of production. Both issue from post-Fordist arrangements: they were made within a small, flexible production unit under the aegis of a large, decentralized corporation. They come, of course, from the same firm. That *Jaws* became a profit center, throwing off many revenue streams (merchandise, video games, sequels), is only incidental to the arrangement of its making even if it fortified such arrangements by abetting the next wave of horizontal conglomeration in which movies would become the riveting image—the "advertising billboard," Elsaesser calls it— synergizing a diversity of media enterprises.[89]

The effort to periodize New Hollywood in aesthetic terms has led critics to report its death arbitrarily and prematurely. For instance, Beverly Walker says in *Sight and Sound* (1971) that the "brief renaissance following *Easy Rider* is now over." It is true that *Easy Rider* (Hopper, Columbia, 1969) had a bewildering effect on the industry, resulting in a giddy hunt to reproduce its return-on-investment ratio, but while pronouncing the end of its moment, Walker points out productions by Clint Eastwood's Malpaso Productions, Peter Fonda's Pando Company, and Jack Lemmon's Jalem. She notes that Cannon Films had produced several movies since the success of *Joe* (Alvidsen, MGM, 1970), but Cinema X had yet "to get a picture into production."[90] In short, in Walker's reporting we see all the signs of the normalized activity of New Hollywood, but she reads them pessimistically as the end of a renaissance. However, when *Variety* surveyed the activity of Zanuck-Brown and Chartoff-Winkler several years later, it observed that the "major resurgence" in the theatrical box office was rooted in the pattern of major studios "recruiting affiliated production units."[91] Hence, the period under analysis in my book—1962 to 1975—is not meant as the period in which New Hollywood existed but rather as the time of its establishment. I conclude my study in 1975 to suggest that patterns of industry that had been initiated in 1962 had, by then, become dominant. And the patterns had been stabilized, moreover, by the aesthetic forms that were the novelty of 1967; by the historic triumphs at the box office such as *The Godfather* (Coppola, Paramount, 1972), *The Exorcist* (Friedkin, Warner Bros., 1973), and *Jaws* in succession; and by the self-theatricalizing of counterculture corporates such as Bert Schneider, whose antiwar speech at the 1976 Academy Awards was meant to divide the audience into the categories of young and old.

## SELF-THEORIZING IN THE CREATIVE ECONOMY

I have stressed the theatrics of this moment, the tendency to make a public show of which side one was on, but if, in the moment, it seemed that what was theatricalized was a "generation gap"—greybeards on one side, upstarts on the other—in hindsight, it seems equally true that a struggle between social classes was being staged. Derek Nystrom describes the auteur theory as an "assertion of professional-managerial class prerogative." He quotes Brian De Palma's justification of nonunion labor on his movie *Hi, Mom!* (Sigma III, 1970): "Suppose I had a union crew here. All those guys are four hundred years old. I would probably have very little rapport with them on any level. You know, 'We come, we do our job, we leave as soon as possible.'"[92] De Palma would say of himself and his collaborators, by contrast, that they were "committed" politically and aesthetically. The upshot of such commitment has been the so-called creative economy, which in its disorganized phase might indeed have been a congeries of the artistically likeminded, but when converted to top-down policy, as Richard Florida has advocated, it has been one name for dismantling welfare provision and rendering labor more precarious.[93] A number of scholars have made such observations. Angela McRobbie notes that "pervasive inequality . . . underpins the growth of the new creative economy at a time when the public sector is being dramatically shrunk." Creative success, she argues, self-selects "those who can take such risks."[94] Sarah Brouillette has defined creativity in such an economy as "the work of flexible, self-managing individuals trained to turn an innate capacity for 'innovation' into saleable properties."[95] Daniel Pink has even made the hyperbolic claim that the MFA is the new MBA.[96] Luc Boltanski and Eve Chiapello root this economic shift in the 1960s, when, in a fragile moment, a confluence of forces allowed factory workers and university students to combine the "social" and "artistic" critiques of capitalist production—the former a critique of wealth concentration and the latter a critique of the loss of meaning in work. But when these critiques were subsequently decoupled, they were shunted onto tracks that were separated by the prerogatives of social class. The post-1968 narrative of political economy, for Boltanski and Chiapello, is found in management literature, and in it, they say that "the small firm" can, for some, "seem like the realm of freedom."[97]

Rooting this narrative in New Hollywood has a methodological advantage in that it grants the double perspective on economic change that Michel Aglietta and the Regulation school economists proposed. In *A Theory of Capitalist Regulation*, Aglietta argues that only by interpreting capitalism "as a social creation" do we correct for the abstract models that imagine a *homo economicus* floating above the contending forces of history.[98] In place of such neoclassical thinking, the Regulation school insists on a dynamic exchange between the "regime of accumulation" (Fordism, flexible accumulation, etc.) and what they have called the "mode of regulation." The former describes a balance between the mode of production and the conditions for reproducing its labor force while the latter describes the set of "norms, habits, laws, regulating networks and so on that ensure the unity of the process," which is, in a word, social.[99] From this standpoint, Aglietta says, a crisis (in Old Hollywood, in the postwar body politic) can be conceived in terms of a "rupture" in "social relations" that will call forth "intense social creation" that effects "an irreversible transformation in the mode of production."[100] Because in such an analysis the social dimension drives change in the economic base just as the economic base is generating social conditions, we can better specify the part played not only by movements in the '60s but by the *textuality* of Hollywood's industrial product. This lines up with the analyses of the Birmingham school and, in particular, John Clarke, Stuart Hall, Tony Jefferson, and Brian Roberts's analyses of postwar subcultures and the special problem of the counterculture in this context. "Working-class subcultures," they note, make a clear division between the parts of "group life still fully under the constraint of dominant or 'parent' institutions (family, home, school, work), and those focused on non-work hours" and hence convert the sites of "leisure-time activities," such as the "street, neighborhood, football ground, seaside town, dance-hall," and so on, into the means of subcultural resistance. But the "middle-class counter-culture" blurs the "distinctions between 'necessary' and 'free' time activities" such that they create "enclaves" within dominant institutions. In consequence, the "control culture," they say, can more easily write off working-class subculture in terms of "delinquency" ("Hooliganism and Vandalism"), whereas the middle-class counterculture more automatically seems political.[101] In virtue of their class, they can self-represent in social institutions. This is to say that as Hollywood personnel who self-identified with the counterculture made their way into the industry, they were able arrogate its textual material—the movies—to theorize their own roles within its institutional crisis. The middle class had this advantage because their lot was to be trained and assumed into the managerial ranks.

Self-theorizing ends up being, in turn, something like a structural feature of knowledge work. "The *sharing* of linguistic and cognitive habits," Paolo Virno argues, "is the constituent element of the post-Fordist process of labor"—and therefore the "culture industry," he continues, becomes "the matrix of post-Fordism"—and when this is so, knowledge qua material is worked over all the more vigorously and expertly.[102] For film and television workers, John Caldwell says, "knowledge about the industry" becomes "highly coded, managed, and inflected." In such work there is an odd tension between the insider's self-reflection and the product pitched to the outside. "The tendency to narrate one's career in public," Caldwell says, becomes "typical of above-the-line creative personnel."[103] In part, what this does for industry personnel is tell the tale of their luck from the artificially constructed standpoint of superior knowledge. They have been saved from the precarity that defines the industry. There must be "someone inside," as J. D. Connor explains, who "is responsible." The "Neoclassical Hollywood," as Connor calls it, makes its name on the wager that "there is no luck, only knowledge."[104] Indeed, Connor calls this period "Neoclassical Hollywood" to signal that a main activity in New Hollywood has been to restore coherence to the studios *imaginatively* after they had lost it *materially*. In such a project, the movies become a vehicle for imagining a connection between themselves as product and the set of arrangements responsible for producing them. Hence, the textuality of New Hollywood is given over to self-examination, veering between self-regarding professionalism (which includes stylistic displays, film-historical allusion, and late-modernist medium specificity); corporate allegory (which issues most often from those who had self-incorporated); and the period's well-known paranoia.

In this light we might return to Frank Yablans. If the Directors Company was a false start, Yablans regained his footing as an independent producer in the late '70s. "Having been liberated from the presidency of a studio," he said, "I fe[lt] free to be more creative."[105] Like Zanuck and Brown at 20th Century Fox, Yablans felt that only by escaping the Paramount hierarchy would he be able to set the terms for his self-regard. In making *The Fury* (De Palma, 20th Century Fox, 1978), Yablans called himself an "auteur producer." On this movie Yablans seems to have learned the value of New Hollywood textuality in claiming one's place in the industry. In it, the government plots to use psychics in its geopolitical projects, but the casting of Hollywood independents Kirk Douglas and John Cassavetes converts its tale of control and paranoia into an industrial allegory. In its story, the psychic mind is analogized to the cinema: "Visualize sitting in an empty theater in front of a blank screen," a prospective psychic is told, "and let that screen fill your mind." Whoever can achieve this "alpha state" can activate the energies of the object world, just—we might think—as De Palma's camera does. Ultimately, the story is concerned with whether Douglas or Cassavetes will control the most powerful psychic, Robin Sandza. If we see it from De Palma's point of view, then, it is an allegory about who will control his cinema. Though both Douglas and Cassavetes were models of independence, Douglas had found his place within the industry, but Cassavetes had found his place outside it. De Palma had clearly struggled with his own independence in his early career. He was "induced to come to Hollywood in 1970" to make *Get to Know Your Rabbit* (Warner Bros., 1972), during which he clashed with the star, Tommy Smothers, and afterward the movie was reedited by a studio executive and released two years later. "You have to be very wary of those situations," he said. "All my other pictures have been made because I was committed to them. It is dangerous to get into a situation where somebody is more powerful than you are." By the time he made *The Fury*, though, he had become "bankable" thanks to *Carrie* (United Artists, 1976).[106] In the last scene, De Palma explodes Cassavetes, and in the gesture, we might think that De Palma has foreclosed the possibility of a career for himself outside the industry.[107]

Here, I am less interested in pressing this particular reading any further than I am in suggesting that this particular movie registers a tendency among filmmakers to sensitize one's textual material to one's industrial situation. Yablans seems to have understood that with independent production comes storytelling of this kind.

In method, my study attends to how filmmakers reconceived their relations to the industry amid the proliferation of small firms and the conglomeration of studios. Chapter 1 begins with Kirk Douglas's establishment of Bryna Productions and the geopolitical evolution of the Hollywood western in the 1950s. The genre was a cathexis for Douglas, for various reasons, but when he called on it in *Lonely Are the Brave* (Miller, Universal International, 1962), he was deploying the cowboy figure not for the older associations it had with a pastoral life removed from modernity but for its resonance with figures of guerrilla organization arising within the post-Fordist phase of modernity that he himself was negotiating. His affinity for the western helped him imagine the ideological stakes in his relation to Universal Pictures as an "independent" producer. Douglas used its narrative to reset his industrial self-understanding. But if he was disappointed with the reception of *Lonely Are the Brave*, I argue that it is because industrial self-understanding would need to be renegotiated not at the level of film narrative but at the level of film form.

In chapter 2, I argue that those movies claiming "outsider" credentials for themselves—such as *The Graduate, Bonnie and Clyde*, and other titles in what I call the genre of defection—did so by way of bravura style and modernist form. To suggest that there were new ways that stories could be told and nonnormative ways that cameras could be used was to repudiate the norms held in place by the guilds and unions and to mark oneself off from the industry. The brandishing of a postclassical style allowed the so-called auteurs to imagine that they were outsiders in the Hollywood industry. Robert Altman, however, deconstructed what I am calling the defection movie in *Brewster McCloud* (MGM, 1970), suggesting that when auteurs imagined they were transcending the grubbiness of the industry, they were only reworking its practices from within. Because Altman was not deceived by the auteurist discourse, he started a company of his own, Lion's Gate, to better control his situation within the industry. In the process, Altman enlisted the ethos of the counterculture to reengineer the corporation.

It is possible that no one learned more from Robert Altman than Richard Zanuck. Altman had made *MASH* (1970) for Richard Zanuck and David Brown when they were first- and second-in-command at 20th Century Fox. *MASH* was a great success, and it reached the newly uncovered "youth market." But its legacy has always been in dispute: Altman has claimed that it succeeded in spite of the studio, whose bosses were distracted enough by their larger productions, *Patton* (Schaffner, 1970) and *Tora! Tora! Tora!* (Fleischer, 1970), that he could escape studio orthodoxies and create an autonomous subunit of his own within the studio. Though *MASH* was produced under Zanuck's aegis, and the risk for undertaking it was his own, in most accounts the credit falls to Altman. When Zanuck and Brown formed their own small production company, the small-unit autonomy that Altman had modeled for them was surely an influence. Because Zanuck-Brown made *Jaws*, the continuity between their company and Altman's at the level of production is lost in the historiography. Moreover, because Steven Spielberg has since become so successful in commercial terms, the continuities between him and his fellow auteurist directors (Scorsese, De Palma, et al.) has often been retroactively downplayed. In her study of the '70s boom in special-effects cinema, Julie Turnock insists that though the work of Steven Spielberg and George Lucas is often considered "the opposite of the auteurist-driven 'personal' film," their films should be understood as "extensions of this ethos, not rejections of it." Critics are now tempted to view "*Star Wars* and *Close Encounters* as the beginning of an end," Turnock notes, but "it is clear from reviews and critical commentary that both films were received enthusiastically as a fresh and exciting development in auteur-driven popular filmmaking."[108]

In chapter 3, I put Spielberg's early career and Zanuck-Brown directly on the heels of Altman in effort to restore them to this historical moment. Indeed, Spielberg's first theatrical feature was a defection movie, *The Sugarland Express*, which he believed fared poorly at the box office because it dropped in the same period as two other defection movies, *Badlands* (Malick, Warner Bros., 1973) and Altman's *Thieves Like Us* (United Artists, 1974). The genre had by then been exhausted, and hence Spielberg combined its impulse with the disaster movie in his next feature, *Jaws*. Turnock astutely notes that not only were Spielberg and Lucas received in the moment as auteurs, but they described their aesthetic projects in terms of avant-garde traditions of "pure cinema" and "graphic dynamism."[109] From the perspective of Zanuck and Brown, who were both eager to reestablish their creative bona fides, Spielberg was avant-garde enough to help them declare the medium specificity of cinema as the Zanuck-Brown Company was being rolled into the corporate structure of Universal, whose media production had largely been given over to television. If *Jaws* reconfigured Hollywood marketing in 1975, the Academy Awards ceremony the next year was the theatrical moment in which New Hollywood declared its own hegemony and consigned Old Hollywood to the past. In that year's ceremony, Bert Schneider received the Best Documentary Oscar for *Hearts and Minds* (Davis, Columbia, 1975) and relayed greetings from the Provisional Revolutionary Government of Vietnam, signaling both that the Vietnam War was over and that the youth movements had taken over in Hollywood and elsewhere.

In chapter 4, I turn to Schneider's BBS Productions, which produced such movies as *Five Easy Pieces* and *The King of Marvin Gardens* (Rafelson, Columbia, 1972), as a case study in this process, demonstrating that its corporate architecture took shape in the seam between the inside and outside of the capitalist system, drawing legitimacy from its association with various countercultural forces such as the Black Panthers. BBS, perhaps more than any other Hollywood firm, squared the circle by converting the counterculture critique of the corporation into its corporate identity. In turn, it was able to solicit an identification between self-regarding artists and corporate culture, which has been prolonged in the management theory of Tom Peters and others in our contemporary period.

It is worth noting, finally, the case studies I could not include. In chapter 4 I gesture to Jane Fonda's IPC Films, but I do not consider her company in depth. In part, this owes to the decision to end my study in 1975, and Fonda's company flowed from the Vietnam documentary she produced with Tom Hayden and Haskell Wexler in late 1974. Her company is nonetheless fascinating for the way it refracts second-wave feminism (which, in general, found little traction in New Hollywood) and the way it helped mainstream Fonda after her radical period in the early '70s. Nor do I make a case study of any of the effects houses or tech boutiques that arose in the period. Though these firms are not production companies per se, they were nonetheless constituted in the post-Fordist image of their era. Robert Abel and Associates, in particular, exhibited many of the traits defining post-Fordist labor. Abel was charismatic and driven by an inner quest to do something beautiful. His studio operated on "a pressurized schedule, twenty-four hours a day, seven days a week," but Sherry McKenna says that while he "worked us to the bone" and "didn't pay us well," his employees "idolized him because for the first time in our lives, and probably the last, we worked for a man who only cared about doing quality work."[110]

The book ends, instead, by skipping to the contemporary moment. In the afterword I reflect on the state of New Hollywood today by offering a brief analysis of Pixar as an avatar of the auteur theory as corporate philosophy in today's creative economy. In Pixar, we see the fusion of the tech boutique and the small production company—its culture seemingly preserved in amber with the vexed status of gender still unresolved.

# 1

# POST (HENRY AND JOHN) FORDISM

## Kirk Douglas and Guerrilla Economy

*For small production companies, however, the militarist strategy is as likely to follow the "special ops" ethos.*

John Caldwell, *Production Culture*

n the concluding scenes of *Billy Jack* (Laughlin, Warner Bros., 1971) the maverick Billy—rather overcoded as cowboy, Native American, Vietnam vet, and martial arts expert—barricades himself inside a church as a fugitive to resist seizure by law enforcement for his murder of the mayor's son. It is a curious move that in such an anti-institutional movie, the hero flees the reach of institutions precisely by hiding *within* one. But what makes it seem less a curiosity than a kind of hermeneutical linchpin is that it recurs throughout this transformational period in several key movies, namely *Cool Hand Luke* (Rosenberg, Warner-Seven, 1967) and *First Blood* (Kotcheff, Orion, 1982). In the former Luke Jackson hides from pursuing officers inside a church, and in the latter John Rambo escapes into the police station itself, but from the former to the latter, the value of what we might call the extrainstitutional figure—Luke, Rambo—has clearly changed. Luke dies; Rambo does not. And though this observation can be complicated by referring to the

Aristotelian functions of death and marriage, I will save that for my chapter 2 analysis of the routinization of death as closure in Hollywood narratives of 1967–1974. For now I limit my focus to the fact that from Luke to Rambo, the outsider becomes an object of recuperation rather than expulsion. It is already at work in movies of the late '60s and early '70s: even if a site like the church seems to operate as an embassy does, outside local jurisdiction, it is only another setting where the same institutional program can be carried out in another register. One only needs to compare the use of the crucifix in *Cool Hand Luke*, where, hovering over the police cruisers, it seems to sanction the law's repression (see fig. 1.1), with *The Graduate* (Nichols, Embassy, 1967), where Benjamin locks everyone behind church doors with it (see fig. 1.2), to see that Luke had always been sealed away in institutional life by his messianic self-image. In the disciplinary society, the age of factories, Michel Foucault called this the "carceral archipelago," wherein "penitentiary techniques" are spread throughout "the entire social body" so as to absorb the "uncertain space" that was once home to the "outlaw"; Gilles Deleuze thought this was superseded in the "society of control," wherein the "enclosure" of the "factory" is replaced by the "mold" of the "corporation," signaling that "one is never finished with anything"; by whatever name, the feeling that "there is no outside" emerges in assorted forms during the postwar period as the culture of Fordism—and its emblem, the factory—lost its sway and a more total, more enveloping structure of modernity took shape in its undoing.[1]

We can return now to the fact that Luke dies while Rambo lives. Kirk Douglas turned down the role of Rambo's mentor, what became Richard Crenna's part, because it did not square with him.[2] Douglas thought Rambo should die. He thought this not because Luke's death cast a permanent destiny for the outsider but because in an earlier movie that *First Blood* insistently recalls—Douglas's *Lonely Are the Brave*, his "favorite movie"—the logic of the material required the protagonist to die. There, Jack Burns (Kirk Douglas) is an outsider because he has been trained in a social code belonging to a world other than the one he inhabits. It is the social code of the westerner; Burns is a cowboy, and he has been displaced by modernity. The movie concludes in a manhunt, with the full

FIGURE 1.1 In *Cool Hand Luke*, Luke seeks refuge in the church, but in this image we see that the church is aligned with the state by the placement of the crucifix above the police cruiser.

FIGURE 1.2 In *The Graduate*, Benjamin locks the church doors with a crucifix.

apparatus of state law enforcement brought to bear on Jack Burns, who eludes it nonetheless. No matter its manpower, no matter its technology, the state is outmatched tactically. There is a lesson here about technologized officers being alienated from nature and in turn rendered unequal to those trained in nature, and it is easy to transpose this lesson, as *First Blood* does, into a story about the Vietnam War. Douglas simplifies the story: "I love the theme that if you try to be an individual, society will crush you."[3] It is the man-against-mass-society theme, in other words, which was so definitive of postwar culture and the 1950s in particular: the smallness of primitive organization against the tendential bigness of modernity. From the other side of the '60s we can see that in telling the story of the holdout cowboy in modernity, Douglas was telling the story of the guerrilla warrior. What we see in the historical defile of Jack Burns/Luke/Billy Jack/Rambo is the transformation of the Hollywood western as the modernist ratio of small to big is socially renegotiated.

Inscribed, too, in their images, those of outsiders made internal to institutional life, is a microhistory of "independent" production in Hollywood. Douglas formed Bryna Productions in 1955, making its debut *The Indian Fighter* (De Toth, United Artists, 1956), which, his publicist Stan Margulies wrote in a press release, concerned an "Indian fighter who finds, as civilization moves westward, that he has more in common with his old enemies, the Indians, than with the white settlers."[4] This dis-identification with the majoritarian politics of Classical Hollywood— its themes of nation building, with the Native American taken for a bogey—was made, it happens, with the "financing and distribution" of United Artists, a key studio within Classical Hollywood. By the time Douglas produced *Lonely Are the Brave*, it was for Universal; the part Universal plays in this history is a main topic of this chapter. But it is worth noting that while United Artists was traditionally the studio to welcome independent producers, by the end of the '50s and into the '60s the same role was filled by all the studios. Jalem Productions had assembled *Cool Hand Luke* before shopping it to Columbia, who were put off by a movie ending in Paul Newman's death, and finally selling it to Warner Bros., who saw in Newman's death an updating of their studio identity, predicated as that was on the regular deaths of the James Cagney and Edward G. Robinson characters. In the same year that *Cool Hand Luke* was released, Joseph E. Levine of Embassy Pictures produced *The Graduate*. Tom Laughlin then famously made *Billy Jack* by the force of his own personality, first losing backing from American International Pictures and then gaining it from Warner Bros. Finally, Anabasis brought the package of *First Blood* to Orion, which was nothing more than the United Artists executives (Arthur Krim, Eric Pleskow, and Robert

Benjamin) regrouped under another name after Transamerica had dismissed them from the studio whose identity they had anchored. This is only a microhistory, as suggested, because it plucks from the dense weave of Hollywood cinema a set of movies in the tradition of "industrial reflexivity."[5]

What this chapter seeks to describe is the way the Hollywood western was arrogated by talent on the make—actors and directors who, unhappy with their portion of industrial power, incorporated and brokered their own deals—and the way the genre came to mirror the political economy between Hollywood and the global order enfolding it. This chapter tracks the western as it changed, globalized as it were, in light of the Second World War. On one hand the genre would bear the preoccupations of individual agents, such as John Ford, George Stevens, and William Wyler, who went to war and then made westerns in relation to it. But on the other hand the genre would float with tendencies inside the industry and outside it, most saliently the rush to deterritorialize production and financialize assets. Doing this long enough spelled the undoing of the genre. In this event, the figure of the cowboy would cede its rhetorical force in legitimizing economic relations to the figure of the artist in what at first blush seems an unlikely succession story. The cowboy was the narrative icon of industrial economy, I argue, but the artist—the manipulator of signs—would become the narrative icon of a fully financialized economy. I give a brief reading of *An Unmarried Woman* (Mazursky, 20th Century Fox, 1978) as a kind of allegory of this process, even something near an insider's account of it. But while at a general level my argument sets up an interpretive schema for the western genre in the '50s, it shifts scales to consider Douglas's western *Lonely Are the Brave* in relation to the broad prerogatives of his company, Bryna, as a particular episode, perhaps even a defining one, in this transformational period of political economy.[6] A collaboration between Kirk Douglas and Dalton Trumbo, derived from a source novel by Edward Abbey, *Lonely Are the Brave* brings into a coherent framework issues that sometimes jar in later movies like *Billy Jack*, such as the pairing of guerrilla warfare and "knowledge work," the army and academia, and B-movie aesthetics and art-cinema values. It does so, significantly, in a manner that illuminates how Hollywood changed in step with—or maybe a step before—the world economy.

## "HOLLYWORLD" AND THE POSTWAR WESTERN

The western genre was clearly a dominant form of postwar culture, as statistics attest.[7] André Bazin, narrating its evolution, claims that before the war, the genre had "reached a definitive stage of perfection" thanks to *Stagecoach* (Ford, United Artists, 1939), and afterward "some new development seemed inevitable" but was "delayed" by "four years of war."[8] This is Bazin the Idealist speaking. The idea of the western, in Bazin's phrasing, was just waiting out the war until Hollywood resources could again be allocated to it. But he leaves space for a materialist account even if he himself only gives it impressionistically: its "evolution" needed explaining not simply in relation to the level the idea had attained "but also in terms of the events of 1941 to 1945."[9] One undeniable effect of *Stagecoach* was that it raised the western to the level of prestige genre, and what the A-picture makers then did, Bazin argues, was appropriate the genre as a means to absorb issues "extrinsic" to it, such as *The Ox-Bow Incident* (Wellman, 20th Century Fox, 1943) did with civil rights or *High Noon* (Zinnemann, United Artists, 1952) did with McCarthyism.[10] This, for Bazin, is tied to the war, but the causality is murky. At best we can imagine that the war forced from filmmakers a different degree of seriousness, and thus the genre was only tolerable to them if they hitched it to other "intellectual or aesthetic alibis."[11]

But I prefer to assay the same question through a narrower aperture. A way to begin this narrowing is to note that John Ford, the genre's self-styled ambassador, left Hollywood shortly after making *Stagecoach* in order to enlist in the navy and form the Field Photo Unit, which was designed to shoot war documentaries. His prewar movies—*Stagecoach* and *The Grapes of Wrath* (20th Century Fox, 1940)—were marked by New Deal populism, but his postwar movies took on another tone, starting with what Scott Simmon calls the noir inflection of his first

western back, *My Darling Clementine* (20th Century Fox, 1946), and culminating in what many deem the genre's valediction, *The Man Who
Shot Liberty Valance* (Paramount, 1962).[12] The point here is to amplify
Mark Harris's argument that Hollywood personnel, changed by their
war experiences, helped in turn to change Hollywood.[13] Following the
war, Harris says, George Stevens looked for projects that "reflected his
changed understanding of the world" and did so because he was among
the first to see Dachau and other camp atrocities.[14] "The war," Frank
Capra said, "had caused American filmmakers to see the movies that
studios had been turning out 'through new eyes' and to recoil from the
'machine-like treatment' that . . . made most pictures look and sound the
same."[15] This led Frank Capra, George Stevens, and William Wyler, to
declare independence from the studios by starting their own company,
Liberty Films. Even if the filmmakers involved in the war had been
assigned to different units (the Field Photo Unit, the Signal Corps), the
experience they had in common was frustration in the face of military
dysfunction. Its scale was too great and its jurisdictions always confused:
George Stevens was sent to Tunisia after action had ceased and there was
nothing left for him to do, William Wyler was stuck waiting in London,
and John Huston was tasked with making a documentary that was then
banned from screening. Stevens complained, "We wait for someone
higher up to tell us what to do. We are never told because no one higher
up presumes to know what to tell us."[16] Ford got things done, namely the
combat record *The Battle of Midway* (1942), only when he ignored protocol; he was otherwise an "officebound bureaucrat," idling away his
time.[17] It was a lesson in organizational culture brought on largely by the
scale of the military, but Huston would say of it that the "same psychol-
ogy prevails" in the army as in his home business, "the movies."[18]

Not only were these directors caught within the internal governance
of a huge organization, the war also called into question any natural
overlap between an organization and a territory. An immediate cause
of this were the Nuremberg trials, which Ford had provisional interest
in filming (though he did not) and for which Stevens made two documentaries, *Nazi Concentration and Prison Camps* and *The Nazi Plan*
(both 1945), assignments which were to be "entered into evidence."

A final documentary from the Field Photo Unit, *That Justice Be Done* (1946)—made after Ford returned to Hollywood, perhaps using footage Stevens had presented in *The Nazi Plan*—tried squaring Nazi war crimes with the jurisprudence of the interstate system: "We cannot translate our traditional concepts of justice," says the voice-over, "into the unprecedented machinery of international law overnight." For this, the UN International Tribunal was chartered, addressed to "crimes so all-embracing" that their status was translocal, being matters of human rights rather than reducible to civil rights. Ford was close to this process since his mentor in the armed forces, Bill Donovan, was part of the tribunal as assistant to the U.S. chief prosecutor, Robert H. Jackson. I contend that this, in combination with other events of war, changed the postwar uptake of the Hollywood western by Ford, Stevens, and Wyler. The war had historically sensitized these filmmakers to the conjuncture of legal rights and territory where the movies had only mythically sensitized them to it. The myth was handled differently henceforth, not discarded altogether but now presumed to hold historical entailments. For Stevens and Wyler, it seems, their war experience had them purge the western of its violence: in *Shane* (Stevens, Paramount, 1953) and *The Big Country* (Wyler, United Artists, 1958) the protagonists foreswear armed violence to the degree that they can. But in Ford's postwar westerns he would radicalize the genre, pressing the logic of its main concepts, sovereignty key among them, until they collapsed into themselves.

The most striking outcome of Ford's rigorous interaction with the genre was the reversal in how he represented Native Americans, what Bazin would call the "political rehabilitation of the Indian."[19] In *Stagecoach*, Indians are there to be shot, showing up as a menacing outcropping of the landscape, the better to consolidate the microcommunity within the coach.[20] But in the heartbreaking late scenes of *Cheyenne Autumn* (Warner Bros., 1964) the alterity imposed on the Native Americans is transferred onto the administrators of community life, whose obedience to chain of command ("orders are orders") leaves them "stark-raving mad." For its wholeness, the community must now fend off the "superior authority" within it, coded as German rationality in Karl Malden's Nazi-ish performance as Captain Oscar Wessels (he tells Dull

Knife, the Cheyenne chief, that he "is brave but no longer *vise*," with wisdom meaning carrying out orders without question). The scenes leading up to the massacre in *Cheyenne Autumn* stay in the perspective of the Cheyenne, and some in the cavalry try speaking on their behalf. "Sir, I only know what those Cheyenne have gone through," reports Captain Archer (Richard Widmark). "If the people had seen it, they wouldn't have liked it." My point is not that Ford had gained sympathy for Native Americans, though it seems he did, but rather that the logic of the western, as he worked it out, suggested that anyone could be deterritorialized, and the Native American was simply a figure for this. Jacques Rancière has similarly interpreted the "Indian turn" in the genre (*Broken Arrow* [Daves, 20th Century Fox, 1950] is an early instance, and *Ulzana's Raid* [Aldrich, Universal, 1972] a late). Maybe what it "really means," Rancière says, is "not the discovery that Indians are also human beings who think, love, and suffer, but rather the feeling that their expropriation spells out a common destiny."[21]

Another figure that comes out of Ford's reckoning with the western is the border raider, bearing out Rancière's modernist concern that we are all potentially deracinated. Ethan Edwards (John Ford) is the most ambiguous and perhaps the most dramatically compelling iteration of this figure. In the opening of *The Searchers* (Warner Bros., 1956), Ethan's arrival at his brother's home with a sack of gold makes him morally suspicious because, if he was once loyal to the Confederacy, he now seems out for personal profit. This question of disloyalty—raised by the war's revealing that borders are a matter of chance anyway—reacted back into the center of postwar westerns. Another movie of the period, *The Law and Jake Wade* (Sturges, MGM, 1958), puts a fine point on the meaning of the border raider. In it, Jake (Robert Taylor) and Clint (Richard Widmark) were "in the same outfit" in the Civil War, "a guerrilla unit raiding Northern border towns." Jake explains, "We'd shoot our way in, loot the town, then shoot our way out." But Jake qualifies, "*I* was doing it as a soldier. Clint did it because, well, that's the same thing he'd always done. The war hadn't changed his life a bit." Clint's response—"It just made it legal" and "During the war they made me an officer and a gentlemen for doing the same things they was gonna hang me for [later on]"—throws into relief the fact that jurisdiction is decided in the state of exception that war creates, a fact that is partially responsible for lending the Hollywood western the intellectual vigor that, in the right hands, made it both a popular and a complex genre in the years following the Second World War.

This complexity, Bazin thinks, derives from the "novelization" of the western, meaning that its characters were treated in terms of their motivation from within and their molding from without rather than in archetypal terms as had been the custom.[22] Anthony Mann is, for Bazin, the director presiding over the transition from national epic to novel. Jeanine Basinger, too, says that Mann "modernized" the genre, which means, I take it, roughly what its novelization means, namely that the natural relation between character and nation that obtained in the epic had been laid bare as a constructed relation, the more in doubt for being understood so.[23] This is what makes Mann's protagonists uneasy and always searching for their land. Here I want to turn to *Bend of the River* (Mann, Universal International, 1952) because, while it is all the things that are implied by "novelistic," its concern with the characterological is equal to its concern with political economy, such that it illuminates genre themes in relation to what Hannah Arendt calls the "decline of the nation-state" on one hand and to Hollywood's industrial reconfiguration (typified by Lew Wasserman's deals with Universal) on the other hand.[24] The main figures in *Bend of the River* are border raiders. Glyn McLyntock (Jimmy Stewart) and Emerson Cole (Arthur Kennedy) are paired opposites, both former border raiders—constituted, it seems, between territories—but each now choosing a different trajectory. Cole cannot believe that "McLyntock of the border" now wants to be "a rancher," committed to the land, because Cole has "picked out another star . . . hanging over California, . . . all full of gold," he says. He refers to the Gold Rush, of course, but the "gold" hanging over California works properly enough within the movie's polyvalent Technicolor schema to suggest the same decoupling of Hollywood finance from California land that the genre's trend toward "runaway production" was facilitating. While McLyntock is helping settlers establish farms in Oregon, Cole ultimately realizes that the food supply being transported to the farms can be shunted instead to the "gold camps," where people will buy the commodity more dearly. The commodity is food, of course, but the movie creates a perspective in which its thingliness will not matter (since its only use is its exchange) just as it creates another, contending perspective in which its speculative exchange will not matter (since you cannot eat a future exchange rate). A paradox of this story, I will show, is that it questions whether the cowboy hero is relevant—that is, whether his ethical commitments still matter—given the economic realities that the movie itself is helping to set in place. But that makes it the kind of self-questioning commodity that in time will define New Hollywood.

Consider this economics lesson in its most immediate sphere of relevance. Jimmy Stewart, like other stars, had begun to realize his value not by way of fixed contracts but by way of short-term speculation. The architects behind this new-style package were Lew Wasserman and the stable of MCA agents over whom Wasserman had assumed control from his former boss, Jules Stein, following the war. When Stewart first teamed with Anthony Mann, Wasserman packaged their effort, *Winchester '73* (Mann, Universal International, 1950), with the more promising *Harvey* (Koster, Universal International, 1950), and he got Stewart net points on *Winchester*'s profit—50 percent, in fact—in exchange for a cut rate ($150,000) on the movie rights to *Harvey*, which had been a Broadway hit.[25] Taking in $2.25 million, *Winchester* did much better in the box office than *Harvey*, and Stewart received $600,000 in its release year rather than what would have been his $200,000 salary. The deal became famous. For the next Stewart-Mann collaboration, *Bend of the River*, MCA got Stewart the same points from Universal International, and into the deal they mixed a script that, while something of a spin on the themes of their other westerns—both *Winchester* and *Naked Spur* (Mann, MGM, 1953)—plays like a commentary on the deal that Universal International had made. But it works, too, to prefigure the fate of Universal (sans International) as a site of production, a fate that Wasserman was busy preparing throughout the 1950s.

If the script allegorizes the inflation of the Hollywood star by way of its financialization, as I shall argue, what it suggests is precisely the way that inflating the star-as-asset would let Wasserman undermine the

integrity of the studio (Universal in this case, but all of them in time) as
a territory-bound entity: capital against country, to put the story in other
terms. There is a constant argument coursing through *Bend of the River*
about whether a commitment to capital or country will make for a more
loyal community. The piety that the western had serviced so long—that
land, cultivated in common, is a people's bond—makes less obvious sense
to the border raiders: "What would you rather have," Cole asks McLyntock, "a hundred thousand dollars or a thank-you somebody will take
back in a few weeks?" The fickle thank-you refers, within the plot, to the
settlers. "Could be they won't take it back," McLyntock says. "If they
don't, I figure that's worth more than a hundred thousand dollars." The
food is worth more than the sum of dollars, McLyntock wagers, if it leads
to long-term community. Heard in another context, this sounds like an
argument for what stars ought to like about studios. Kirk Douglas recalls
the days "when everyone was dying to be under contract because it was
safe, it was guaranteed income." But those days had passed for him,
because when he was making his career, "it was like slavery."[26] Like
Jimmy Stewart, Kirk Douglas is something of a transitional figure.
But if Stewart's McLyntock seems to uphold the values of the settlers,
and if in the final shot-countershot he is shown clasping the hand of
their community's matriarch, his green jacket matching her green
shirt and the green grass and water lilies behind her, he is, for all that,
less surely the pure hero he appears to be. The argument about loyalty
earlier in the movie was cast in this Technicolor schema, with the deep
greens connoting land and the lush colors its yield. Jeremy, the settler
patriarch, says that since Cole was a border raider, he "can't change"—
"When an apple's rotten," he tells McLyntock as the two men gather red
apples in a barrel, "there's nothing you can do except throw it away or
it'll spoil the whole barrel." For McLyntock, constituted between territories, the concern is that he can now no longer belong to any land.
When we assume this as the deep background for McLyntock's debate
with Cole ("a hundred thousand dollars or a thank-you somebody will
take back in a few weeks"), we in turn restore the complexity of Stewart's own situation. When the money was offered to him, he was without the guarantees of his earlier MGM contract, and his star, like that

of his benefactor Frank Capra, was on the wane.[27] He took the $100,000—or six times that, thanks to Lew Wasserman's engineering—and it constituted him as a star between studios, seemingly in the dubious position that Emerson Cole recommends. But in a late scene in *Bend of the River*, it is Jeremy who has a change of heart, assuring Stewart qua McLyntock, "There is a difference between apples and men." Men do not grow from soil, suggests the "modernized" western.

The point to make is that first John Ford and then Anthony Mann were refashioning the genre's principles in a way that would comport with the changing Hollywood industry. Jimmy Stewart could drift from studio to studio, since he was a man and not an apple, and his drifting fit into the movement away from "the studio" as a place and toward it functioning strictly as a concept. Universal best exemplifies this. When Stewart and Mann made *Bend of the River*, they shot the exteriors on Mount Hood in Oregon, as their Technicolor, wide-screen production was the closest Universal-International had to a "prestige picture." Universal was otherwise profiting increasingly from renting its lot to Revue for telefilm productions. Wasserman's MCA was the parent company of Revue, which meant that Universal was afloat on his capital, and in 1958 he and MCA took the next step and proposed to "buy everything but the studio—the land, the soundstages, the sets, the warehouses, the vaults, and the offices."[28] On the face of it, this seems strange, because what was Universal if not its land, sound stages, offices, and so on?

Its essence, in fact, was laid bare in this transaction: it was a corporation, a capital structure, and a brand, in no way reducible to any one of its concrete holdings. In this—its capital structure, its strategies for expansion—MCA pledged no interference. They bought the land and leased it back to Universal for "a fee of $1 million a year."[29] Studio president Milton Rackmil made the deal because Universal needed the capital if it was going to compete with the other studios, which had always been better leveraged than it was. But, as Dennis McDougal establishes, the MCA purchase of Universal's real estate did not signal their commitment to production; they wanted the brand, the corporate entity itself, but Wasserman knew that Rackmil would not sell it outright. MCA did finally buy Universal in 1962, and by then the point had been made—across Hollywood, as Fox, Paramount, and others sold off real estate—that "the studio" was not a site of production but a framework for internalizing transactions. This first stage of horizontally reintegrating what the studio system had famously held together vertically, Aida Hozic argues, "represents the key point of distinction between the manufacturers' economy of the Hollywood studio era and the contemporary merchant economy."[30] The shift, in Hozic's analysis, is from making things to selling things. However, what she calls a "merchant economy," I prefer to call the process of financialization, a mode of economy in which the work of production no longer drives value but rather is the far-removed source of underlying assets that are now cycling through new ensembles of valuation.[31] The film libraries, of course, furnish the ideal example of this because, in the hands of circumspect studios such as Paramount, their sale was timed, like a stock, for the highest yield.[32]

The hollowing out of Hollywood production—the selling of studio real estate and libraries—can look like a couple of things. From one perspective, it can simply look like the relocation of jobs. Universal had less need for its lots because more and more movies were made on location, whether in Mount Hood, Oregon, or increasingly, in Europe. After the studios were broken up as places, in other words, they were reassembled as global networks that were held fast, if I can invoke Peter Drucker's phrase, by the "concept of the corporation."[33] The factory was a place, but the corporation, Drucker argues, was a way to conceptualize "human relationships" that would grant "social purpose" in the degree that it refused factory organization.[34] The Hollywood western, in this sense, resonates with the "diffusion of production and the opening of the postwar economy in general," as Hozic puts it, because it evokes what Paolo Virno calls the mid-nineteenth-century "mass exodus from the regime of the factory" that let "American workers" venture into the "'frontier' to colonize inexpensive land" and "reverse their own initial condition."[35] But the relocation of jobs to Europe tended to benefit above-the-line talent, what I have called "talent on the make," at the expense of the crews and technicians and craftspeople. What Hozic has called "Hollyworld"— the "transformation of Hollywood from a company town into a global factory"—was "directly related to increasing labor costs."[36] Hollywood unions themselves recognized that by the end of the '50s, "wages in Europe were approximately 50 percent lower than in the United States."[37]

We can dramatize the difference between above-the-line talent and the crafts by foreshadowing the case study that will bind this chapter: Kirk Douglas. Douglas was offered $1.5 million by the Bronston Group to do a Roman epic in Spain because the cost of extras was cheap enough to mount epic-scale productions. Douglas turned down the role, but not because its labor implications worried him. When his Bryna Productions shot *The Vikings* (Fleischer, United Artists, 1958) in Norway, after all, the crew went on strike for higher wages. "I was shocked," Douglas claimed, because he had thrown them a big party with an open bar. They were friends, he had thought. "After this wonderful party of camaraderie," he said, "this infuriated me."[38] Rather than negotiate with them, he determined that the remaining shots could be done on sound stages in Munich (which was destitute and desperate for movies after the war), so he packed up his production and left Norway in favor of lower costs. Hence, Hozic's retention of the term "factory"—"global factory"—is correct enough if indexed to "workers" who remained within its regime as opposed to "talent" who had putatively escaped it.

In another, more world-historical perspective, a hollowed-out Hollywood looks like an expected phase of political economy. Giovanni Arrighi shows that within the "*longue durée*" of capitalist development, the "relocation of processes of capital accumulation from high-income to low-income countries" signals that the commitment to fixed production has flagged as it always will.[39] Whatever profits Hollywood had secured under a certain configuration—what we call the "classical" moment—had gone into terminal decline. The means of production will be liquidated at such times, Arrighi says, and returned to their money form, free to pursue more eclectic channels of valorization.[40] Among the major studios, Paramount over the course of the 1950s furnishes an explicit case of the turn from fixed production toward finance capital. Timothy White explains that after settling with the Justice Department, Paramount chose not to intensify production—which is to say not do more of what it did, *make movies*—but to fortify its capital structure.[41]

Throughout the '50s Paramount began buying back its stock to control both its price and the amount of it outstanding. By March 1960, "the company spent about $44 million to purchase 1,631,000 shares," White notes, cutting the amount of its stock nearly in half.[42] One effect was that it held steady the level of its annual dividend; another was that it "increased the value of the stock at a slow but steady rate."[43] Rather than double down on new productions, Paramount began in this period to reissue its popular older movies such as *The Lady Eve* (Sturges, 1941) and *Holiday Inn* (Sandrich, 1942) and thus "capitalized on an asset which was valuable but not producing revenue."[44] In short, Paramount curbed production and financialized itself. This phase, which Arrighi suggests is a "recurrent world-systemic tendency," was supported by the breakdown in another of what Charles Tilly calls the "master processes" of modernity, namely the cogency of the nation-state as organizing principle.[45] Hannah Arendt argues that the two world wars had induced a "rise of stateless people," whose very existence impeached the sufficiency of the nation-state as a legal framework and threw into crisis "the old trinity of state-people-territory."[46] The state form, Arendt argues, had been transformed from "an instrument of law into an instrument of the nation."[47] In this context, then, the concept of the corporation asserted itself as the more cogent device because people were already defining themselves in relation to a concept—nation—rather than a territory. What this means, in sum, is that when this or that studio relocated jobs to low-income regions, it only particularized what the world economy did on the whole to regenerate itself. It did it as a kind of proof that the suasion of a corporate identity such as Paramount was just as able as a nation or state in organizing what Drucker calls social purpose.

## BRYNA PRODUCTIONS AND THE GUERRILLA WARRIOR

As true as it may be that in postwar geopolitics the corporation grabbed power from the nation-state, the corporation hardly had automatic

legitimacy. By the time Kirk Douglas began to work in studio Hollywood, in fact, Paramount had begun to suffer from its bigness. When
Douglas got to the Paramount lot for his first movie, *The Strange Love
of Martha Ivers* (Milestone, 1946), he saw "picket lines everywhere, people waving clubs, yelling, and pounding on the car."[48] Much like the Disney studios after their move to Burbank, the size of Paramount had
tipped the studio into social disorder marked by labor unrest.[49] Douglas says he was "afraid" that for him, "Hollywood would end" before his
career there could begin. Part of his response was to resist a long-term
contract with the studio. When Douglas founded Bryna in the midfifties, however, he was not opposed to the bigness of the major studios,
nor did he want to smash the system. True, he said the long-term contract was a kind of "slavery," and perhaps what Douglas later meant for
*Spartacus* (Kubrick, Universal International, 1960) to demonstrate was
that the studios, in their decadent phase, needed a vitality that only their
"slaves" had. It is easy to imagine Douglas thinking in these terms when
one hears him recall taking on Arthur Krim at United Artists, who had
planned a movie on the same topic with Yul Brynner called *The Gladi-
ators*. Rather than concede to UA, Douglas wanted to best them. Krim
took out a *Variety* ad saying that UA's movie was budgeted at $5.5 mil-
lion, and Douglas sent him a telegram saying he was "spending five million five hundred thousand and two dollars on Spartacus. Your move."[50]
Krim backed down. Douglas could engage in gamesmanship of this kind
because, by then, he had Wasserman and Universal backing him. But
he was careful in his rhetoric to establish that it was not a revolution but
the redistribution of power that interested him. His publicist, Stan Margulies, found a Thomas Jefferson quote that Bryna might use to defend
*Spartacus* against "the church groups": "Rebellion to Tyrants Is Obedience to God."[51] But who are the tyrants? The movie is ambiguous enough
on this question that it could be a "big hit" with both President Kennedy
and moviegoers in Russia ("They saw it as their revolution," Douglas
claims, "the uprising of the slaves against the masters").[52] To mute the
suggestion that the major studios were the tyrants, Douglas toned down
the language of "revolution" and "rebellion" because, as a Bryna memo
admits, the "industry cannot survive without the majors."[53]

If the industry needed the majors for its infrastructure, it needed the independents, Douglas thought, to adjust its corporate interior to the needs of Hollywood talent. When founding Bryna, the impulse came from Douglas's talent agency, Famous Artists, where they were busy finding ways for him to retain more salary, first through the "eighteen months exemption," which forgave "income taxes on monies earned" if the earner were abroad for "seventeen out of eighteen consecutive months" (an incentive meant not for Hollywood talent but for "construction and oil workers working abroad in the postwar years"), and second through the formation of an independent company.[54] In Bryna's early publicity, they made no bones about this motivation: "As for [Douglas's] reasons for entering the independent field, he is the only performer ever to state, flatly, that the first consideration was financial."[55] The marginal tax rate would have been 90 percent if Douglas's income were personal, but, Stan Margulies explained, it had only a "26 percent bite on a capital gains basis."[56] The idea of forming an independent company had come from his agent and his lawyer—Ray Stark and Sam Norton respectively—as early as 1953, though Bryna did not incorporate until 1954. "If the pictures can be made [for less than $500,000]," Stark told him, "you really have an opportunity to make a killing."[57] But Douglas was always careful to note that in this, both reward and risk were democratized. In some cases, such as one Stark tried working out with Elia Kazan and Budd Schulberg, the independent deal was structured such that "everyone defers for a large percentage of the profits," and the "picture could be made independently for very little money, avoiding studio overhead charges" in order to give the participants "a chance to make a killing."[58] For Bryna to become a company, however, it required the kind of "cooperation and camaraderie," Stark would say, that he had with Douglas's lawyer, Sam Norton; together they could have "a really well integrated organization."[59] What made the company well integrated, ultimately, as it added Stan Margulies and Edward Lewis, was that it developed a culture that made it unlike the studios on one hand and unlike the talent agencies on the other hand. Denise Mann notes that while the talent agencies helped break the studios' monopoly, they did nothing but reproduce, perhaps even intensify, the studios' culture. MCA's culture, for instance, insisted on "uniformity of dress—the requisite dark suit, white shirt, and dark tie—long hours, and a detached, unemotional demeanor" that squared with the "gray flannel" ethos of corporate culture at large.[60] Hence, one of the first Bryna movies, *Spring Reunion* (Pirosh, United Artists, 1957), was meant to be "a white-collar 'Marty,'" Margulies said, aimed, it seems, at the soullessness of corporate labor. When Margulies and Douglas joked with each other about Bryna's culture, they did so in terms of how it undid the company-man style. "Are you wearing ties these days, or playing it cool?" Douglas asked. Margulies responded, "I haven't worn a tie in weeks."[61]

What Bryna allowed Douglas and his staff was the range of choice that a studio would not. Choice in dress code and manner, choice in the material they pursued.[62] Douglas routinely cited his interest in choosing material. "The most exciting part of movie production—and frequently the most creative aspect of the entire process," said his publicist, "comes in finding and selecting story material."[63] Early in his career, when Douglas defied his talent agency and chose his own projects, he found rewards other than the narrow ones imposed on him. When MGM offered him a role in *The Great Sinner*, costarring with Ava Gardner and Gregory Peck, the assured money of it appealed to him less than the opportunity to star in Stanley Kramer's *Champion* (United Artists, 1949) on a "deferred-payment basis."[64] What Kramer offered was not only a lead part but an open, collaborative work relationship. Douglas says of the experience, "We all sat around at my house at Vado Place eating sandwiches and working on the script. Everyone made suggestions. That's the way I like to make a film."[65] The advantage gained in labor environments such as Kramer's would seem obvious to Douglas and his company members: they could work without a script, instead developing one from their assembled interests, and they could get the project together very cheaply. Here was Bryna's business identity as Margulies understood it, the "low overhead, fluidity and mobility of operation."[66] This was their self-understanding. Douglas's lawyer encouraged the firm to "operate with a skeleton staff at a minimum expense."[67] This led at times to their noncompliance with Hollywood unions. In a letter to the firm, Ben Nathanson, legal counsel in Hollywood collective bargaining, warned Bryna that they had been guilty of a pattern found in independent production of hiring "Publicists who are not members of this Local and Publicity Agencies which do not have contracts with the Publicists Association, IATSE [International Alliance of Theatrical Stage Employees] Local 818."[68] Producer Jerry Bresler complained while making *The Vikings* that Douglas's disregard for unions placed Bryna "in an embarrassing position" with the crafts and guilds whose personnel he required.[69] This too would come to characterize New Hollywood production in general, as the small production firm made itself increasingly essential to the major studios by weakening organized labor in relation to them.[70]

Slipping unionized labor was, for Douglas and others following him, a means of slipping Hollywood's regime of labor. Only by attaining organizational smallness could companies like Bryna compete with majors like United Artists. Margulies remarked that Bryna had "no desire to wake up and find you are that worst of all things—a small major studio." Their ambition, as he put it, "to be successful and *small*" made *Spartacus* resonant story material, though the way in which it resonated with discourses of guerrilla warfare exceeded Douglas's control in the moment of its making.[71] Hence, both sides of the Cold War—the Kennedys and the Russians—could read their message from it. Douglas understood this, I argue, and hence he made *Lonely Are the Brave* as part of a theme-and-variation experiment, which allowed him to refine his deployment of the figure of the guerrilla warrior. The "years of 1959 to 1979," according to Max Booth, were the "golden years" for the romanticization of guerrilla war.[72] In 1965 Robert Taber would publish his "widely read paean to guerrillas," *The War of the Flea*, which imputed virtue in battle to the small guerrilla units (the "fleas") because their large opponents had "too much to defend" against an assailant that was "too small . . . and agile . . . to come to grips with."[73] In the moment of *Spartacus*, however, the guerrilla warrior was a polyvalent figure, evoking everything from Mao Tse-tung and the Huk Rebellion in the Philippines to "freedom fighters" in the American tradition. A sign of how equivocal a figure it was appears in the rather unmotivated scene from another 1960 movie, *The Apartment* (Wilder, United Artists), in which the company man C. C. Baxter is asked by a fellow carouser on New Year's Eve what he thinks of Fidel Castro. In this scene it would have been a year since the *fidelistas* had seized Havana, and the throwaway question suggests the unsettling fascination with their revolution. The fidelistas exerted fascination, I believe, not for ideological reasons per se but because they were an object lesson in organizational theory. How did their scruffy band of fighters take down Fulgencio Batista? A commitment to smallness, the theory went, might compel conviction in participants in ways that were unavailable to large organizations, which were typically top-down in their command. That is, Fidel's fighters were not company men. As Douglas would say in the character of Spartacus, "One gladiator is worth any two Roman soldiers that ever lived." The sense that the small army kept its soldiers fitter because they were more invested in their cause certainly helped orient Douglas's own business philosophy. In dealing with Arthur Krim, for instance, he signed off a letter with a jocular wish that at United Artists they not become "fat, successful, and reactionary" in contrast to himself, "a lean, unsuccessful liberal."[74] Hence, for Douglas, the appeal of the guerrilla fighter was that it simultaneously demonstrated a way to remain the more "lean" competitor and a disregard for the rules of engagement (between capital and labor) as Hollywood had established them.

In that perspective *Spartacus* is an interesting, vexed movie because it fuses the topic of slave revolt with Hollywood capital-labor relations that had tipped, in the saga of the blacklist, more and more toward capital.[75] Famously, Douglas contracted one of the Unfriendly Ten— screenwriter Dalton Trumbo—to adapt Howard Fast's 1951 novel, *Spartacus*, when the novelist himself proved unsuited to the task.[76] One can understand Trumbo's prison term and subsequent banishment from Hollywood as simply the upshot of Cold War paranoia; Jon Lewis, however, argues that for the studios, anti-Communist sentiment became a fulcrum for "industry management" at the moment when their absolute hold over it had been ended by the Paramount decree.[77] The strikes that Douglas had seen outside the Paramount lot should be understood, then, as part of the story leading to the incorporation of Bryna first and to the employment of Dalton Trumbo second. Douglas asserted his industry prerogative in the legal form of Bryna, but this legal form, insofar as it was antiestablishment—even insurgent—would require narrative support if it were to gain legitimacy. For this purpose, Dalton Trumbo became Bryna's house narrator. He was the figure of the labor that Hollywood could not integrate, yet could not wholly eject either. Hence, his work was done for a period under pseudonyms (true too for Abraham Polonsky, a.k.a. Ira Wolfert, and Ring Lardner Jr., a.k.a. Philip Rush), which means that such labor was formally valorized by Hollywood all the while that it substantively yielded little for these writers. Trumbo was hardly paid on these assignments, and for several he was awarded Oscars that he could not accept. What *Spartacus* gave him (other than his name in the credit sequence) was story material with allegorical resonance. In it he could examine the gap between formal and substantive authority. But the next movie he wrote for Bryna, *Lonely Are the Brave*, would make the case for the new authority that Douglas's firm represented in much richer terms, largely because it cast those terms in aesthetic and geopolitical idioms whose time was arriving rather than already passing. That is, *Spartacus* marked the end of the '50s and the wide-screen epics that sustained Hollywood's business model in that period; *Lonely Are the Brave* hailed the '60s and the genre revisionism designed to reckon with that business model.

Of course, the genre Bryna chose to revise was the western, its bread-and-butter genre, the one that could be made on the cheap (unlike the wide-screen epic) and still attract large audiences. Throughout the '50s, indeed, the western had become the Hollywood genre of choice for representing the guerrilla warrior, and in particular, the subgenre that Richard Slotkin calls the "Mexico Western" moved "in step with the development of American policy in the struggle for hearts and minds in the Third World and reached its height of popularity in the Vietnam War."[78] Noël Carroll has suggested, moreover, that the Mexico Western is a variant of what Will Wright had called the "Professional Western," which makes it something of a self-divided narrative, insofar as the Professional Western had vehiculated the concerns of the U.S. technocratic class but the Mexico Western variant would put this class in service of Third World revolution.[79] The movies to most insistently stake out this contradictory position, *The Professionals* (Brooks, Columbia, 1966) and *The Wild Bunch* (Peckinpah, Warner-Seven, 1969), arrived later in the '60s in the efflorescence of the so-called Hollywood Renaissance, but a set of movies prefiguring this turn was released in 1962. Michael Coyne says that in that year, the genre began to elegize itself. The output of western movies was at an all-time low (only eleven, including indie productions) and even the production of western television series had been halved since the previous year. For all its quantitative depreciation, though, Coyne says that from a qualitative standpoint, it was "the genre's most remarkable year" owing to the release of *The Man Who Shot Liberty Valance*, *Lonely Are the Brave*, *Ride the High Country* (Peckinpah, MGM), and *How the West Was Won* (Ford, Hathaway, and Marshall, MGM).[80] These movies, each in its own way, signaled the obsolescence of the cowboy hero, but it is worth pairing *The Man Who Shot Liberty Valance* in particular with *Lonely Are the Brave*. In both films a hero of yesteryear must cede his place to a new, more appropriate hero within the present arrangements. In the former Tom Doniphon must lend his force to Ransom Stoddard's legitimacy and, in the process, lose the hand of his beloved Hallie because Stoddard's legitimacy entitles him to the future and therefore a wife. The marriage is symbolic more than romantically pleasing because it represents the possibility of juridical community. In the latter movie, *Lonely Are the Brave*, Jack Burns has always been in love with Jerri, but rather than pursue her, he has approved her marriage to his best friend, Paul Bondi. Again, it is self-sacrifice in the name of juridical community. "It's God's own blessing I didn't get you," Burns tells Jerri, and when she asks why, he gives the rather stock response that he's "a loner clear down deep to my very guts." But here Burns gives an adequate account of cowboy sovereignty—he can "only live with himself," as he puts it—and this amounts to a denial of juridical community. Cowboys are so much themselves, this implies, that no one else can share in their liberties. This is the "man against mass society" theme, as noted previously, but as in *Liberty Valance*, the theme of the "loner" is open to criticism because the movie embeds it in a new context. Both movies provide a foil for the figure of natural law (the loner, the cowboy hero) in the figure of positive law—an abstract law that, though we might mourn the vanishing romance of the sui generis hero, lets us imagine, in compensation, that matters of individual right might sponsor inclusionary rather than exclusionary projects.

This was the project of the'60s, I argue, and it was a fraught project. For all the movies such as *Liberty Valance* and *Lonely Are the Brave* that couple the figures of natural law and positive law, there are also their opposite numbers, that is, movies such as *Advise & Consent* (Preminger, Columbia, 1962), *Dr. Strangelove*, *Seven Days in May* (Frankenheimer, Paramount, 1964), and *Fail-Safe* (Lumet, Columbia, 1964) that show only the figure of positive law in its monstrous extremes. The terror of modernization, these movies suggest, comes after we are lifted from the state of nature. In part, what these movies are reflecting is the rise of the Kennedy men, the Walt Rostows and Mac Bundys, those men whose faith in superior ratiocination led to a basic acceptance of "modernization theory" within JFK's cabinet. This is the technocrat unbound. In *Lonely Are the Brave* the character of Paul Bondi works as a kind of registering apparatus for the fears provoked by modernization. Bondi is a figure whose emergence seems to carry with it the problems that came to a head in the '60s and then defined the decades that followed. I shall call him a knowledge worker. But here I will focus on the cowboy hero, Jack Burns, not because he is the movie's elegiac figure—he is, in qualified form— but because it is clear that there is still some use for him even if the movie, and postwar society generally, does not know yet what it will be. The movie does find one telling use for him: upon escaping jail, Burns and his horse climb a mountain that will admit them into Mexico, and in the manhunt to detain him, the military calls the local sheriff to see whether they can deploy a helicopter in order to give their "personnel a little practical experience." Burns, they think, is the kind of soldier the military will face again, and they need better training to fight his kind. What this means is that Burns is not simply a cowboy whose time has passed but is rather a figure of uneven development—a guerrilla, that is to say—whose time is now. Indeed, the military helicopter is no match for Burns as he downs it with a couple of rifle shots to the tail rotor. The contest between Burns and the helicopter is meant to stage the hubris of the technologized, bureaucratically elaborated military force. The pilot relays intelligence over the radio to the sheriff on the ground, remarking that Burns is "not mad, but he's awful smart," as though surprised that this cowboy can think strategically. The hubris of the big would have resonated at the time with the popular images of Fidel Castro and the *barbudos* in the Sierra Maestra and the more recent routing of the CIA invasion at the Bay of Pigs. Moreover, its resonance would deepen as the U.S. military became more embroiled in the Vietnam conflict over the course of the '60s. Robert Taber would call guerrilla war the "political phenomenon" of the midcentury, and French activist and intellectual Régis Debray would raise it into a philosophical order. It could become philosophical, according to Taber, because it arises from no cause, as such, but from an insight into "the *will to act*," and hence, it need not have, as Cuba was sometimes said not to have had, a set of demands, but only a horizon of "*potentiality*."[81] It was not political, then, but philosophical. Norman Mailer would marvel at Cuba because it "created the revolution first and learned from it."[82] This learning simply came from organizing the will to act.

My argument here has nothing to say about the changing military or about what Mailer called the "political aesthetic" that the New Left adapted from guerrilla combat. Instead I suggest that the lesson of guerrilla war, once understood, in Taber's words, as "nothing more than *the ability to inspire this state of mind in others*"—a state of quickness and eagerness, that is, a mood of "*here is something we can do . . . simply by acting*"—was immediately transferable into the vernacular of business management.[83] In that field there evolved a "literature on small business and military tactics," with essays such as "How Business Strategists Can Use Guerrilla Warfare Tactics."[84] In a narrower application, though, I am claiming not simply that corporations would learn how to decentralize their structure by observing certain guerrilla campaigns in the midcentury but rather that small firms used their self-regard as "guerrilla outfits" to recalibrate theories of corporate personhood, the logic of which, namely the monopartite charter, had lost its suasion in the age of business conglomeration. In short, I am arguing that the notion of guerrilla warfare was instrumentalized and emptied of content by U.S.

business culture and that Hollywood is a main locus in this process because its product has time and again enabled the narrative conversion of geopolitical menace into commercial wherewithal. Bryna did this, pressing its cause by arrogating the commercial cinema as a forum for corporate theorizing. The "most creative aspect" of the moviemaking process, according to Bryna, "comes in finding and selecting story material," after all, and we can speculate that this is because Bryna created itself through its selection of stories. Narrating the ideal of the cowboy hero as it mutates into the figure of the guerrilla warrior, then, is not what it seems on the surface, whether that is considered to be a lament of bygone values or of the agrarian society; more obliquely, it is an allegorical act whose true object of interest—submerged in the genre of the western and in the specter of guerrilla war—is the ideological project of so-called small business.

My argument is predicated on Bryna's oblique representation of guerrilla war even though other movies of this era, such as *Merrill's Marauders* (Fuller, Warner Bros., 1962), *The Battle of Algiers* (Pontecorvo, Rialto, 1966), and *The Green Berets* (Wayne et al., Warner-Seven, 1968), addressed the topic directly. These movies, each in its own way, made guerrilla war their central concern. Sam Fuller hired Yay Marking of the Filipino unit Marking's Guerrillas as a consultant for his movie; *The Battle of Algiers* was taken up broadly by New Left insurgent groups such as the Black Panthers and later the Baader-Meinhof Group in Germany; and *The Green Berets* is often considered the first Hollywood movie to address the Vietnam War and the deployment of Special Forces to counter guerrilla methods. For my argument, though, the oblique address is what matters. *Lonely Are the Brave* does not address guerrilla war but simply resembles it. Being an elegiac western, it means to narrate the eclipsing of the agrarian order within a fully realized modernity, but what motivates its concern with the residual figure of the past order—the cowboy hero—is a gnawing sense that this figure's reserves, its creaturely self-sufficiency, will not be outstripped after all in the comfortably teleological narration of modern progress. Hence, it must be either repressed (resulting in so many Castros) or mobilized (resulting in so many Rambos).

## KNOWLEDGE WORK AND POSTMODERN WAR

In *Lonely Are the Brave* we are meant to understand that Jack Burns has let his best friend, Paul Bondi, marry his love interest, Jerri. He lets this happen because he cannot make a home in this world, and marriage in this movie is simply the figure for making a home within the modern state. Paul Bondi, on the other hand, *can* make a home in this world, and it seems implied that this is a matter of professional self-definition: Bondi is a professor; he is hard at work writing a book. "He finish his book?" Burns asks Jerri. "Half of it," she responds. "The other half'll have to wait two years." Writing a book, it seems, is one means of making a home for oneself in modernity. The fact that Bondi's work on his book will be interrupted for two years—because he will serve a two-year sentence in prison—suggests how attenuated agency is within an information economy. This attenuated agency is what gives the movie its tension, rested as it is on the equipoise of the cowboy hero's "contemporary actionism," as Theodor Adorno would call it, and the knowledge worker's power to mete out and give shape to a world confected from information.[85] The tension is dramatized when Burns walks in from the wilderness and into what we will come to understand is Paul Bondi's home but is greeted by Jerri in a wifely role straight from 1950s television. "Welcome home," she greets Burns. We assume this is their romantic reunion. But we soon learn that Jerri and Paul Bondi have been married seven years and together have a son, Seth. The tension between Burns and Bondi is sublated in their agreement that "you got to hate fences." In a genre cliché, Burns tells Jerri she will never understand Paul because she is "still an Easterner," and within the genre discourse, the Eastern United States is still in the shadow of Westphalian sovereignty, but what shakes up the cliché here is that Paul Bondi, the knowledge worker, and not Jack Burns, the cowboy, is the one capable of establishing a deterritorialized, borderless social order. "How come Paul got mixed up smuggling those wetbacks across the border?" Burns asks Jerri. "He didn't smuggle anybody," she says. "He just helped them after they got here: he hid them and fed them and gave them directions about where to find work." Burns approves—"Good for him," he says—but seems unable to help his friend realize this borderless world. My point, as already demonstrated, is that Kirk Douglas thought in these terms (he ignored borders in his productions and focused instead on labor relations), and rather than accept the agency attenuated within an information economy, he augmented it by constituting himself as a corporate person.

By and large, I argue, the case for this borderless world will be made through the appeal of the artist rather than the corporate person in the abstract. Douglas would later defend his role in the Australian production, *The Man from Snowy River* (Miller, Hoyts/20th Century Fox, 1982), which met with efforts to keep Douglas from entering the country on "legal grounds" by questioning whether he "could work under their union rules": Banjo Patterson, the author of the national poem from which the movie derived, "wasn't just an Australian," Douglas said. "As a great artist he belonged to the world."[86] Before weighing the appeal of the artist-as-icon, though, I want to consider how figures of political economy such as the knowledge worker and the cowboy are paired in what Deak Nabers has called the "martial imagination" prior to their being sanitized in the form of popular iconography.[87] Conjoined, these icons redound to the stratagems of war, and this is the insight that *Lonely Are the Brave* preserves in narrative form. Studies of the Hollywood western suggest how this might be true for the cowboy.[88] And, too, a set of movies pegged to the Kennedy administration and the rise of "expertise-based culture" suggests how this might be true for the knowledge worker.[89] But these icons are typically viewed in parallax. If our perspective is rooted in the civilian economy, it is easy to see why one displaces the other in a kind of succession story. Peter Drucker observed that "the center of gravity has shifted to the knowledge worker, the man who puts to work what he has between his ears rather than the brawn of his muscles or the skill of his hands."[90] Mutatis mutandis, this is how *Lonely Are the Brave* narrates it, ending with Paul Bondi alive, if incarcerated, and Jack Burns dead, if memorialized. But the patness of its linear narration is complicated, even undermined, by the fact that its perspective on the "story material" is rooted in the military-industrial complex. The movie presumes, in short, that the military apparatus—its organizational model, its capital structure—is imbricated in the economy and that there can be no such thing as a purely civilian economy. The movie illustrates this, as mentioned, when a military helicopter is put to use domestically as a simulated operation for its pilots. And elsewhere, when asked whether he is a veteran, Jack Burns responds, "Wasn't everybody who could stand up straight for five minutes without falling over backwards?" Every civilian, no matter the profession nor the iconographic representation, is always already militarized. The strongest claim for *Lonely Are the Brave* as a New Hollywood movie, in fact, is that it had a share in enunciating this perspective, one in which the knowledge sector, and the university most conspicuously, is locked into partnership with military "brawn." Paul Bondi is left alive as the theorist of a social order that Jack Burns is killed (a metaphor for hidden) enforcing.

The story is not of these two terms in succession, wherein the premodern cowboy cedes his place to the postindustrial knowledge worker, but of these terms in combination. In the previous year President Eisenhower had seen it this way, cautioning against the "unwarranted influence" of the military-industrial complex, and in the next years the Free Speech Movement would see it this way. Douglas himself did not seem to see in precisely this way, hence he would say of the movie and its cowboy individualism that if you are an outsider, "society will crush you." This is just to say that "selecting story material" is not identical to understanding its portent. Despite Douglas's corporate agency, the story is not altogether his. The portent of the story, rather, is attached to the writers involved, Dalton Trumbo, the screenwriter, and Edward Abbey, the novelist. Each was drawn as an actant into the perpetual war that seems to have unfolded from the historical conjuncture of the knowledge worker and the cowboy. Trumbo had been imprisoned for his communist ideas, but in particular for having them in a knowledge industry—Hollywood— with the power to seed such ideas in national culture. Abbey would go on to write a novel, *The Monkey Wrench Gang*, which was widely credited as a beta model for ecoterrorism and as an inspiration for the radical organization Earth First! At the heart of Abbey's novel is George Hayduke, a Vietnam veteran trained in munitions who has found domestic application for skills he learned as a Green Beret. Hayduke was based on Abbey's friend, Doug Peacock, whose own reintegration into U.S. society after the Vietnam War is a case study for the generalized fear that those trained for irregular combat in Vietnam and those who then suffered the experience would neither be reabsorbed into civilian life nor otherwise disappear; they would, it was feared, inject into U.S. society whatever had gone afoul in Vietnam. This foreshadows Rambo in *First Blood*, but it is a fear we first see in independent movies such as *Hi, Mom!* and *Tracks* (Jaglom, Trio, 1977). What is interesting about the fear of domestic terrorism is that it is prefigured in *Lonely Are the Brave*. In a letter from Abbey to the film's director, David Miller, he gives a character biography for Jack Burns, noting that Burns and Bondi were "comrades" in World War II and that Burns, though he "hates the military discipline," nonetheless "makes a pretty good soldier, especially in guerrilla-type warfare." But what Burns cannot do, according to Abbey, is expect justice when he returns from the war, and though he might wish to remain aloof from domestic society, "he is still drawn back to the human pack, again and again, though each return becomes more dangerous for him, as the omnipresent forces of law, organization, industry, the Machine State, close off, one by one, most of the traditional pathways of escape."[91] While Abbey's story concludes in Burns's death, he seemed to understand that the storytelling possibilities, or the future of Burns's cowboyism as an ideologeme, depended on the coarticulation of the cowboy and the knowledge worker: "Bondi and Burns are each attracted by the other, even though unable to fully share it—in fact, this difference, this tension, is what makes their friendship vital and alive: each man senses in the other a quality which he does not possess in sufficient degree, himself."[92] The one does not escape, then, not even by the pathway of death, but is rather absorbed into the other. In short, the portent of the story is controlled by an insight that the writers had (but Douglas did not) into the perpetual war whose separate phases can be said to include the Cold War and the war on terror, themselves indicating that postmodern war brooks no hard distinction between civilian and combatant, between war in the abstract (its simulation and its means-end reconfiguration) and its concrete instantiation.

# THE ARTIST AS CORPORATE PERSON

The insight Douglas did have—the counterpart to the insight that, in the factory enclosure, one might deem the cowboy a fantasy—is that knowledge work might only cathect one's laboring energy when redescribed as art. This is a conflict that Douglas obviously felt himself as he set up a schematic self-understanding of the corporate and the creative person: "Kirk does not consider himself a business man," his publicist Margulies stated, "but is chiefly concerned with the creative aspects." Douglas would stage a hokey dual image of himself, such as a 1960 television interview between two versions of himself, Douglas the Producer and Douglas the Actor, in order to manage the troublesome fact that he had established himself as a corporate person legally even if he still identified himself as a creative person psychologically. "I am not a corporation," he claimed. "I am an actor first, last and always. The corporation exists because it enables me to be creative."[93] But if the corporation propertizes his creativity and, in doing so, sets conditions to augment it, then it is hard to see how his work is much different from labor as it was everywhere reconfigured in support of what alternately has been called the information economy, cognitive capitalism, and post-Fordism. Douglas would say of acting, "Our profession is a very personal thing. We feel more passionately about our job than a banker, say, does about his."[94] The notion of professionalizing what is most personal, one's personality—for Douglas, "a certain amount of the identifiable quality which makes people willing to pay to see him in a picture"—is at the core of C. Wright Mills's famous disquisition on white-collar labor. "The employer of many white-collar services," Mills says, "buys the employees' social personalities."[95] Douglas understands the actor's job in precisely these terms: "Their basic merchandise," he says, "is themselves." But Douglas does not consider this to be the general condition for white-collar labor as Mills does. "When an accountant balances his books at the end of the month," Douglas says, "he doesn't boast about it. Another man with similar training could have done as well. Not so with an actor."[96] For him, the actor's craft is separate from the white-collar economy in the main, but for Mills it is the merger of a host of pursuits which could be categorized as "intellectual"—and the accompanying logic that one professionalize one's passions—that defines the white-collar economy tout court. "Intellectuals cannot be defined as a single social unit," Mills argues, "but rather as a scattered set of grouplets." They are "people who specialize in symbols" and "produce, distribute, and preserve distinct forms of consciousness." Further, as "the immediate carriers of art and of ideas," Mills says, certain advance-guard ventures such as the "New Deal, Hollywood, and the Luce enterprises" have helped instrumentalize "the cultural and marketing life of the intellectual."[97]

What Mills detects is the condition of post-Fordism. In Paolo Virno's diagnosis, post-Fordism overcomes the Fordist split between brain and brawn, what I designate as the knowledge worker and the cowboy, by claiming the "general intellect" as the unitary source of economy. He believes the "*sharing* of linguistic and cognitive habits is the constituent element of the post-Fordist process of labor," and hence "all the workers enter into production in as much as they are speaking-thinking." For the sake of productivity, "what really counts is the original sharing of linguistic-cognitive talents, since it is this sharing which guarantees readiness, adaptability, etc., in reacting to innovation."[98] Virno refers to the latter model of "Toyotaism," which in deploying "the productive mobilization of the cognitive faculties" trumps Fordism.[99] But Virno also builds on Mills's insight that Hollywood is the advance guard. He argues that the "role the culture industry assumed with relation to overcoming the Ford/Taylor model" was that its model of labor required "a certain space that was informal, not programmed, one which was open to the unforeseen spark, to communicative and creative improvisation," not, Virno says, "to favor human creativity . . . but in order to achieve satisfactory levels of corporate productivity," which was made both "exemplary and pervasive."[100]

Alan Liu agrees with Virno that "knowledge work is primarily a linguistic habit," but he thinks that what allows it to pervade the economy is a "culture of cool" that it has given rise to, one which "originates in schooling to inculcate habits of analytical distance, judgment through rationality (as opposed to authority), technical mastery, professional autonomy, and other ultimately class practices."[101] Kirk Douglas, we might say, was simply an emissary of this culture. He understood that his job was attractive because he was an artist and not a businessman and that bankers and accountants, such as they have been depicted, were but the soulless white-collar workers whose self-understanding still derived from Fordist tenets. It might be a fantasy of the banker, Douglas thought, to be an artist. The Bryna movie *Seconds* (Frankenheimer, Paramount, 1966) would float such a scenario, as the "second" life its banker protagonist purchases is an artist's life. What we find in Douglas's career, in short, is that just as John Ford found it necessary to flee the factory conditions of Hollywood for the vistas onto which he might overlay a western imaginary, so Douglas found it necessary to flee the white-collar conditions of Hollywood for the domain of "aestheticism unbound," in Liu's words.[102] This explains, I believe, Douglas's interest in artist biopics such as *Young Man with a Horn* (Curtiz, Warner Bros., 1950) and *Lust for Life* (Minnelli, MGM, 1956). It explains, too, why Douglas, a friend of John Wayne's, was unperturbed when after a private screening of *Lust for Life*, Wayne admonished him, "Christ, Kirk! How can you play a part like that? There's so goddamn few of us left. We got to play strong, tough characters. Not those weak queers." Douglas says he took it "as a compliment," though we might imagine he did so because he understood that Bryna had a better ideological orientation on the economy than Wayne's Batjac Productions did.[103] Cowboys were yesterday, he intuited, and artists tomorrow.

In this way Douglas foretold New Hollywood in the more updated, progressive form it would take later in the '60s in a movie such as *Midnight Cowboy* (Schlesinger, United Artists, 1969), where the cowboy icon is somewhat self-reflexively masqueraded. In it, Dustin Hoffman tells Jon Voight, "In New York no rich lady with any class buys that cowboy crap anymore." They do buy the artist, however, as *An Unmarried Woman* suggests. It is worth considering this movie, though, as the culminating form of independence that New Hollywood's talent-on-the-make had been asserting through their ceaseless innovation of form. Its director, Paul Mazursky, had been pegged as the *kulturträger* since his *Bob & Carol & Ted & Alice* (Columbia, 1969) had converted the sexual revolution into a box-office hit, and his next movie, *Alex in Wonderland* (MGM, 1970), dramatized his casting about for material that befits his filmmaking independence. Alex (Donald Sutherland), the screen surrogate for Mazursky, visits an MGM executive to talk about his next movie. As Alex walks down a hallway lined with the framed photographs of Hollywood royalty of yesteryear, among the last, most prominent photographs we see are Burt Lancaster and Kirk Douglas, meant to indicate their pastness on one hand, but on the other hand to recognize them as the forbears of New Hollywood independence. Though Alex cites European cinema as his influence, and Mazursky underlines it with cameos from Federico Fellini and Jeanne Moreau, Hollywood independence is nonetheless what Alex negotiates when the executive asks him, "Can you get personally involved with a project that will make fifty million dollars?" If he can call himself an artist and make a profit too, the executive suggests, then his self-image can be supported and given amplitude within MGM. *An Unmarried Woman* is the upshot of what, in the years of the Hollywood Renaissance (1967–1974), had been a source of industry restlessness. In its broad scenario, Erica (Jill Clayburgh) goes from her routinized marriage with a banker husband to her spirited, less predictable relationship with an artist boyfriend. Her husband, Martin, is not thrown overboard so much as he needs to be replaced, which he seems to understand on his own. He tells Erica that he has fantasized "about changing [his] life" and that he might "quit Wall Street and go be a disc jockey somewhere." He has an affair and leaves her and in short order is replaced by an artist, Saul. One might simply think that the tired figure of finance has willed himself into the form of the modern artist.

The outcome of replacing money with art is twofold. First, it seems that doing so shifts the ground of class identity from labor to lifestyle. Stanley Corkin has focused on *An Unmarried Woman* in reference to New York City's emergence as the center of finance capital because in it, the arts are an agent of gentrification, and the annexing of Soho lofts, for instance, lets the Upper East Side protagonist think in terms of "class-as-lifestyle."[104] This acculturation of capital leads to what Liu calls "a fuzzy, lifestyle version of economic class" that is "weakly formed" insofar as its basis in culture—in knowledge and preferences—is vast and inclusive since culture is "locally everywhere."[105] Second, once class is a matter of lifestyle, one never knows where one's work ends. Once Erica is dating an artist, he is working all the time. "If I stop painting for a few days," he worries, "I may stop painting altogether." Hence, after Saul and Erica's first night together, they wake up to work; he pours paint on a canvas and she cooks breakfast. In fact, the point is made that their leisure and work are seamlessly integrated through intercuts between running paint and running egg yolks. She likes the arrangement. "I feel great," Erica says. "I feel happy." Saul scarcely stops his painting to eat the breakfast Erica has made him; he also drinks liquor, and they begin kissing, all while he finishes his canvas. "Living with me is work," he tells her, and though this seems to mean that Saul is a handful, in another register it means that he is always working.

My point is that Kirk Douglas anticipated this. "There's a value," he says, "in being willing to work like a horse to do a better job." And "no one is willing to work harder," he thinks, "than an actor—to the end of his endurance, if need be."[106] But the value, according to Douglas, derives not from being remunerated but from being able to commit one's person to the job. In his memoirs, Douglas thinks something like this to himself when his driver asks why "a rich man like you" continues to work so hard. "How odd that he would equate working hard only with making money," Douglas writes, "not with liking your work."[107] The driver's question is less odd, historically, than Douglas's willingness to imagine that he works for a reason other than money. It cuts against the orthodoxies of management theory, after all, for which a main premise is that a single brain farther up the line must incentivize the labor below by means of reward. If the job is intrinsically the reward, as Douglas suggests, this might mark the beginning of a democratization of the "managerial demiurge," as Mills calls it, wherein one now introjects what once was an extrinsic call to labor. This is the threshold of post-Fordism, where it is no longer possible, Virno argues, "to establish an actual distinction between a stable 'inside' and an uncertain and telluric 'outside.'"[108]

It should not surprise us, then, that in this moment the figure of the outside emerges again in Hollywood movies. When Erica first separates from her husband, she is set up on a blind date with a Hollywood press agent. They go for dim sum with friends, and her date tells the table that the picture he is presently working on is about "an ex–Vietnam vet who comes back to a small Midwestern town and shoots three hundred people." Erica responds, "That should make a fortune." A friend claims he has seen the movie. But her date corrects him, "I don't think so, Hal." Yet the friend persists, "I saw it, I'm telling you." Finally, her date shuts down the conversation, "You couldn't, they haven't made it yet." The scene is strange in that the dialogue is throwaway but is nonetheless so topical as to be nearly insider information. Though the Vietnam War was everywhere in the media throughout the late '60s and early '70s, and though Saigon had fallen in 1975, it was only in the release year of *An Unmarried Woman*, 1978, that Hollywood had begun to make Vietnam movies. Early in the year *Coming Home* (Ashby, United Artists) and *The Boys in Company C* (Furie, Columbia) had been released, and later in the year *The Deer Hunter* (Cimino, Universal) was released. The friend's name is Hal, so maybe it alludes to Hal Ashby's movie. But the movie described is less like *Coming Home* than *First Blood*, and Hal is played by Paul Mazursky himself in what might be taken as an insider's report on the scripts that were then circulating in Hollywood. Hal's final word on the subject is that it "sounds familiar," which it surely would for Mazursky because the novel that was its source material, David Morrell's *First Blood*, had been acquired by Columbia in 1972. It had kicked around the industry, with Warner Bros. developing it in the early '70s only to decide that it was too risky to portray Vietnam in the midst of its unfolding. Every actor had at one time been offered the role. It finally went to Sylvester Stallone after his success in the *Rocky* franchise. It is hard to know whether Erica seriously thinks the movie will make a "fortune," since it seems a sarcastic response to the dark subject, but indeed, *First Blood* broke opening weekend records for October and was among the highest-grossing movies of its release year. Kirk Douglas, as noted, rejected the movie because it ended with the extrajuridical figure's reintegration into society, specialized now and deployed only in Third World special ops. This rejection might be seen in a different way, however, not from the perspective of which movies will make a fortune but from the self-understanding of the new class, who recognized this outsider as their repressed other.

# NEW HOLLYWOOD AESTHETICS AND
# THE EMANCIPATED SPECTATOR

Though I have been making a case for *Lonely Are the Brave* as an early movie or a prefiguration of New Hollywood, in closing I want to remark on the irony that *Lonely Are the Brave* went largely unrecognized in this regime. *First Blood*, the movie Douglas later rejected, became the kind of hit he had been seeking. The bleak ending of *Lonely Are the Brave* is typical of that first wave of movies in the Hollywood Renaissance—*The Graduate*, *Bonnie and Clyde*, and so on—and yet, over the long term, it would be the case that turning away from such bleak endings, as *First Blood* would do, gave New Hollywood its permanent footing. The irony is this: the story of the outsider who is incorporated is what wins the box office, and the impulse that led to the New Hollywood was what ulti- mately would be banished from it. Perhaps Douglas simply loved his work, as he claimed, and cared less about the money it made. But the record shows that he found it hard to accept the weak earnings of *Lonely Are the Brave* and laid the blame on Lew Wasserman and Universal.[109] Because Universal did not recognize the kind of movie it was, Douglas complained, they did not devise the correct release strategy. In a June 1962 letter from his publicist was a review clipped from *Cosmopolitan* showing how "great" they thought *Lonely Are the Brave* was, and Dick Guttman adds, "Apparently everybody else does except Universal- International."[110] In March and April, Bryna struggled with a market- ing campaign for the movie. By its May release, everyone associated with Douglas felt that Universal had "dumped" it by "its non-Broadway theater release pattern."[111] On June 13 the movie's producer, Edward Lewis, wrote a nine-page single-spaced letter to the president of Univer- sal, Milton Rackmil, in which he accused Universal of having reneged on an agreement to give the movie "special handling."[112] Bryna wanted what we now call a "platform release." The movie "would surely receive excellent word of mouth," Lewis explained, "and, if opened slowly, could build to an important grosser." Through this strategy, they could aim at niche audiences. Lewis explained that they had made one " 'total action' ad" because a certain "unsophisticated audience responds only to this kind of picture," but then this ad—he was surprised to learn—"was the only one being used." *Lonely Are the Brave* opened at "the biggest house in San Francisco" when, had it opened "at one of the smaller houses that attracts a different audience," one exhibitor told him, it "could well have run many months."[113]

Kirk Douglas believed, in short, that Universal ought to have "put the picture in an art house."[114] In his view *Lonely Are the Brave* was an American version of the New Wave movies coming out of Europe and should in turn have reached the same audiences being uncovered by Andrew Sarris, journals such as *Film Culture*, and the art-house boom of the 1950s. Friends told him, Douglas wrote, "that 'Lonely Are the Brave' is 'an artistic gem' and it has that 'new wave feeling.'"[115] Among the appreciative responses that Douglas saved is a July 2, 1962, letter from Curtis Harrington. Harrington, I think, remains an interesting figure in the coming of New Hollywood: he had begun his career in the West Coast avant-garde, making "trance films" of his own such as *A Fragment of Seeking* (1946) and working with Kenneth Anger on *Puce Moment* (1949) and *Inauguration of the Pleasure Dome* (1954) but had moved into the exploitation industry when his *Night Tide* (AIP, 1961) was released by American International Pictures thanks to Roger Corman. Harrington wrote to Douglas that because he was "a member of this Industry," he was "very proud when a film of this calibre [*sic*] is made. It brings credit and honor to all of us." He assured Douglas, "It ranks with some of the finest films we've been receiving from Europe."[116] Harrington's letterhead was from Jerry Wald Productions, where he was then working, but I lay stress on his letter because his emergence into the industry, such as it was, traced a path through the exploitation sector that was not only a common one for many of the renowned talents of New Hollywood such as Francis Ford Coppola, Peter Bogdanovich, Peter Fonda, and Jack Nicholson, it was also arguably the path by which this personnel was able to forge what might be called New Hollywood textuality. Such textuality, in a gloss, is characterized by the crossing of New Wave form and sensationalized, formerly verboten subject matter. At the time that Douglas received Harrington's letter, he seemed conflicted by the "Europeanness" of his movie, deeming it "a terrible cross to bear for a picture that hasn't been made overseas."[117] *Lonely Are the Brave*, in fact, did great business in London, "shatter[ing] all previous U-I records at the start of its world premiere engagement," but, he asked, how might it reach an American audience, "which looks to Europe for depth in film entertainment?"[118] Douglas joked that had they shot in "the Himalayas," the "chase would have been more avant garde," and that his solution was "to dub it in Italian and release it with sub titles." What Douglas was struggling with here and would in fact continue to struggle with throughout the early years of New Hollywood was the problem of matching the themes of the new cinema with its proper textuality. "Perhaps," he said of his movie, "we should give it the chi-chi touch. Everyone who has ever seen a new wave picture or read a new wave review knows that chi-chi is an indispensable European monopoly." But in this telling, he seems to think "chi-chi" lies not in the textuality but rather in the provenance. "A poorly lighted foreign picture" would be celebrated, he believed, but a Hollywood picture with the same trait would be panned.[119]

My object is not to adjudicate Douglas's belief but rather to suggest that in it lies the germ of New Hollywood aesthetics. The notion that the textuality of a movie should be tuned to its provenance, that its style, in short, should bear the mark of its production situation, was an article of faith among the cinephiles then coming of age. Appealing to that belief would turn out to be an essential term in the compact between filmmakers and their audiences, both having become more educated in film and in general thanks to the democratizing of higher education. So now a figure such as Curtis Harrington (who wrote a book on Josef von Sternberg) was closer to the center of the audience than to its margins. Such audiences were primed for a textual signal, something within the movie explaining its orientation on the medium as such and on the cinema as an institution. Such signals might be "visual obscurities, jump cuts, time changes," as David Newman and Robert Benton would write, "bizarre opticals, so-called inconsistencies of plot."[120] The emblematic moment for them is when Anna Karina "suddenly winks *at the audience*" in *Une femme est une femme* (Godard, Unidex, 1961).[121] Here is Douglas's "chi-chi." The rules are broken, but in this they are acknowledged, all for the sake of an audience that is highly versed in them. Perhaps the defining tension of cinephilia, as Nico Baumbach contends, was its at-once "aristocratic and proletarian" character: one must be university educated in "the rules" to find pleasure in their violation.[122] Hence, the cinema for this generation helped combat "the bourgeois museumification of art," and the "lower genres" (the western, the gangster movie) would furnish an idiom of New Hollywood mastery.[123] In the lower genres one might tap "something other than or, at the very least, oblique to the classical norm," and this, for Miriam Hansen, is the source of a "vernacular modernism" that had long been cinema's claim.[124] Its domain, Hansen says, was "external appearance, the sensual, material surface," and the power these possessed to upset any codified aesthetics.[125] Difficult though it might be to formulate such textuality—and my point, indeed, is that Douglas found that the "chi-chi" was difficult, elusive—Harrington found it in *Lonely Are the Brave* because it did not give its themes the A treatment as, for instance, *Stagecoach* had, but only the B treatment. In the debased form of the B movie, that is, Douglas stashed a commentary on the cowboy icon that is personal in the degree that it jars against convention. What frustrated Douglas was that Bryna knew they had to distinguish the movie in this way ("Our policy is to avoid, wherever possible, any hint that this is a conventional western") but nonetheless could not find an audience for it.[126]

Douglas continued to petition Lew Wasserman throughout the '60s for a rerelease of the movie that would better exploit its merits. In a January 1967 letter to Wasserman, he suggested they reissue the movie under the title *The Last Cowboy* because they had used the title in Europe "with great success."[127] By the end of that year David Newman and Robert Benton would find the audience that Douglas could not with their screenplay *Bonnie and Clyde*, which they had shopped around to New Wave filmmakers François Truffaut and Jean-Luc Godard before making the movie with Arthur Penn and Warren Beatty. Their movie brought to a head what Bryna had been doing in *Lonely Are the Brave*, then in *The List of Adrian Messenger* (Huston, Universal International, 1963), and finally in *Seconds*, each time in more aggressive textuality. But even though *Bonnie and Clyde* was ultimately celebrated as the herald of New Hollywood, it too was "dumped" by its distributor and had to be rereleased before it found its audience. Newman and Benton admitted how much was left to chance. "The students are responding to works of art," they wrote, "only when they can somehow relate the movies to their own *outside* experiences, ideas, life." But the filmmaker "can't do anything about it," they thought, "and so must be just as good and inventive as he can, send the picture out into the world and *see what the reverberations are*."[128] This observation would seem unremarkable, since it has surely always been the case that knowledge of audience taste is imperfect, and only when a work lines up, by chance, with an audience's outside interests does it gain the kind of traction that makes it culturally significant. What makes it remarkable, though, is that the audience, specified as "students," was measured differently according to the new profile of students. The hierarchy implied in the student-teacher relationship was unsettled in the sit-ins of the early '60s and then in the teach-ins and be-ins throughout the decade, and this model, displaced in the cinema, resulted in what Jacques Rancière would call the "emancipated spectator." In this model, though the "director does not know what she wants the spectator to do, she at least knows one thing," says Rancière, and that is to "overcome the gulf separating activity from passivity."[129] If the impulse to democratized control, to equal shares in creativity—or "equality of intelligence," as Rancière puts it—was what moved Kirk Douglas to form his own company (owning a company, he said, is "the difference between doing something and sitting back and waiting for the right thing to come along"), in the project of finding an audience, he would turn, finally, to Newman and Benton. "I have been a fan of yours since I first saw *Bonnie and Clyde*," he wrote them. "I would love to do a project with you. I have some thoughts I would like to knock around with you, and perhaps you have some."[130] He wrote them this while starring in their movie, *There Was a Crooked Man* (Mankiewicz, Warner Bros., 1970), another western that, for all its B-movie aesthetics, failed to hook Douglas up with the New Hollywood audience he desired.

# 2

# THE CINEMA OF DEFECTION

## The Corporate Counterculture and Robert Altman's Lion's Gate

**Interviewer:** They weren't just drop-out kids who hadn't been able to make it?

**Arthur Penn:** Oh no, anything but. The intellectual level of the group was quite high, I would say.

Joseph Gelmis, *The Film Director as Superstar*

At the very center of *Taxi Driver* (Scorsese, Columbia, 1976) we can find the most prominent, if undertheorized, genre of late 1960s and early 1970s Hollywood: the "defection" movie. Embodying the counterculture dropout, Iris (Jodie Foster) lives a precarious life in New York City, having left home due to differences with her parents, differences she imputes to "women's lib." She dreams of joining "one of them communes in Vermont." But the signal of this genre—the defection genre—is nearly lost in the noise of other genres. Robin Wood calls the movie incoherent because, in crossing the generic cues of the western and the horror movie, it never grants a settled perspective on its protagonist, Travis Bickle (Robert De Niro).[1] Travis, a Special Forces veteran of Vietnam (his jacket patch says "King Kong Company, 1968–1970"), is at once cowboy hero and monster. Though Wood considers this an unsettled perspective, it is more accurate to say that Travis is just the figuration of a fear, one that had been settling for some time, that guerrilla warfare might react back into domestic society. Trained in unconventional fighting, traumatized by his experience of it, Travis tries to restart his life in New York City but can only see what are for him its social problems in terms of military solutions. He mistakenly believes his violent solutions serve a social good that is otherwise entrusted—negligently, he believes—to an ongoing political campaign; what he plans to do, Travis thinks, will safeguard the innocent from the "whores, skunk pussies, buggers, queens, fairies, dopers, junkies." In short, from the city as it would appear from a conservative standpoint in the wake of the movements (Black Power, feminism, gay rights, and the New Left in its militant phase). That Travis is mistakenly celebrated as a hero instead of the monster the movie reveals him to be is not incoherence, pace Robin Wood, but a critique of both the reactionary backlash against the '60s and the vigilantism of '70s cinema such as *Dirty Harry* (Siegel, Warner Bros., 1971).

We ought to note that Brian De Palma's *Hi, Mom!* similarly imagined the guerrilla battles of the so-called Third World brought back to U.S. cities, but there it is not imagined through the optic of the Hollywood western.[2] Part of why the western matters is that Iris, the defector, is recaptured by Travis and returned to her parents, who report they "have taken steps to see that she has never cause to run away again"—her future escape is foreclosed—in a twist on the captivity plot of John Ford's *The Searchers*. In this twist, *Taxi Driver* draws out and intensifies the complicated sense of "captivity" in Ford's movie: Who is the captor, who is capable of rescue? For Ford the relation had been flipping, as I argue in chapter 1, and whatever moral neatness had once obtained in an us-against-them opposition had been largely undone within youth culture by the time of the '60s. *Taxi Driver* indexes this. Travis is referred to as a "real cowboy," and at one point the movie's version of cowboyism is aligned with *Lonely Are the Brave*. "I had a horse in Coney Island," Sport tells Travis. "It got hit by a car." In *Lonely Are the Brave*, Kirk Douglas and his horse are struck by a tractor trailer on the expressway, and the horse dies. Nothing suggests that *Taxi Driver* is directly alluding to this, but it is clear that the theme of the cowboy's displacement in modernity is what both *Lonely Are the Brave* and *Taxi Driver* find relevant in the western tradition. Though an anachronism, the cowboy is nonetheless put to contemporary use in the revanchist project of nullifying the dream of escape that had sustained youth-culture utopianism.

This dream, however troubled from the start, is the stuff worked over in a cycle of Hollywood movies whose generic formulation in the years 1967–1974 is something like an aesthetic shadow thrown by the political project of the New Left. In what follows I will call this the genre of defection—the term applies literally to draft dodgers and figuratively to independent movie producers—and I will demonstrate how the genre became a means for reckoning with the philosophical shift from the Old Left to the New Left. In turn, I will suggest that many of the filmmakers responsible for the developing genre were using it to resist imaginatively the structure they were folded into materially, namely the corporation. The genre seems to have been bred of a fear that within the transpersonal structure of the corporation, they, the filmmakers, were stripped of agency as they presumed it had once been configured for persons. Such notions of personhood, though, are more equivocal than New Left discourses might allow for, since, as Walter Benn Michaels argues, the corporation might best be understood as "the embodiment of figurality that makes personhood possible" (in a certain moment) rather than "as a figurative extension of personhood," and as Fredric Jameson qualifies, the process thus construed is something like a displaced version of "class consciousness."[3] The nub of the problem, put simply, is that all forms of personal agency may finally be nothing more than preferred ways of camouflaging the social power enabling individual acts. Hence, when the New Left denied class consciousness its preferential status, the problem remaining was which source of social power it would prefer instead.

Here, I want to consider the Hollywood refraction of New Left discourses. At the levels of production and aesthetics alike, there was a hum of dissonance in 1960s Hollywood, generated by the break from studio Hollywood. What emerged from the break is something we tend to call—rather indefinitely—poststudio Hollywood. Part of the reason to imagine a supersession of the studios, indeed, is that the kind of work

Hollywood talent did was organized differently (movies were shot on location, stars began their own companies) and the resulting work looked different (technicians might now flaunt their style, the production code was often ignored). Directors Mike Nichols and Arthur Penn did not come up through the studios as did, say, John Ford and Howard Hawks. This is not to say that they did not work for the studios; it just means that their work, in its most immediate sphere, was insulated from them. Nichols and Penn both made their way to Hollywood by way of New York and, most significantly, by way of its bohemian life, which by then only weakly survived in its old form. Michael Harrington described the bohemia of the '30s and '40s as "small, organized on a human scale."[4] Nichols and his comedy partner, Elaine May, participated in its tail end in their Village Vanguard shows. And Arthur Penn, an alum of Black Mountain College, directed Nichols and May when their show moved to Broadway. This was the start of a drift that took them to Hollywood, where Nichols's *The Graduate* and Penn's *Bonnie and Clyde* helped convert bohemia into the counterculture. Preparing the way for a "mass counterculture," Harrington said, "destroyed the possibility of Bohemia," for a "Bohemia that enrolls a good portion of a generation is no longer a Bohemia." The genre of defection, which *The Graduate* and *Bonnie and Clyde* gave shape to, derived from the fact that "the counterculture freaks falling off the margin of society," as Harrington said, "have such a difficult task."[5] It was difficult to find the margins, that is, when corporations converted them into sites of mass consumption. What the genre seemed to narrativize was the more or less nonnarrative condition of negation, a rejection (of "society," of "institutions") implying no positive recommendation of its own. It is a version of the American romance, I will suggest, but inverted. In what follows I will track this effort to quiet Hollywood's narrative engine across a series of movies, many of them high profile, but I do so in part to observe that many of these movies were directed by so-called auteurs who had invested in the genre's fantasy of escape to deflect from the fact that they themselves—in their most personal, aesthetic projects—were being integrated into corporate culture.

Robert Altman, however, is a counterpoint. He accepted the corporation as the main force in media production. Altman's experience was first
in industrial film, next in television, and then in feature-length movies,
and early in his Hollywood dealings, he formed Lion's Gate in order to
infuse the corporation with his values rather than be subject to the corporation's. Hence, he might be said to have bodied forth the "corporate
person," and he did so, crucially, in the heat of its historical transformation. His values were those of the counterculture, broadly speaking,
and he presided over Lion's Gate as "the big, immoderate, pot-smoking,
scotch-chugging, cuddly, counter-culture daddy" in such a way that his
"commune in Westwood" became the site of "grand, crazy parties which
just happen[ed] to become movies."[6] He understood the corporation as a
"social system," it seems, knowing that his own firm could arrange the
relations of those within it—could set up its own culture—in other ways
than the large firms of the midcentury had.[7] He was, in consequence,
frank about his relation to corporate Hollywood, and it is in this light
that I turn to his movie *Brewster McCloud* in the last section of this chapter. In *Brewster McCloud*, indeed, Altman deconstructed the genre of
defection, sending up its pieties in the same manner as he would those of
many other Hollywood genres. I turn first, however, to the origins of the
genre and the members of it to show how it outlined a sensibility and a
philosophical disposition, because the significance of *Brewster McCloud*,
a box-office failure, can only be restored if the genre is reconstructed.


## DEFECTS OF CLASSICAL HOLLYWOOD

In his 1975 essay, "The Pathos of Failure," Thomas Elsaesser identifies
"examples of a shift, no doubt historically significant," in movies such
as *Two-Lane Blacktop* (Hellman, Universal, 1971), *Five Easy Pieces* (Rafelson, Columbia, 1970), *The Last Detail* (Ashby, Columbia, 1973), and *California Split* (Altman, Columbia, 1974).[8] The historic shift lay in the
"architecture of film narrative": though the movies were concerned with

"mapping out journeys as were" the movies of "the classical American cinema," Elsaesser says, they placed an "unmotivated hero" at their narrative centers. A tension thus arose, a kind of formal frustration from "the combination of the unmotivated hero and the motif of the journey." Rather than form their own journeys, these characters were formed by them. They were made from without, in an ideological twist, not from within. What Elsaesser is identifying, in other words, is the emergence of postclassical form. In the strongest formulation of Hollywood classicality, David Bordwell argues that form of this kind is rooted in "psychological causality."[9] Cause and effect, that is, flow from "psychologically defined individuals who struggle to solve a clear-cut problem or to attain specific goals."[10] These characters make things happen, but in what Elsaesser observes, the reason why things happen is less easy to discern. Gone is the "affirmative attitude to the world," he says, gone the "a-priori optimism."[11]

For scholars, a lot has turned on whether Hollywood classicality has ever been overcome.[12] I am less concerned with a totalizing assessment of Hollywood's program, I admit, since I agree with Richard Maltby's argument that the industry has been "too opportunistic" to commit itself to a set of poetic norms.[13] However, it is worth noting Elsaesser's admission that "his choice of films is selective."[14] He has selected out a postclassical genre, I believe, but has not elaborated its features. To take up where he leaves off, we first need to dwell on the "unmotivated hero"— the rightness of the phrase—and from there we can elaborate the generic schema. Retaining the term "hero" seems fair, since Bonnie and Clyde and Benjamin Braddock did become culture heroes of a sort for young audiences.[15] But "unmotivated" misses the point. Many of these movies drew such round protagonists that they seemed more like character studies than narratives, with questions of motivation often eclipsing the importance of plotted events.[16] The formal asymmetry between hero and journey, in fact, suggests that at stake in the genre is an actantial problem, a problem (at once narrative and philosophical) with the unit of agency at its most basic. It is a social problem, not a psychological one, but there are two ways to cast the problem. On one hand, we can say that society is simply not geared to recognize the protagonist's motivations, that they are of such a novel kind that as yet there are no social coordinates in place for their realization. Call this the generation gap. On the other hand, we can say that the movies reveal the insufficiency of the protagonist as an actant. Given the scale of modernity, the protagonist, traditionally understood, makes nothing happen. That is, upon the modern transition into gesellschaft, whoever is not cognizant of the associative being (here, corporations) that functions as a "social level between political states and individual people" will seem only like a person adrift, atomized, "unmotivated."[17] Call this social alienation. The point of this, as it relates to classicality, is that Hollywood movies had been evolved by corporations as a means of integrating a population, but as they themselves became implicated in a mode of production in which employees might count as mere "inputs," these corporations, as the auteur theory would suggest, were agents of alienation instead.

But corporations were social agents, make no mistake, and when Nichols (for Embassy) or Penn (for Warner Bros.) made movie worlds that imaginatively subtracted their agency, what came from that subtraction was a genre that is rightly called postclassical. In it, the goal-oriented journey is converted into mere drifting. The narrative parts of the genre were under formation early in the '60s in movies such as *David and Lisa* (Perry, Continental Film, 1962) and *Mickey One*, but only in what critics have called the "watershed year" of 1967 did the parts get assembled into the narrative syntax iterated in *The Graduate, Bonnie and Clyde*, and *Cool Hand Luke*.[18] In *Five Easy Pieces* the genre was stitched together, as it were, in that it articulates the problem at the heart of the midcentury corporation, what I will later work out as a quantity-quality dialectic. The movie follows Robert Dupea (Jack Nicholson) as he turns away from his family, all of whom are classically trained musicians, toward a working-class community. In a late scene, Robert guides his father's wheelchair to a clearing on their estate because the two of them, according to his sister Partita, need to "reach an understanding." The father-son relationship is the broken filial connection. Robert tries holding a conversation with his father, though it will be one-sided since his father was stricken mute by a stroke. Robert says, "I don't know if you'd be particularly interested in hearing about me. My life, most of it doesn't

add up to much that I could relay as a way of life that you'd approve of."
The language here, his reliance in this moment on quantitative terms
("add up"), evokes the corporate ethos that BBS Productions—the maker
of this movie and *Easy Rider* before it—was trying to replace. It was an
ethos of accumulation, and if addition was its status quo, then in these
movies, subtraction would start to look like resistance. Robert explains,
"I move around a lot, not because I'm looking for anything really, but
because I'm getting away from things that get bad if I stay." Theodore
Roszak would claim that this typified the counterculture. The unique
problem of a "high-consumption, leisure-wealthy society," Roszak says,
is that for young people intent on "epochal transformation" political
activity could only be figured negatively. Theirs, he says, was "much more
a flight *from* than *toward*."[19] Or, as Clyde Barrow says, "At this point, we
ain't heading to nowhere; we just running from." Indeed, the popular
slogans of the New Left—Nicola Chiaromonte's "total rejection" and
Herbert Marcuse's "Great Refusal"—traded on the premise that within
the "affluent society" one must devise a political project in negative
terms.[20]

The genre elaborated its logic in a sequence including *Midnight Cowboy, Easy Rider, Brewster McCloud, Harold and Maude* (Ashby, Paramount, 1970), *Two-Lane Blacktop, The Panic in Needle Park* (Schatzberg,
20th Century Fox, 1971), *Straw Dogs* (Peckinpah, Cinerama, 1971), *Wanda*
(Loden, Bardene International, 1971), *The Heartbreak Kid* (May,
20th Century Fox, 1972), *Scarecrow* (Schatzberg, Warner Bros., 1973),
*Badlands, The Last Detail, Cockfighter* (Hellman, New World Pictures,
1974), *Thunderbolt and Lightfoot* (Cimino, United Artists, 1974), and *The
Sugarland Express*. The studios, it is worth noting, did not mean to
develop a genre. To the extent that they perceived some similarity
between these movies, they did so rather superficially, producing in turn
what Derek Nystrom calls the "youth-cult cycle," which would include
movies such as *The Strawberry Statement* (Hagmann, MGM, 1970) and
*Getting Straight* (Rush, Columbia, 1970) that, though aimed at the youth
demographic, did not capture it as *Easy Rider* had. Rather than understand the genre as studio codified, then, it is better to call on Stanley
Cavell's definition of genre as movies that are what they are in view of

each other, bearing a "family resemblance" because they "share the inheritance of certain conditions, procedures and subjects and goals of composition."[21] Sharing this inheritance, they must work out "its internal consequences."[22] At minimum, directors in poststudio Hollywood had inherited the condition of classicality, or anyway, a form that had once performed the classical requirement, as Robin Wood describes it, of making the artist "at one with at least the finest values of his culture."[23] One way to cancel out this harmony textually was to deny the Hollywood couple its marriage, signaling in the gesture that society had neither hope of integration nor chance of reproduction. Nothing had been more definitive of the "smooth, careful linearity" of Hollywood narrative than the "heterosexual romance" and in particular the way its private success became an emblem—even a precondition—of public order and stability.[24] Some movies in the genre avoided the reproductive couple by putting male "buddies" at the center of the story (*Midnight Cowboy, Easy Rider, Two-Lane Blacktop, The Last Detail*).[25] Some movies kept the heterosexual couple but disabled its reproduction, in this way or that, as *Harold and Maude* does via menopause or *The Panic in Needle Park* via a delibidinizing drug habit. Still other movies, such as *Bonnie and Clyde*, preferred to complicate the matter by making the couple eligible, both glamorous and young, but yet unable to consummate the relationship. For those unable to consummate, and for those adrift, their stories often end in death.

Toggling between the impossible marriage and abrupt death, it seems, was a means for these movies to contemplate the limits of genre. Not only is this genre a study of classicality, that is, its failure to hold, it is also a version of the American romance. What Leo Marx once analyzed as a perdurable mode of storytelling, with a special inflection in American letters, the romance meant "to withdraw from the great world and begin a new life in a fresh, green landscape."[26] This is largely true of, but troubled in, the genre of defection. Such that this is its "inheritance," it does not come straight from Nathaniel Hawthorne but is more recently mediated by Jack Kerouac and the Beats. If this withdrawal into nature once called up oneness of a less "artificial kind," however, it is not preserved in the "ritual marriage" of "pastoral romance" but rather is stashed in "the landscape of the psyche."[27] Northrop Frye suggests that the upshot of this failure to "incorporate a central character" is pathos, because the "isolate mind," separated from society, is the object of study. When Frye says the "root idea of pathos is the exclusion of an individual on our level from a social group to which he is trying to belong," though, it is fair to bet that "an individual on our level" is construed on the model of gemeinschaft, on the order of the face-to-face, where the interpersonal encounter presumes two individual beings with "isolate minds" that, no matter their social positions, might be harmonized.[28] But the genre of defection, in contradistinction, confronts a personhood that is now legally reconstituted by corporations, the effect of which is to frustrate any kind of methodological individualism—dramaturgical, sociological, or philosophical. Denying the corporation its status as postwar society's "representative institution," the genre's protagonists are unintelligibly motivated; they are "broken by a conflict between the inner and outer world, between imaginative reality and the sort of reality which is established by a social consensus."[29] Hence, their broken drifting hangs as a question, one no longer answerable in the terms of the American romance, as to where one goes when fleeing society. "When we started out, I thought we was really going somewhere," Bonnie tells Clyde. "But this is it—we just going."

This can take us several directions. In one, the very notion that the romance had reached its imaginative limits can shunt us, in a political register, into New Left discourses subtended by the belief that institutions had no more safe "middle ground," as Leo Marx calls it, none of the spaces once set aside for a public sphere.[30] "The very isolation of the individual," according to "The Port Huron Statement," "means the rise of a democracy without publics."[31] Historically, it was the function of the university to tend such space, but it had been penetrated—so thought the New Left—by the combined imperatives of state and corporation, known in its byword, the "military-industrial complex." Hence, defection from institutional life as such would start to count, increasingly, as a political stratagem. One can track the genealogy of this politics through strains of Old Left thought, such as David Riesman's critique of "groupism" or C. Wright Mills's critique of white-collar conformity.

William H. Whyte helped mainstream these anxieties in his account of the "organization man."[32] In response, the New Left set its face against "dominant conceptions" that "man" is a "thing to be manipulated" by the institutional ensemble of "Big Business," "big labor," and "big government."[33] What is most remarkable in their formulation, in their fear, as they put it, of a "depersonalization that reduces human beings to the status of things," is that it marks a conceptual problem that, at root, might invite a symbolic rather than a practical resolution.[34]

In another, related direction, then, we can say that New Hollywood defined itself as a transfer of energy between the New Left and the "cultural apparatus," as Mills would call it, and for this, the genre of defection was a main node. When the New Left objected that no doctrines from "the past seem adequate to the forms of the present," New Hollywood could imagine, in turn, that it was taking on political problems when it renovated Classical Hollywood form. In *The Graduate*, *Bonnie and Clyde*, and *Five Easy Pieces*, what we can track is the "new class" that the university delimits, the so-called knowledge workers, as well as the organ of expression that this class would claim in the cultural apparatus and how, by way of acculturation of the social sphere, the condition of "objecthood" (to borrow from Michael Fried) would set the terms for a postindividual politics.[35] These key movies in the genre represent an aesthetic response to a political impasse.

In still another direction, it is possible to say that New Left antiinstitutional politics and New Hollywood objecthood, taken together, would redound to management theory and corporate form. In the field of management studies, a field legitimated by the MBA boom of the '60s, Douglas McGregor insisted that the old theory (Theory X) of top-down control be replaced by a model of employee "self-direction" that allowed "for realizing one's own potentialities, for continued self-development, for being creative in the broadest sense of that term."[36] McGregor's theory fit with Peter Drucker's ongoing call for a new corporate form, one attending to the centers of specialized knowledge within the firm, such that it might grant them the "greatest divisional autonomy and responsibility."[37] In the field of film studies, a field being legitimated by the development of film schools in the '60s, Andrew Sarris formulated the auteur theory to similar effect. That is the reason, I contend, that the genre of defection was epochal: it performed a New Hollywood self-understanding that, peeled back, revealed the so-called auteurs as agents of industrial reconfiguration, and while they put themselves across, textually, as "independent," even "maverick," the work they did, industrially, was to ensconce within a corporate structure the autonomous units—units such as Tatira-Hiller, Jalem, and BBS—that, thanks to them, made the structure more limber, more sustainable. What hand the auteur theory had in this is the story hidden in the genre of defection.

## BENJAMIN BRADDOCK AND BERKELEY

It is not obvious that *The Graduate* has something to do with the American romance, not in the same way that, say, *Easy Rider* or *Scarecrow* or *Badlands* so obviously relates to its thematic. It is easier to understand *The Graduate* in this way, though, when we consider how central the pastoral imagination is to the design of both American universities and suburbs. They are, we could say, pastoralism institutionalized, and they are the backdrop of *The Graduate* and the ground against which the figure of Benjamin Braddock (Dustin Hoffman) is struck. In a later scene when Benjamin visits the Berkeley campus, he is followed at a great distance by a crane shot that loses him for a moment in tree cover (see fig. 2.1). In what was for the time an unconventional establishing shot, the trees become the foreground, and the protagonist is out of sight, implying a dissolution of figure into ground. When Benjamin emerges, he sits on the lip of a fountain—an Arcadian scene at the water's edge—but it all happens beneath the seal of the American flag, which now dominates the foreground of the image (see fig. 2.2). What the movie indicates in this and other scenes is that the university is not a deliberative space where, as Marcuse would say, the "inner dimension" negotiates the "outer," where a "man may become and remain 'himself,'" but rather is an institution that is hooked into state functions.[38] The New Left was disappointed by this, by the "$40,000-a-year anthropologists and sociologists

**FIGURE 2.1**  In *The Graduate*, Benjamin strolls through Berkeley's faux-pastoral campus.

**FIGURE 2.2**  Benjamin arrives at the fountain, under the sign of the state.

for the AID program of the CIA," because, as Kirkpatrick Sale says, "they expected more from the university than they did from most other institutions because of its own claims."[39]

In this, the choice of Berkeley is perfect. Its president in those years, Clark Kerr, had been viewed by the student radicals as a "kept-apologist" for corporate liberalism.[40] In his *The Uses of the University*, a book known to the students, Kerr explains that the postwar university had come "to merge its activities with industry as never before." The university was "bait" for industry, he says, and the "intellect" had become "an instrument of national purpose, a component part of the 'military-industrial complex.'"[41] Benjamin was being shuttled along this "approved track," as Todd Gitlin describes it, and his graduation would look, in this view, like the minting of a product.[42] His consent to the system was a priori, secured by its very affluence, by its "increasing standard of living," as Marcuse would say, by the Alfa Romeo the Braddocks will give him on graduation and the ridiculous wet suit on his birthday.[43] This sense was familiar to those students who would form the New Left. Ronald Aronson, Marcuse's student at Brandeis and later the editor of *Studies on the Left*, describes himself in these terms: "Somehow I had gotten on this machine in motion, had become the machine, acting on behalf of some enormous power I couldn't even begin to fathom."[44] In *The Graduate* we see this from the start. In the first scenes Benjamin flies into Los Angeles and in the airport is conveyed along a moving walkway, which, in a visual pun, is matched in a parallel shot to luggage on a conveyor belt (see figs. 2.3 and 2.4). Benjamin is conveyed, his luggage is conveyed, and they join together—Benjamin lifts his luggage—only after we are shown a sign reading "Do They Match?" They *match*, as the pun goes, because they are both objects on a "machine in motion."

In this way, the movie was pitched to a young audience, an audience that had politicized in the university because it believed there it was being machine-fitted for corporate imperatives. And the audience

**FIGURE 2.3** Benjamin is carried along by the moving walkway.

**FIGURE 2.4** In a matching shot, Benjamin's suitcase is carried along by a similar conveyance.

responded in kind. Andrew Sarris recalls that while the National Society of Film Critics gathered to decide their annual awards, they looked down on the street below where an "endless" line of "young, shaggy moviegoers" waited outside the Coronet for *The Graduate*. "It wasn't lost on us," he said. "The line looked different from other lines. It felt quite symbolic."[45]

Benjamin Braddock, however, does not resemble the student radicals in either appearance or activity. The character, Mike Nichols said, "doesn't have the moral or intellectual resources to do what a large percentage of other kids like him do—to rebel, to march, to demonstrate, to turn on."[46] The radicalism of the movie is aesthetic, not political. Nichols took a comic scenario (a love triangle involving a young man and a mother and daughter) that lent itself to screwball conventions, such as it had in *The Moon Is Blue* (Preminger, United Artists, 1953), and he rendered it by nonverbal means. "People used to think that comedy meant talking very fast," Nichols said.[47] But for *The Graduate* he "cut long passages of dialogue" from Charles Webb's novel.[48] He wanted to convert the dynamic proper to screwball—the intersubjective battle for recognition—into a comedy of objecthood. Benjamin, according to Nichols, is "drowning in objects" and "in danger of becoming an object" and indeed "thought of himself as an object."[49] In fact, the real joke of the sets of tracking shots—of Benjamin on the moving walkway and his luggage on the belt—is that in the shot of Benjamin, he gradually moves from right to left in the frame, and as he exits it, there is a cut to the luggage at the extreme right of the frame: Benjamin has been transformed, it seems, into a piece of luggage. In short, the movie reduces a social problem into a condition of the film medium, which is defined, for André Bazin, by its leveling of the difference between subjects and objects and its granting "no a priori privilege" to the former over the latter.[50] This visual design is given special stress by the audacious use of the telephoto lens. The cinematographer, Robert Surtees, had been trained in classical methods during the studio era, but in Nichols's account, he "loved the idea of turning things upside down."[51] It is possible, then, to think that overturning classicality was a matter of dethroning subjectivity and installing in its place a poetics of objecthood. In part, Surtees's camera work was designed to disorient, to deprive the viewer of her hold on spatial relations and the subject position of knowledge it entails. Take, for instance, the graduation party that the Braddocks throw for Benjamin. The sequence involves a long handheld shot following Benjamin, beginning in his room, where he is placed before an aquarium in a close-up, framed so that his head seems like a strange outcropping of the sea floor, and from there his parents usher him in a tightly framed shot to the top of the stairs (see figs. 2.5 and 2.6). Then a cut. Unconventionally, rather than cut to a shot at the foot of the stairs, which might more properly establish the scene—taking in Benjamin from a distance and displaying the guests awaiting him below—the next shot yet again tightly frames him and his parents and holds them in a crowded frame as they descend the staircase (see fig. 2.7). Benjamin is being moved about, and the viewer cannot anticipate where he will be placed next or by whom.

The long take of Benjamin emerging into his parents' circle of friends famously culminates in Mr. McGuire's one-word counsel, "Plastics," which, however cryptic, seemed to make obvious sense for young audiences. One way to explain it is as a code word for the artifice of suburban happiness. Another, more specific explanation is that "plastics" is code for the underside of suburban affluence, the way it depends on a

**FIGURE 2.5** Benjamin's bust, planted in the aquarium.

**FIGURE 2.6** Benjamin being ushered along by his parents.

**FIGURE 2.7** In a crowded frame, Benjamin is met on the staircase by partygoers.

tripartite relation of state, industry, and not just the university but the class of knowledge workers it produces. Those corporations, then, known to play dual roles in a domestic and wartime economy, such as DuPont, the manufacturer of both nylons and plutonium, or Dow, the manufacturer of plastics and napalm, would be evoked by McGuire's advice.[52] The word "plastics" describes a class protocol predicated on disorientation, we might say, on the concealment of cause and effect in a knowledge economy. Benjamin later confesses to Elaine that he feels he is "playing some kind of game, but the rules don't make sense" to him. "They're being made up by all the wrong people. No, I mean no one makes them up; they seem to have made themselves up." Here, he is struggling with the issue of transpersonal agency, much like Ronald Aronson did, and in doing so, he gives form to what seems to be the paradox that within a knowledge economy, one is not the subject but the object of knowledge. At Berkeley, student radicals had taken this as the formal problem of their university experience, and they tried to figure out, dialectically, whether one could be both if one were to trace causality throughout a corporate structure. Mario Savio, orator of the Free Speech Movement, argued that if the university "is a firm, and if the Board of Regents are the board of directors, and if President Kerr is in fact the manager," then the faculty were just "a bunch of employees" and the students nothing but "raw material."[53] The solution, Savio thought, was to become a material that was resistant to processing. "You've got to put your bodies upon the gears and upon the wheels, upon the levers, upon all the apparatus," he commanded, "and you've got to make it stop."[54] What he advocated, in short, were the sit-in tactics recently used in Greensboro by blacks students who were protesting the denial of their basic citizenship. If they were objects, they reasoned, why not get in the way as objects do? Following suit, Berkeley students surrounded a police car in Sproul Plaza, and by simply *not moving* they prevented the police from hauling off Jack Newfield, a fellow protester. For Savio, what the sit-ins suggested was a mode of expression that was more politically effective than the liberal "speech" that "has no consequences" in the face of the "depersonalized, unresponsive bureaucracy" of institutions.[55]

While Nichols is right to say that Benjamin does not "turn on" politically as Mario Savio and the Berkeley students did, the movie offers the same analysis of institutions and likewise concludes that a mode of resisting institutions is simply to remain unprocessed raw material. In the final scenes, Benjamin shows his disregard of a main social institution—marriage—when he steals away with Elaine just after her marriage rite has been taken. Nichols was careful to make this change from Charles Webb's novel, wherein Benjamin arrives just before Elaine says her vows. In fact, Webb complained that in the book, Benjamin's "moral attitudes" make it necessary "for him to reach the girl before she becomes the wife of someone else" whereas in the "film version," to his chagrin, it makes "little difference whether he gets there in time or not."[56] The couple embarks on a city bus, then, and sits at the back, each one with a Mona Lisa expression that seems to invite a genre to answer the question, Did they succeed? Having fled the reach of institutions, do they form new ones more amenable to their interests? Will they have children? That is, will they reproduce sociality of this kind, or is this the end of the line?

## ALONG LEFTIST LINES

When Todd Gitlin called *The Graduate* "the blander" companion to *Bonnie and Clyde*, what he perhaps meant is that the latter seemed to take Mario Savio at his word when he declared that his generation would "die rather than be standardized, replaceable, and irrelevant."[57] This is what raised the genre of defection into another order, and it is also what split *Bonnie and Clyde*'s reception in half, precisely along generational lines. The most powerful establishment critic, Bosley Crowther, denounced the movie's "camp-tinctured travesties," and in trying to bury it in three separate reviews, he in effect ended his career.[58] Pauline Kael, by contrast, made her career by explaining that *Bonnie and Clyde* worked on the principle of the "put-on," which Jerome Christensen has argued is another name for postmodernism, and what the put-on could do most efficiently, Kael said, was select out an audience, an "educated, or 'knowing,' group," and for this audience "there is an excitement in hearing its own private thoughts expressed out loud and in seeing something of its own sensibility become part of our common culture."[59] It is Harrington's bohemia become mass culture, a minoritarian style—a "style of radical will," to crib from Susan Sontag—made available in the mainstream. *Newsweek* film critic Joseph Morgenstern, in an "unprecedented" gesture, filed a second review to rescind his first.[60] What we might say of its polarized reception, though, is that it restaged a political aporia in the terms of cultural debate. Gitlin's claim that Arthur Penn's Bonnie and Clyde were "children of the sixties set three decades back" suggests that reconfigured in them is the snarled transmission of values from the Old to the New Left, from the condition of depression to affluence.

Irwin Unger has described the shift from Old to New Left in terms of "the defection of the intellectual and academic communities from the left's vision of society and history," an outcome, arguably, of the internalization of Old Left members such as Daniel Bell and Irving Kristol in what C. Wright Mills delineates as the "establishment," namely that "zone of at least semiofficial prestige" where "culture and authority . . . overlap."[61] Their message to the New Left that "modern America was the best of all possible worlds" made the young prefer "radical banditry" to what seemed the acquiescence of their elders.[62] Quite often, the difference between the Old and the New Left seemed to boil down to questions of personal style. Irving Howe, an Old Leftist who retained his socialist convictions even as Bell and Kristol abandoned theirs, thought the New Left's leading light, Tom Hayden, had an "authoritarian personality."[63] Likewise, Dwight Macdonald criticized the New Left for not having "the same intellectual and moral style, as you might say, that my own generation had." We might gloss this to mean that they did not have faith in history, particularly in an evolving class self-understanding, as the engine of social change.[64] They displayed instead, Macdonald worried, a "principled refusal to learn from the past, from history, because you have to go to the library, probably, and look up all those big dull books."[65] The crux of their difference, however much it might be attributed to "style," lay more in the form that their dependency on institutions took. In a public exchange between representative members— Dwight Macdonald and Richard Rovere on behalf of the Old Left, Tom Hayden and Ivanhoe Donaldson of the New—Hayden's significant complaint was with how institutions had circumscribed their power, such that it was. "The only space for people who want to change the system," he said, "seems to be in theaters like this, or in magazines, but not in the world where power is accumulated."[66] His mention of "magazines" no doubt registered for Macdonald and colleagues as an attack on the "little magazines" such as *Partisan Review*, *Politics*, and *Commentary*, which had been a main avenue for the authority of the Old Left.

But in this attack, Hayden did not exactly exempt the New Left. He worried that accepting such institutional space meant there would not "be any operating room for any Left, New or Old." The New Left itself, he argued, risked "being swallowed up as a cultural artifact." The country did not want social change, he thought, but it wanted "the image of being tolerant and friendly toward protest." Activists spend such "considerable amounts" of time self-interpreting for "the mass media," he explained, that they become "a piece of fiction or a cut-out caricature."[67] Though Daniel Aaron accused the New Left of having "a certain ahistorical attitude," what he overlooked was that implicit in New Left style was a historical sensitivity to the "cultural apparatus," as Mills would call it, and what flowed from it was a strategy of outfoxing or staying a beat ahead of the cultural apparatus.[68] This animated the New Left's sense of institutions tout court, as Donaldson would suggest, of "the entire institution called America."[69] Hence Rovere's comment that "there is on the New Left a spirit of undiscriminating rejection of society" whereas the Old Left had "a kind of selective hostility toward political institutions" but not toward institutions per se. The Old Left, in fact, exploited the "health in particular institutions" for their political ends.[70] Rovere's assessment, on the face of it, seems right. Hayden was known to put challenges to the SDS at the level of institutional form. In the midst of debate, he would ask, "What if we were to stay here for six years and not come to a decision?" Or, "Suppose parliamentary democracy . . . were a contrivance of nineteenth-century imperialism and merely a tool of enslavement?" Hayden believed, according to Kirkpatrick Sale, "that SDS was caught in the bind of trying to create a new world with the tools of the old."[71] Right as Rovere's assessment seems, though, it does not capture how vexed the New Left was in their effort to put their politics in different relations to the cultural apparatus than the Old Left had put theirs.

On this point *Bonnie and Clyde* was clarifying. Consider, in its opening frames, the slide-show presentation of old black-and-white photographs. From the first, these photographs of Depression-era hardship in the style of Walker Evans raise the issue of culture in relation to the state, evoking as they do the Works Progress Administration and its support of what Mills called "cultural workers" in the 1930s vis-à-vis their counterparts in the 1960s, whose dependency on the culture industry was total. It polemicizes. Were Evans's images of poverty, it asks, politically agitating or culturally gratifying? Sorted into these photographs, eventually, are the images of stars Faye Dunaway and Warren Beatty dressed as Bonnie and Clyde. Then the slide show, complete with clicking sounds one might hear in a lecture hall, gives way not only to the moving image (twenty-four frames per second) but to the cinema (Bonnie, framed by her second-story window, for Clyde, the spectator below). Telescoped in this medium change, from photography to cinema, from education to titillation, is a recent history of cultural politics that the movie later works out in more explicit terms. In the later scene, Bonnie and Clyde are camped in an abandoned farmhouse when the dispossessed owner happens upon them. "Me and him put in the years," the farmer says gesturing to a black tenant farmer, but the "bank took it." In this, there is a leveling of race relations, as though the white and black farmer were in partnership, and whatever the movie means by it, we can be assured that it indexes the internal dynamics of the movements—where civil rights authorizes a set of other causes—more than it does Depression-era solidarity. In response, Clyde turns to the foreclosure sign ("Property of Midlothian Citizens Bank") and shoots holes in it. He offers the farmers the chance to do the same. This plays as catharsis for the farmers, but for Clyde, who to their bemusement says, "We rob banks," it performs a transaction of another kind. They have licensed Clyde, he thinks, to act *in their name.* He can cloak his vanity campaign with moral authority. What the scene captures is the unacknowledged moment when the real politics of a situation, understood as a difference in access to institutional resources, is absorbed into culture. Here, attention pivots from the situation to the person who represents it, from those who are oppressed to the person who acts on their behalf. In what follows, Clyde's claim to be "just folks"—when what he seems to mean is "folk heroes"—is the conversion of politics into cultural capital, which, for the New Left, was the Old Left's fault. Witness Ivanhoe Donaldson's frustration, for instance, with Michael Harrington legitimating poverty as a cause, which "does not relate to society as it is among the poor," Donaldson argues, but "relates to society as middle-class America thinks it is among the poor."[72]

Clyde means to curate their image, as we are shown. "I bet you're a movie star," he tells Bonnie, but then he demands that she comb the curlicue out of her hair when he sees the diner waitress wearing the same hairstyle. He is the film director to her starlet, and he wants her not to be a working-class waitress but an image of one. The image, however, at once enables and bedevils the New Left. When SDS activist Rennie Davis undertook to "organize with mirrors"—to make a *real* political movement by first producing its *image*—he was heeding C. Wright Mills's advice.[73] In his "Letter to the New Left," Mills suggests that with the "collapse of our historic agencies of change," namely "the working class" and those "acting in its name," the "young intelligentsia" might turn to "the cultural apparatus" as "a possible, immediate, radical agency of change."[74] The cultural apparatus, Gitlin argues, was precisely the source of the New Left's undoing, because the media would "certify" the "noteworthy 'personalities'" and hence reduce substantive "leadership" into hollow "*celebrity.*"[75] There, the personality "floated in a kind of artificial space," tempting "the follower or the fan" with entrance that would, in nearly all cases, be debarred to them.[76] In some sense, this is just what Marcuse warned that "affirmative culture" would do so efficiently, that is, store the "individual's claim to happiness" in a deathless image, in an immaterial stratum, "without freeing him from his factual debasement."[77] Celebrity, as the mechanism for this, solicits "admiration, not merely envy."[78]

What makes *Bonnie and Clyde* especially rich is that it harnesses this "deathlessness" to what will become the interdiction on reproduction in the genre of defection. Bonnie and Clyde, however idealized a couple, will not have children but will die. Yet the image of their death, the image for which the movie reserves its most spectacular treatment, will keep them alive at the level of culture rather than biology. Clyde's brother, Buck (Gene Hackman), representing the family-man's perspective, has different assumptions when he asks about Bonnie, "Tell me true, is she as good as she looks?" It is a carefully scripted question meant to underscore Clyde's contrarian notion that you are only as good as you look; there is no higher mark. Bonnie is less quick to accept this. Early on, Clyde rebuffs her sexual advances, "I ain't much of a loverboy." She is surprised—it seems so obviously one of the thrills his lifestyle promises—as are we; he is Warren Beatty, after all, well known by then *as* a loverboy. "Your advertising is just dandy," Bonnie quips. "Folks would never guess you don't have a thing to sell." Again, the dialogue is precise, setting her critique of his "peculiar ideas of love making" in the idiom of marketing. In it, the very art is to decouple image from substance, the "put-on," as Kael calls it, and Clyde's every gesture is characterized by it, as is their entire campaign. When Clyde drinks Coca-Cola, for instance, he takes a hearty pull from the bottle, but after his display, it seems no soda has been consumed (see figs. 2.8 and 2.9). There is a Freudian joke underneath this—his being unable to drink from the bottle, her fondling his gun, his having shot off his toes in prison—but the true rift in manifest-latent content is formed by advertising culture, by what Guy Debord would call the "society of the spectacle."

If all Bonnie wants is "a stud service," he tells her, she can go back to West Dallas and "stay there for the rest of [her] life." Have kids, he implies, reproduce what you know. But she is "worth more than that," Clyde argues, and he can show her how to accrue value in another way. "Let me take one of Bonnie alone," he says when Buck brings a Kodak. Bonnie then becomes instantly iconic, consumable but never fully consumed, when she takes Clyde's cigar and holds a pistol at her hip, cocking it toward the ground (see fig. 2.10). Clyde's commitment to their image is so thoroughgoing, in fact, that when they detain a lawman, he celebrates, "We got you!" when in truth they only take his picture and then release

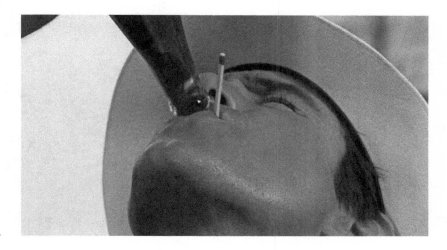

**FIGURE 2.8**  In *Bonnie and Clyde*, Clyde makes a great show of drinking soda.

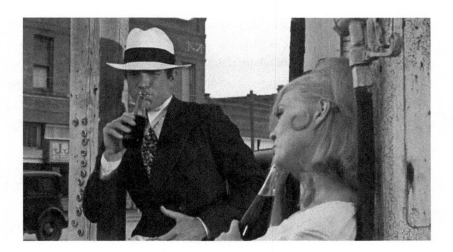

**FIGURE 2.9**  But after drinking, very little soda has been consumed.

him so that he can spread their legend. They got his image, and now it can be added to theirs. In this way Clyde guarantees their death, since this is the lawman who eventually brings them down.

By these outcomes combined, their deaths assured and their images preserved, they are now free to make love. Bonnie has narrated their

**FIGURE 2.10** Clyde makes Bonnie a cultural icon.

legend in a bit of doggerel sent to the newspaper, and Clyde commends her. "You know what you've done there?" he says. "You've told my story." It is an odd but telling formulation. Bonnie and Clyde, both, are the protagonists, but it is "his" story because he knew that the medium to carry it forward would be culture, not children. Now potent, Clyde makes love to her in the grass, and as he does, the newspaper is blown away by the wind, and then there is a jump cut on the newspaper to punctuate that *by it* they are reproduced. It is a fairly obvious gesture. However, while the movie lets Clyde enact his ideas, and by turns enacts them for him, it is not a blank endorsement for them. A voracious cultural apparatus, the movie suggests, is not progressive but repetitive. "What would you do," Bonnie asks Clyde, if by "some miracle" he "could start all over again, clean, with no record and nobody after us?" Clyde replies, as her face falls, that he would do it the same, but this time he would knock over banks in one state and live in another. She understands for good— hence her fallen face—that by the terms of their escape, they are doomed to static legend, playing the same roles over and over, forever sealed away in their deathlessness.

# THE ART OF OBJECTHOOD

When Nichols was making *The Graduate* and Penn *Bonnie and Clyde*, they had no way to know that their separate movies would amplify each other. But once their movies hit, they established a Rubicon, on one side of which was Old Hollywood and on the other, New Hollywood. The genre of defection formed in recognition of this. In *Midnight Cowboy*, Dustin Hoffman was once again placed at the back of a bus next to his partner, this time failed stud Joe Buck (Jon Voight), but rather than leave his destiny vague, as *The Graduate* does Benjamin Braddock's, this time it is made plain—his character, Ratso Rizzo, dies (see figs. 2.11 and 2.12). His escape to Miami is doomed, his defection a dead letter. Sam Peckinpah, having already answered the bell by re-creating the slow-motion, balletic deaths of Bonnie and Clyde on expanded scales in *The Wild Bunch*, would then riff on the trope of the defecting couple in *Straw Dogs*, only this time Dustin Hoffman's character more literally "defects" from the United States to rural England and is placed, finally, in the front seat of a car in a somewhat perverse coupling with the "village idiot" (see fig. 2.13).

It is easy to see why Peckinpah would try out the genre of defection, given that his métier was to unmake and remake another version of the pastoral romance, the Hollywood western. In fact, if we rooted our study of this genre in its most successful instance, *Easy Rider*, we might be led to call it residue from the western's generic exhaustion. Peter Fonda meant *Easy Rider* to be a modern western, with motorcycles instead of horses. But *Easy Rider*, for all that it shored up the genre and made it a cause célèbre, interpreted its requirements less subtly than *Five Easy Pieces* did. One thing we might say, though, is that the two movies, taken together, attest to the stake that BBS Productions had in the theme of defection. BBS, started by Bert Schneider and Bob Rafelson, established itself by way of *Easy Rider* but used *Five Easy Pieces* to refine its theme and make a study of the philosophy underlying it. In this sense, *Five Easy Pieces* works as what Jacques Lacan would call a "quilting point" (*point*

**FIGURE 2.11** In the iconic final scene of *The Graduate*, Benjamin and Elaine sit in the rear of a bus, heading nowhere in particular.

**FIGURE 2.12** In *Midnight Cowboy*, Dustin Hoffman reprises Benjamin and Elaine's escape by bus, this time with Joe Buck, and this time he dies.

*de capiton*) for the genre insofar as it seems to fix its meaning in place for the moment.[79] To talk about a genre—in this way, at least—is always to talk retroactively, hence it is best to consider it a as group of terms that only looks to be complete in view of its last term.

First we shall consider the final scene of *Five Easy Pieces*, since the question of endings is central to the genre. The screenwriter, Carole

**FIGURE 2.13** In *Straw Dogs*, Dustin Hoffman again flees in the final scenes, this time with the "village idiot."

Eastman (credited as Adrien Joyce), had written one ending, but Bob Rafelson shot a different one. In the original, Robert Dupea and his girl-friend, Rayette (Karen Black), would drive off a bridge to their deaths. This would have been a tribute to *Jules and Jim* (Truffaut, Janus, 1962), and it would have declared its doomed romanticism to be foundational to the genre. In the earlier movie's final scenes, Jim tells Catherine (Jeanne Moreau), "I agree with you that in love, a couple is not ideal. . . . You wanted to invent something better by rejecting hypocrisy and res-ignation." But when Jim tells her, "We failed"—as later in *Easy Rider*, Captain America (Peter Fonda) will say, "We blew it"—the only solution left to Catherine is to drive them off a bridge to their deaths. Indeed, before writing *Bonnie and Clyde*, Robert Benton had watched *Jules and Jim* more than ten times, and the original idea that Bonnie, Clyde, and C. W. Moss would have a ménage à trois had derived from Truffaut's love triangle. What is more, Jeanne Moreau remained a figure of fascination for the genre. Nichols had tried casting her for the part of Mrs. Robin-son, and Carole Eastman wrote her next movie after *Five Easy Pieces* for Jeanne Moreau and Jack Nicholson.[80] Moreau's final lament in *Jules and*

*Jim*—"What about the children I wanted?" she asks Jim; "they would have been beautiful"—puts a fine point on the genre's concern with non-reproductivity. But Rafelson preferred another interpretation. Hence, in the final scene, Robert Dupea leaves Rayette and their car at a gas station and gets a lift in a tractor trailer heading for Canada. Because the driver tells him, "Where we're going it's gonna get colder than hell," some have suggested that Robert is "heading for death."[81] But reading it this way says less than does the more literal reading that he is heading for Canada, a destination for many resisting the draft. This is defection by the book, and when he leaves his wallet with Rayette and his jacket in the bathroom—which is to say, his driver's license and legal tender—the movie is carefully underlining that what he is doing is disavowing his national personhood. This contrasts with the opening scene of Robert and Rayette in their living room, seated beneath a painting of JFK with the White House and Capitol to his left. There, Robert was still under the sign of citizenship, and in particular, the exuberant citizenship that the Kennedy administration had promised, but on the other end of the '60s, the channels of political belonging that had then enjoyed official sanction were foreclosed.

In its compressed imagery, *Five Easy Pieces* tracks the career of the New Left over the course of the '60s, from its reinvigorated citizenship to its renunciation, but in a perspective shift it tells the story in relation to the cultural apparatus, not the political sphere. Squint, and you might think it is about politics—this explains, I think, its passionate reception by young audiences—but seen head-on, it is hard to say that Robert is anything but apolitical. What Robert escapes from is the making of culture. His family lives in retreat from society on a Pacific Northwest island, each of them a virtuoso on one instrument or another, but the plot withholds this background, such that we might first take a position, seemingly a naturalized one, on culture making. In the first scenes, we see Robert working on an oil rig, coming home with a six-pack, and listening to his girlfriend as she sings verses to country songs. She hints that he has the wherewithal to make her more musical ("your whole damn family can play on some type of musical instrument," and she wants him to help her "pick a song"), but his concern is the next beer, sex, a night out bowling with friends. Derek Nystrom observes that Robert has given himself over to "proletarian physicality."[82] This describes his impulse to violence, for Nystrom, but it applies just as well to his sexual promiscuity and his general commitment to sensuous life. He commits to a proletarian lifestyle, we see, but not its class identity. The latter commitment, in the movie's account, gathers around a couple's reproductivity. While visiting friends Elton and Stoney, Robert and Rayette experience working-class family life at a remove. Rayette holds their baby and then passes it to Robert, as if to tempt him, and though he seems unmoved, upon leaving, Rayette suggests, "You just love that little baby, don't you?" Cut to a conversation on the oil rig, perhaps the next day. Elton tells Robert that Rayette is pregnant, that she confided as much to him, and that Robert should face up to his responsibility. "It's ridiculous," Robert objects. "I'm sitting here listening to some cracker asshole, lives in a trailer park, compare his life to mine." He makes it clear—in his most unlikeable moment—that he might try on the culture but has no interest in reproducing the social structure of the working class. The culture is not an agency of political change for Robert but a resource of creaturely pleasure.

When in the final scene Robert tells the truck driver, "All I've got is what I've got on," he makes a sidelong philosophical statement that lines up with aesthetic debates of the moment. Susan Sontag was the popular spokesperson for this position. "For we are what we are able to see (hear, taste, smell, feel)," she writes, "even more powerfully and profoundly than we are what furniture of ideas we have stocked in our heads."[83] What he has "got on" is his sensory equipment, his very bodiliness, and this is his point of conflict with his family. His brother, Carl, the most unapologetic bearer of high-culture values, has been physically disabled, making him less body and more mind. He "crashe[d] into a jeep and total[ed] his neck," Robert jokes. He has the "furniture of ideas," but— his injury implies—they do not arise from the immediacy of the sensorium. Carl's feeling, this suggests, is on loan; he stewards ruling-class values. Robert makes his point in a key scene with Catherine, Carl's fiancée and an eager student of the high culture he represents. She asks Robert to play the piano for her. As he starts a Chopin etude, a long tracking shot surveys the room, from the sheet music to the gallery of portraits, which sorts photographs of the Dupea children into the famous composers, and then back to Catherine, whose eyes are wet. "I was really very moved," she tells him, and he laughs because it was the "easiest piece" he could pick, and he played it better when he was "eight years old." It was not the technical prowess, she explains, but the "feeling" that she "was affected by." Robert counters that he "didn't have any," and she confesses that if he, the artist, had no "inner feeling," then she "must have been supplying it." What Robert denies her is a notion of art as a preserve and model of subjectivity; as a kind of structure into which the singularity of feeling can be deposited and sheltered for interpersonal exchange; and as a shield, importantly, against any grossly commercial transaction. It is a shell game, Robert thinks, this guessing of how much personality is found in the structure. For him, "the work of art is reasserting its existence as 'object,'" as Sontag argues, not dissimulating itself as "individual personal expression."[84] He chooses Chopin for this because, as he is a figurehead of Romanticism, his aesthetic claim turns on the transference of such feeling.

Robert implies that because Catherine wants the class lifestyle ("Some bath oil? How 'bout some avocado or some of this? Or some of this jasmine. . . . What are you doing screwing around with all this crap?"), she goes through the motions of music appreciation. He faked some Chopin, he says; she "faked a big response." Robert draws no bright line between high and low culture. When asked how he could turn away from "this incredible background in music," Robert says, "I've played a little bit here and there," once as "a rehearsal pianist" for a "Las Vegas musical revue." She objects, "You don't call that music." "Oh yes I do," he says. "It's music." He disdains those who depend on this hierarchy. When a family friend belittles Rayette, for instance, Robert asks, "What the hell gives you the ass to tell anybody anything about class or who the hell's got it or what she typifies?" On one hand, he is disputing the authority that Carl and his friends, as a group of artists and intellectuals, take for granted. But in deploying the word "class," with its double meaning, he makes their taste ("classy") identical with their class privilege. On the other hand, by telling the friend she does not have "the ass," he is telling her she lacks the only true source of authority, her bodiliness. Hence, once Robert tells Carl's friends, "You're totally full of shit, you're all full of shit," that is, once he tells them that their ideas are insubstantial, it makes sense that he goes off to encounter a body that gives him resistance. He then gets into a fight with Spicer, his father's nurse. The problem with Carl, as Catherine says, is that Robert does not think he is "substantial." This is the problem Robert has with all Carl's friends; they are moving pieces programmed by class values, and it seems the movie has meant them to resemble the New York Intellectuals. One character, in fact, looks conspicuously like Dwight Macdonald. Their ideas, moreover, sound like his. "But there is always hope for the few," says Carl's friend as she denounces instrumental rationality. Here, she echoes Macdonald's belief in the old avant-garde "from Rimbaud to Picasso," which "made a desperate effort to fence off some area within which the serious artist could still function." It was an "elite community, a rather snobbish one," Macdonald concedes, but it was "based not on wealth or birth but on common tastes." For Macdonald, the defeat of the "masscult" would come from the elite "insisting on higher standards and setting itself off— joyously, implacably—from most of its fellow citizens."[85] It is like the Dupea island, only accessible by ferry. The island, however, in Robert's perspective, is like an Easter Island of the bourgeoisie, just so many monuments to class life. If Carl's body is breaking down, his neck permanently in a brace, it is because, like his father, he is degrading into an object state. The father, Nicholas, now sits "there like a stone," Robert says. Indeed, when Robert first sees his father after his stroke, Nicholas is wheeled around like a bust, designed, it would seem, to fit among the dead composers adorning his home (see figs. 2.14 and 2.15).

For *Five Easy Pieces* this seems to be the outcome of the cultural apparatus, with country and classical music fitted cheek by jowl in its criticism. If modernist subjectivity has lapsed, it supposes, the one thing left to a person is his objecthood. Michael Fried attacks this position in his 1967 essay, "Art and Objecthood." In it, he designates as "literalists" those artists who believe the artwork cannot bear subjectivity nor suggest anything beyond itself. Robert Dupea assumes this position, I have argued, as he has only what he has "got on"; he is a literalist. For Fried, however,

**FIGURE 2.14** In *Five Easy Pieces*, Robert's father has been reduced to object state.

**FIGURE 2.15** He is an object like the busts of composers adorning the family home.

to give up on the modernist project is to give up on sociality in a non-dominating mode. There is a social project tied, necessarily, to aesthetic principles. What "literalists" reject is "the relational character of almost all painting." The fact that a painting is "made part by part, by addition," requires that the painter, and the painting's beholder, attend to the relation of the parts within it in a way that allegorically mirrors the relations without (the foremost relation being the one between painter and beholder). The "literalist" prefers instead "the wholeness, singleness, and indivisibility" of the object.[86] Denied any interiority, the artworks are perceived as "hollow," as indeed Catherine seems to worry Robert is. "If a person has no love of himself, no respect for himself, no love of his friends, family, work, something," she asks him, "what will you come to?" That she perceives in him no self-relation makes her worry that he can sustain no relation to her. This is in keeping with the "distancing" effect of objecthood, its power to structure the "non-personal or public mode" of interaction. Such artworks are simply in a room with a beholder—"They must," Fried says, "be placed not just in his space but in his *way*." Encountering "such objects" is not "entirely unlike being distanced, or crowded, by the silent presence of another *person*."[87] But the interpersonal agon is gone and any negotiation beside the point. What the other thing or person does is heighten one's awareness, light up one's sensorium, in the aesthetic mode known for "modifying our consciousness and sensibility," as Sontag says.[88] One is hence "against interpretation" if one is for experience.

So Robert must leave. My point, here, is less about the modernism-postmodernism debate than it is about *Five Easy Pieces* working through the logic of the genre. Moreover, it is most compelling that this logic is worked out by the first Hollywood directors to embrace and benefit from auteur theory. Denying relationality—which is the core of defection—is a fraught matter for the so-called auteur director, because Nichols, for instance, would have to deny or be shielded from Joseph Levine and Embassy Pictures, and Penn likewise would insulate himself from Warner Bros., which he could do, in fact, thanks to the intervention of Warren Beatty, who suggested to Jack Warner that the "WB" could as easily stand for Warren Beatty as for Warner Bros.[89] The firm BBS seems to approach a solution, or at least name the problem, by integrating art-world debates into its corporate culture (perhaps the effect of Dennis Hopper's intimacy with the art world) in order to reject the culture of its parent company, Columbia.[90] In this, they played their qualitative method off Columbia's quantitative one. BBS head Bert Schneider's father, Abe, president of Columbia, was, after all, an accountant. Call-ing the movie *Five Easy Pieces* put the stress on number ("five") and tech-nicity ("easy") in order to suggest that movies that would matter to people, namely young people, could not be made in an accountant's per-spective or by a group of technicians. When *Easy Rider* proved as much with a small budget ($375,000) and a huge return ($60 million), the Columbia accountants questioned which means would accomplish their ends. The studio contracted BBS to deliver six titles (*Five Easy Pieces* plus five more) produced without studio meddling so long as they came in under $1 million. BBS began, in *Five Easy Pieces*, to imagine that it was in their relation to Columbia that a problem lay. In later BBS movies they squarely address this, but in *Five Easy Pieces* they approach it asymp-totically by addressing, instead, the genre of defection. The genre, I believe, was a device for imagining industrial problems at one remove. If the genre imagined them in terms of political theory or aesthetic inno-vation, it is easy to transpose that imagination into the more practical, more immediate industrial context in which these directors worked. In turn, we can see how these themes of escape and augmented personal style became for them a mechanism for blotting out the corporate infra-structure without which their personal authority—however much they might think its force is intrinsic—would be radically scaled back.

## ROBERT ALTMAN MEETS LEO THE LION

For Robert Altman, there was no need to address the industry "at a remove" when he could do it head-on; no need, then, for defection movies, no need for auteur theory. "Are you a big believer in the auteur theory, of the director as author?" an interviewer asked Altman. "Uh, no," he replied; there is no "one author." "It's totally collaborative," he said. "Somebody has to show up to turn the switch on, that's all." Altman was not alone in his suspicion of auteur theory. Kirk Douglas claimed that whereas "the *auteur* theory holds that the director is the creator of the film," it is in fact a "collaborative effort," and it is "rare that a movie is ever one person's film."[91] And Warren Beatty would say the same: "To attribute [movies] wholly to their directors—not to the actors, not to the producers . . . well, that's bullshit!" Beatty objected, "Those pictures were made by directors, writers, and sound men and cameramen and actors and so forth, but suddenly, it's 'Otto Preminger's *Hurry Sundown.*' . . . It's not healthy."[92] It is not "healthy," in Altman's assessment, because it cannot "accept" cooperative activity without imagining that it is controlled by a "genius." In auteur theory we find an economy of genius, which replaces, or is a permutation of, the spirit that was dominating studio Hollywood, the "genius of the system." The notion that one form of domination must succeed another is, for Altman, simply "not true." "You can start an idea," he says, "but the idea can come from somebody else." When Altman concedes that "somebody has to show up to turn the switch on," however, he is saying, in effect, that "somebody" organizes the operation.[93] Organize, Altman suggests, but minimally. "The less I have to do with [my films]," he says, "the better they get." For him, it works as a management style—"somebody else picks up what they think that I want because their ambition and desire to do something" drives them to think, "he'll let me do that." According to Altman, "That's really all I do, is allow things to happen."[94] This form of liberation management is common, as it happens, to those movies we now lump together in the auteurist moment of New Hollywood. Liberated, people worked harder because their own "ambition and desire" were now at stake, whereas before, they had not been. "Everyone connected with [*Bonnie and Clyde*] felt just a little bit insulted by the movie business before they went into it," Beatty would say. "Everybody had something they knew they could do better, and they all showed up and did it."[95] Robert Towne concurred, "There was no department on that film where there wasn't somebody who was simply extraordinary being given the opportunity to do their job in a way that they had rarely if ever been given an opportunity to do it before."[96]

Altman did not care to present himself as a Romantic artist contending with an unfeeling institution—which was then the mythicizing function of auteur theory—and this was in part because, ever the pragmatist, he had accepted the corporation as the unit of agency within Hollywood and had in turn incorporated himself. Hence, his power would be of the same kind (if not the same count) as the studio's. On November 18, 1969, as his movie *MASH* was about to be released, Altman filed an article of incorporation for Lion's Gate, and on December 8 he was given consent papers. "I use the capitalistic system," he explained. "We all do."[97] If Altman did not need the auteur theory to set himself off from the Hollywood studios, he would use it nonetheless to change up their corporate protocols. "We stay away from the standardized way most of the studios work," he explained. "Our company philosophy, if we have any, is to break patterns. We say, 'Let's see if we can do it a different way'—not necessarily a *better* way. Just a different way, to find out why we do it that way. It may be perfectly logical for Twentieth-Century Fox to do it one way, but there may be no reason for *us* to do it that way."[98] For him, then, the defection movie (with its Romantic, pastoral imagination) was as committed to mythmaking as traditional genres such as the western and the detective story were, and just as he would deconstruct those genres, he also did so with the defection movie. In *Brewster McCloud*, Altman makes a study of the defection movie, at once underlining and undermining its generic features. But given that the genre was only then unfolding itself (*Cool Hand Luke, The Graduate, Bonnie and Clyde, Midnight Cowboy,* and *Easy Rider* had already been hits, but other genre members were still to come), his spoof of it was too "inside" for most audiences, so inside, in fact, that one presumes its true audience was the Hollywood studios themselves. For Altman, *Brewster McCloud* became the occasion to expose the fantasized relation of defection filmmakers to their corporate aegis, which he did in the very moment that he was constructing a corporate alternative of his own, Lion's Gate, which would not wish away the corporate studios but transform them.

Let us start with *Brewster McCloud*'s first frame: its studio logo. We see the MGM logo card, with the "Ars Gratia Artis" paper scroll encircling Leo the Lion, the same as every other MGM movie; but as Leo the Lion dips back his head to roar, we hear nothing. Then, instead of a roar, we hear, "I forgot the opening line," as though the lion is nothing more than a disinterested, unrehearsed actor. It is more than a swipe at MGM having lost its roar; it is a denaturing of what the animal—in this case, the corporation, MGM—seems most naturally to do.[99] The logo card is made continuous with the first scene, then, by the laughter of the crowd at the lion's flubbed line, which bridges the two frames. J. D. Connor explains that "logo bleed" such as this is "the privileged sign of the intentional integration of studio and story" and argues that it is a device that became increasingly common once the studios lost their identities (their "roars") and the stories they told seemed in no obvious way connected to their corporate cultures.[100] Scored to crowd laughter, the first scene begins with René Auberjonois, an actor in Altman's company, entering a university classroom and addressing the camera with a lecture on "the flight of bird" and "the flight of man." In a fully Brechtian mode, he seems to outline for us what will be the thesis of the movie: "These are the subjects at hand," he says. "We will deal with them for the next hour or so and hope that we draw no conclusions, elsewise the subject shall cease to fascinate us and, alas, another dream shall be lost—there are far too few." The thesis of the movie thus concerns the movies themselves, the "dreams" they give form to, and though it is clear that Altman means to deconstruct their mechanism here, he wants somehow to keep their charm intact. The charm of this dream, however, man's dream of flight, puts us in mind of the defection movie and its impulse to transcend the social world. In the "next hour or so," the movie will analyze this; it will, in short, deconstruct the defection movie. It will include Margaret Hamilton reprising her Wicked Witch of the West from *The Wizard of Oz* (Fleming, MGM, 1939), this time as a nasty, racist dowager, and in a curtain call Jennifer Salt's character reappears as Dorothy. This is to say that the defection movie that *Brewster McCloud* has acted out for us, what we had thought was a hippie staple filled with counterculture types, is no more than a variant of *The Wizard of Oz* (see fig. 2.16). In that movie, Dorothy's urge to transcend her social world is satisfied by a whirl through Technicolor—*by the movies*, as it were—and once her urge is satisfied, she is resettled in her Kansas home. Altman's critique of the defection movie, therefore, is not only that it is old hat but that its protestation is autotelic, concerned not with changing the social world but only with expressing itself.

**FIGURE 2.16** In the curtain call for *Brewster McCloud*, the defection movie is revealed as a version of *The Wizard of Oz*, as Jennifer Salt takes her bow as Dorothy, with the Tin Man and the Cowardly Lion visible behind her.

Altman was not criticizing the movies for opening their expressive ambit, if that is in fact all the defection movie was doing (i.e., now movies can be negative instead of positive, critical instead of affirmative). He favored movies in that expressive key, after all, as *MASH* had shown. His objection was that movie corporations, such as MGM, had forgotten what they did most naturally: make movies. In this period MGM and the other studios had shifted into real estate and other ventures as they either managed their financial structures or were folded into conglomerates. In 1969 Kirk Kerkorian had bought MGM, at least in part because its real estate was attractive and also because the symbolic value of its logo could be attached to his other ventures (Vegas hotels, chiefly). Hence, Altman's criticism was that this self-styled movie company was no longer even a movie company. It now looked outside itself to see what it ought to be doing. According to Doran William Cannon, the original screenwriter of *Brewster McCloud*, the studio "people who hated the script in 1967 have come over to the other camp and love it now" because, in his judgment, the "businessmen types . . . find it profitable to 'like' such works now."[101] They did not care what it was as a movie, Cannon implied, they cared that it could make money. Counterculture style, for their purposes, might as well have been prime real estate. In reviewing

*Brewster McCloud*, Vincent Canby claimed that it made him "uneasy," much as he would be inclined to be upon meeting a "$150,000-a-year movie executive whose newly freed spirit is expressed by his custom-made dungarees, his shoulder-length, 'styled' hair and his love beads. It's imitation hip."[102] Altman likely shared Canby's disdain for ersatz counterculture, but the intent of *Brewster McCloud* was not to reproduce it but rather critique it. Canby seemed to mistake it for just another iteration of *Skidoo* (Preminger, Paramount, 1968), Doran William Cannon's previous movie, when in fact it was looking inward at the anti-corporate spirit of the counterculture instead of simply having outward fun with it. It might be best to say that Cannon wrote *Brewster McCloud* in earnest, and the studio was hoping to peddle it in these terms, but Altman satirized it in its making. If studios hoped a counterculture veneer would cover up their failing business model, Altman had no sympathy for their lack of imagination. "All studios are going broke," he said, "and I love it."[103] Richard Zanuck wrote him a note in response: "Dear Bob, Thanks a lot."[104]

Zanuck had reason to be hurt. As production head at 20th Century Fox, he was the one to give Altman the chance to direct *MASH*. If Peter Biskind is to be believed, though, Zanuck was "appalled" by Altman's work, "groaned" at it in dailies, and "wanted to reedit" *MASH* until a test screening suggested it could be a hit.[105] The personal animus between Altman and Zanuck, if any obtained, is less important for my purposes than the systemic critique implicit in all of Altman's "anti-s," particularly his anti-studio-management culture.[106] He had to shoot *MASH* on Fox's Malibu Ranch rather than on location as he had with *That Cold Day in the Park* (Commonwealth United, 1969), but he believed the studio's much larger pictures that year, *Patton* and *Tora! Tora! Tora!*, would deflect attention from him as long as *MASH* "stayed under budget."[107] His production was annealed as a self-contained unit, a sort of portable commune, by what he imagined to be the outside antagonism to it. He would later learn, it is worth noting, that there was dissension *within* it. Elliott Gould said that he and Donald Sutherland had a problem with Altman for "being lax in terms of what our expectations were," and since they shared CMA agent Richard Shepard, they "went in and had a meeting and complained." They were, Gould has confessed, "two elitist, arrogant actors who really weren't getting Altman's genius."[108] His genius, of course, was to flatten whatever hierarchies had once elevated some on the set at the expense of others. Those who gained from this deemed it workplace democracy; those who lost deemed it anarchy. "Free yourself up," Altman would say. "We're all in this together. Yeah, I'm the captain of the ship, but we're all guiding the ship through the fog, and the fog is the movie system."[109] Richard Zanuck, for better or worse, embodied better than anyone the "movie system" that Altman and company were navigating. He was the son of Darryl Zanuck, one of the moguls of the studio system, and had been reared on the 20th Century Fox lot, learning it one department at a time. When still in his twenties, he took over as production chief, and by the time he green-lighted *MASH*, he was associated with boondoggle projects such as *Doctor Dolittle* and *Star!* that spelled Old Hollywood's breakdown. Zanuck was management, and Altman "had an enormous disagreement"—abstractly, as it were—with "the management."[110]

The management situation he devised in response was a kind of utopian enclave, a "ship" guided through a "movie system." With *MASH* he did this by hiding in plain sight, on the backlot but overshadowed by *Patton* and *Tora! Tora! Tora!* But with *Brewster McCloud*, *McCabe & Mrs. Miller* (Warner Bros., 1971), *Nashville* (Paramount, 1975)—and the list goes on—he did it by taking productions to distant locations. There, a business culture would be improvised. In a certain sense, the improvisation that became Altman's calling card was simply the textual equivalent (in script, character, dialogue, etc.) of his more structural impulse to improvise the corporation at a new site each time. That he could do it as efficiently as he did, improvising labor regimes while bringing in productions on budget, might stand as his signal innovation on corporate form; it should be noted, though, that Lion's Gate had a more or less permanent site. In April 1971, Altman took a lease on a "cluster of eclectically decorated offices that used to be small 'artsy-craftsy' shops in a courtyard" at 1334 Westwood Boulevard in Los Angeles.[111] This was his studio, Lion's Gate. The emphasis on architecture ("'artsy-craftsy' shops in a courtyard") is key—as if recalling the open-air plan of the Cadbury brothers or foretelling the "campus" layouts of Silicon Valley—and we shall see that for Altman, that is where the communitarian ethos is always inscribed, from *Brewster McCloud* to *McCabe & Mrs. Miller* to *Quintet* (20th Century Fox, 1979) and down the line.[112] Building a place to work is building a place to work *pleasurably*. Hence, when you walked into Lion's Gate, there was "a full-scale pinball machine, which [was] always being played by one or another of Altman's young staff."[113] There was a bar, and there was a pool table in Altman's office. He "converted one of the garages in the back alleyway into an illegal screening room" per city ordinances. Jan Stuart describes it as "a fantasy of masculine Old World charm." Actor Scott Glenn considered it "just sort of a hangout place for friends of Bob's," a place he would drop by after work "to see who was there." Activity was constant, "the bar was open, and they'd schmooze."[114]

Altman's management style, in brief, was characterized by the blurring of work and fun in a mode that Tom Peters calls liberation management. Innumerable collaborators recall the freewheeling time they spent working with Altman. Carol Burnett said *A Wedding* (20th Century Fox, 1978) "was like summer camp. We all had our kids with us and we had a hoot. Best summer vacation I ever had."[115] Michael Murphy claimed it was "upsetting" not to work on one of Altman's movies "because you knew there were a lot of people out there having a hell of a good time and you weren't."[116] Bud Cort said, "It was bonding, like actually a family."[117] But the work did not disappear into fun for everyone. Donald Sutherland, for one, held out from the bacchanal. George Segal said working for Altman "was like visiting Mars. . . . You visit his world. Welcome to it. Lion's Gate Productions. He's the lion. Hi. Have a good time. It's a very secure world."[118] According to Wayne Grigsby, "Some find the camaraderie cloying, others find it exploitative."[119] The fun—the "enthusiasm," Altman calls it—ended up being a substitute for compensation of other kinds. "All of them could get better jobs," Altman said of his employees. "They could improve their incomes, their status by working somewhere else."[120] If they are not doing it for the money or status, he believes, they do it for love of the project. When building the sets of *McCabe & Mrs. Miller*, Altman recounts taking Warren Beatty to the location. "We drove up to this little site," he says, "and there is a guy up to his waist in dirty water and he's pulling a lot through the thing and he's got a beard and tattoos on him." Altman realized that the man was completing a job that he had first rejected, building a bridge for Altman. "I said, 'Hey, you're gonna do my bridge after all.' . . . And he came up to me and said, 'I figured out a way to make your bridge, because there are two trees that happen to be there that would work.' He put a whole little structure in that allows for this bridge I wanted to be there. So he's up to his ass in mud and water building this bridge with some other guy, and I mean this is really hard work," Altman notes. "Those people up there—and I know they're not on dope, so they're not just up there stoned—they really love what they're doing."[121] The work they did, in short, had returns for them only to the degree that they were invested in the project. Altman expressed it in canny terms: "The total energy goes toward the center of a product."[122] What is so canny about this is that the same terms can be used to describe the corporation. The "grand, crazy parties" that Neal Gabler says "happen[ed] to become movies" just as easily became a corporation; the "center" of "total energy" expressed either way, in fact, would become a peculiar emblem of the new economy. It is an economic order that, decades later, Tom Peters says offers "unending personal liberation and total business fun." But Christopher Newfield is right to point out that Peters's latter-day "new economy" fantasies have a long tradition for "probusiness liberals" of being nurtured "only within the borders of the firm."[123]

It is this sense of enclosure, I contend, that Altman thinks the defection movie depends on. Its spatial imagination, in his diagnosis, is predicated on corporate territory, and so whenever a defection movie imagines escape, it is not escaping but only deterritorializing the firm. As *Brewster McCloud* begins with a pan across downtown Houston, René Auberjonois's ornithological lecturer says, "It may someday be necessary to build enormous environmental enclosures," and the image of the Astrodome appears at the phrase "enormous environmental enclosures." The Astrodome will constitute, for Brewster McCloud, his arena for action. Its corporate markings are accentuated: outsize Texaco signs are featured prominently above the stadium's outfield seats, and the assorted facilities of the Astroworld complex in general fill out the movie's mise-en-scène. Thanks to MGM leverage, Altman was able to negotiate "the use of the entire Astrodomain which includes the Astroworld Hotel, the Astroworld Amusement Park and the Astrohall, a huge convention pavilion which housed production facilities, including a projection room, and served as a studio for the construction and housing of the film's three major interior sets."[124] In return, MGM promised "to strike a special 70 mm print" and for the Astrodome to foot the bill for a lavish world premiere "to kick off festivities for the Astro Blue Bonnet Bowl football game."[125] Though Altman would use this setup to "eliminate any shooting on the coast" and thereby insulate from its parent company the Lion's Gate crew—a kind of ad hoc corporate fiefdom, themselves—he made much of the corporate enclosure of Astroworld and the branded universe it supplied.[126] "Whole scenes," said producer Lou Adler, "were created and improvised on the spot when Altman was intrigued by a particular situation or fascinated by a portion of the Astrodome's architecture."[127] Adler would say it was "like an adult Disney picture," and though in this he only reiterates Altman's notion that "it's either going to be an R-rated children's picture or an adult children's film," in short, that it had "turned into a kind of cartoon," it is likely, too, that Adler was saying that its action fit properly within a corporate theme park.[128] What Altman did, logistically, was broker an agreement between large entities—MGM and Astrodomain—that allowed his small firm a space to act without fettering.

At the root of *Brewster McCloud*, then, is Altman's observation that it is "a difficult task," as Michael Harrington had argued, to fall off "the margin of society" because it is in that margin that so much commercial activity is generated. Hence, fleeing for the margin—or dropping off it—is seldom the same as escaping the corporate framework of social experience. Often, Altman thinks, it is a form of resizing the corporate framework. The movie begins as an essay (Altman says his movies are either "essay films or interior films") on flight as a concept. "We must isolate the dream," the lecturer tells us. "Was the dream to attain the ability to fly, or was the dream the freedom that true flight seemed to offer man?" Because the ability to fly, he continues, does not imply freedom from social hierarchy but simply hierarchy of a different kind. "Schjelderup-Ebbe first used the word 'dominance,'" he tells us, "in describing his observations on the social hierarchies of birds. He concluded that within a flock composed of a single species there exists a definite order of social distinction." Following this preamble, we are introduced to Abraham Wright, a capitalist in the tradition of Lionel Barrymore's Mr. Potter; we learn in due course that Abraham is a descendant of Orville and Wilbur Wright, and his wealth—we infer—derives from patenting the means of flight. Flight therefore promises commerce and thus social hierarchy, not freedom. Our protagonist, Brewster McCloud, shortly kills off Abraham Wright, and perhaps too the social hierarchy he upholds, but in the drama stemming from Brewster's own designs for a "flying machine," we scarcely get the sense that he intends social good over individual profit.

It is hard to know his intent, though, because he is building his wings at the behest of Louise (Sally Kellerman), a Glinda the Good Witch to Margaret Hamilton's opposite number. Brewster, if he is a cipher dramatically, is meant to stand in for the counterculture, and hence Louise counsels him against what might be considered its illusory emancipation. What Louise tells Brewster is a stock criticism of the counterculture. "People like Hope accept what's been told to them," she says. "They don't think they can be free . . . their sex is the closest thing they have to . . ." And Brewster finishes the thought: "Flying." That is to say, they accept sensuous pleasure as a trade-off for more principled forms of freedom. The stock criticism, as Paul Monaco phrases it, is that "the late 1960s in the United States proved far more revolutionary culturally than politically."[129] Louise cautions Brewster that if the horizon for most people's ambitions is first political, "something happens to them as they grow; they turn more and more toward Earth, and when they experience sex, they simply settle for it and procreate more of their own kind." Here the movie explicitly names the interdiction on reproductive couplehood. It suggests, in turn, that the interdiction is in place because the status quo is so inexorable that only it can be reproduced. The point is driven home when Brewster meets Suzanne (Shelly Duvall), has sex with her, shares details of his flying machine with her, and invites her to fly away with him. "Fly away?" she objects. "You could be a millionaire. I've got to get you a good lawyer, to protect you. And you'll need a patent." She uses sex, much as Louise warned Brewster, as one among many commercial stratagems. In the final scenes, then, we are not at all surprised when Brewster straps on his wings and takes flight in the Astrodome only to crash in a heap on the artificial turf below.

It is no surprise that Brewster cannot fly beyond the Astrodome, given its enclosure, just as Altman is saying it is no surprise that he flies not beyond but within the corporate framework set for him by MGM and other media companies. "Someone has suggested that with Lion's Gate you're founding a mini-MGM," an interviewer told him.[130] Comparing Lion's Gate to MGM at the time seemed irresistible thanks to Leo the Lion. A *Film Comment* article began, "While the roar of MGM's Leo has been reduced to little more than a whimper, another lion is roaring more loudly than ever. That's the lion of Robert Altman's film production company."[131] Altman conceded, "If I am" founding a mini-MGM, "it's in self-defense."[132] By 1977 his company had grown to the point where "bigness" came to seem the "natural end of an operation" such as his.[133] In that year he made *3 Women* (20th Century Fox) and produced *Welcome to L. A.* (Rudolph, United Artists) and *The Late Show* (Benton, Warner Bros.) and had figured out by then that "our nut is $660,000 a year roughly," he said. "Fifty thousand a month is what we have to generate in income to keep the thing going."[134] Once Lion's Gate was a fully realized corporate fiefdom, Mike Kaplan's comment that Altman was not "a dictator" but a "commander" makes sense of the strange position he had evolved for himself.[135] It was the nature of his managerial role, which he would come to terms with throughout the corporate maturation of Lion's Gate, but most explicitly in *Brewster McCloud*.

In this period, Altman and his advisers had debated whether his firm should be a C or an S corporation, and recondite as their debate was, it turned on whether Lion's Gate was merely a legal shield for Altman's "personal talents" or whether its "operational organization" was "broader and more permanent."[136] Though the firm had in fact innovated sound equipment and become known in the production community for its services, the rental of this equipment was classified as income from a personal holding company. "In the Lions Gate situation," his lawyers advised, "while some of the equipment was designed by Lions Gate and built to its specification, it is not clear that such equipment would qualify as being 'manufactured' by Lions Gate."[137] Hence, in their recommendation, all the year's income would need to be paid to Altman "either in the form of compensation or in the form of dividends" lest it be assessed as "the corporation's retained earnings" and levied an 85 percent surtax.[138]

What is relevant, here, is that the legal standing Altman had would necessarily bear on how he worked with others, and the question of whether they subserved his vision (i.e., the auteur theory conventionally understood) or whether a corporate spirit might remain unattached to a person and be spread to all members of the firm (i.e., the auteur theory reconfigured as management theory) was a distressing matter for Altman. The fear that his was a "beneficent monarchy" seemed to be a function of his company lapsing into subchapter S status or of being always on this verge, and in *Brewster McCloud* the rawness of this fear is lampooned in the character of Frank Shaft (Michael Murphy), a send-up of the police detective that Steve McQueen played in *Bullitt* (Yates, Warner-Seven, 1968).

Shaft is an investigator imported from San Francisco on the assumption that his renegade methods are more effective than those of the hidebound police department to solve the serial murders happening in Houston. His hipness distinguishes him: "If keeping your cool and being totally composed makes for a better detective," a radio voice says of Shaft as he unpacks a suitcase of turtleneck sweaters—just after our lecturer has described the "matchless plumage" of the crested peacock—"then this Shaft is one whale of a cop." The counterpoint between Shaft's West Coast ways and the local police department's Southern ways is established again and again. "I don't know how it is in San Francisco, sir," says Officer Johnson (John Schuck), "but here in Houston, Captain Crandall is head of homicide, and he rules that department with an iron fist." Throughout the movie, Shaft will insist that Officer Johnson call him Frank—"That's my name," he says—whereas Captain Crandall, in a running gag, never remembers the name of his subordinate (he calls him Haynes, but his name is Hines). But Shaft's faux chumminess, we see, is only a technique by which he exploits his workplace relationships. He imagines that he and Officer Johnson are friends but sits in the back seat of Johnson's cruiser because, he says, "There's no point in them knowing we're friends." Yet it is on the basis of their friendship that Frank calls Johnson during off hours and asks that he do legwork on their case. "I need somebody I can trust on this," Shaft tells him. Ultimately, the movie satirizes the "beneficent monarchy" of Frank Shaft in the same amount it does the top-down authoritarianism of Captain Crandall.

Altman at times called his "working philosophy" a "beneficent monarchy" in recognition that, although his command structure was "uncommonly open to suggestions and alternative solutions," it was nonetheless the case that the "funky live-in/work-in manner" of Lion's Gate would return its yield to corporate form.[139] And it was Altman qua corporate person who stood to gain. A refrain that sounds throughout *Brewster McCloud*—"Are you happy in your work?"—suggests that we do not find our happiness in the idyllic spaces outside the centers of power but rather within them. Altman was dialed in to this, and he used *Brewster McCloud* to caution youth culture that its dreams of liberation will simply redound to power in its newer, more companionable permutations. Part of his enterprise, indeed, was to extract work from the centers of power that would stymie it, and relocate it (literally, to Canada, Houston, and elsewhere; figuratively, from factory to playground) so that the energies that enabled it could be unbound. In his own habits, Altman was notorious for brooking no difference between work and its other. "My work is the only thing I live for," he said. "From getting up in the morning until I go to bed."[140] He came to work every day, he said, "whether there's anything to do or not. . . . I can be here in the office, get drunk, go next door and edit out a piece of film. It's terrific, like owning the world's biggest erector set."[141]

The corporation as "the world's biggest erector set," in Altman's view, is a more honest way to see the setting for our labors than the pastoral romance imagined in the defection movie. Participating in this world—self-incorporating, that is, acquiring an erector set of one's own—does not limit one's political agency but rather enables it. But if the exploitation of resources were simply the terms of corporate enterprise, it would always be a risk that the resource most likely to be exploited in the utopianized firm (such as Altman's) would be the labor of its members. It was a risk Altman was willing to bear because he believed that the alternative—the youthful dream of escape—was more vulnerable to exploitation still.

# 3

# TELEVISION TOTALITIES

## Zanuck-Brown and the Privately Held Company

*Television has not only affected the economic structures of film-making, it has also brought ideologically less representative groups into the cinemas, notably the young who now see the cinema as an escape from television.*

Thomas Elsaesser

Although the genre of defection was ripe for Robert Altman's satire in 1970, it continued nonetheless to be generative for the next several years, culminating in its peak years of 1973–1974. In that moment, Steven Spielberg's *The Sugarland Express* failed theatrically, and he believed it was due to genre fatigue. "The main failing of the *The Sugarland Express*," Spielberg said, "was the fact that we came out with two other films thematically similar—*Badlands* and *Thieves Like Us*—and that the audiences were wrapping all three of them into one bundle."[1] Their "bundling" kept audiences from understanding how "essentially different" these "motion pictures" were. This was Spielberg's sense, at least, and it is not altogether wrong. It is just hard to say whether they are different in their essence or their features. Spielberg claimed that Terrence Malick's movie, *Badlands*, was different because it was "a great downer."² Insofar as both movies (Malick's and his) narrate the failure of romance to produce family, though, they seem alike; that is to say, they seem like defection movies, which in essence are "downers." In Spielberg's movie the couple has a child, it is true, but the child has been taken from them by the state, and in their flight from the state's agents, the husband, Clovis (William Atherton), is gunned down. But the difference for Spielberg is that the audience was not meant to root for the fleeing couple but rather the cops pursuing them. "But I think the heroes are the police," he said, though he conceded that "nobody else sees it that way." What we might assume is that the difference is garbled, in part because Spielberg was caught in the generic habit of seeing "the picture through Goldie Hawn's eyes"—i.e., the defector's point of view—even though he wouldn't grant her character, Lou Jean, his sympathy.³ It is not in the mechanics of storytelling to see through the eyes of the pursued but root nonetheless for the pursuers.

But neither Spielberg nor Malick was occupied with the mechanics of storytelling so much as he was with reestablishing what is properly "cinematic." In both cases, I argue, they were marshaling proof of cinema, so to speak, in the teeth of television's encroachment as a dominant medium. This preoccupation suggests to me that one thing the defection movie was trying to separate itself from was television: that is, if the defection movie was the auteurist genre, and auteurs liked to imagine themselves defecting from "the system," then for them, television was a metonym for the system. Spielberg effectively did this in *Jaws* when, according to Judith Crist, he "stuck to the heart of the art . . . rendering unto cinema the things that are peculiarly its own."⁴ In *The Sugarland Express*, however, the agon between cinema and television remains a theme more than a formal challenge. Spielberg thought its "villains are the well-wishers that wished a little too much for these people," and of course these wishes are channeled by television coverage; Clovis and Lou Jean's flight is broadcast as a media event.⁵ In *Badlands*, too, Malick stages the difference between private media and public broadcast: Kit and Holly document their experiences by way of a series of private devices, such as the Voice-O-Graph, a "private recording studio," and a time capsule of written "vows" and "tokens" of their life together. But their private experience is hemmed in at each turn by public broadcast. Even when they escape civilization and build their "house in the trees, with tamarisk walls and willows laid side by side to make a floor," they have a radio piping in the pop songs of the day. In one scene they dance to Mickey & Sylvia's "Love Is Strange"; in another Kit leads Holly through a forced box step to Nat King Cole. For Malick, it seems, the system of broadcasting is the enemy. It is the transpersonal system that reaches into and transforms personal experience. Ultimately, we see that Kit was interested in escaping the civilized world to the extent that his feat would be amplified within it. The closing line—"You're quite an individual, Kit"—is the movie's wry commentary on how monstrous a category this has become in the media age. In the face of this, Malick evokes the cinema as a private mediation of experience. When Holly looks at "vistas" through a stereopticon, for instance, it hits her that she is "just this little girl, born in Texas, whose father was a sign painter, who had only just so many years to live." As a protocinematic device, the stereopticon sparks an epiphany and induces in Holly a sense of the smallness of her being. The cinema is a "personal" medium of this kind, Malick suggests, in contrast to broadcast media.

Making the cinema personal, which is one way to describe turning away from industrial conventions, was a byword of New Hollywood modernism as it set itself against television. It passed as a term of art from avant-gardists such as Maya Deren and Jonas Mekas to movie brats such as Francis Ford Coppola and George Lucas, and in that passage, one can track the institutionalization of modernism. Fredric Jameson calls this the "ideology of modernism," the way, in effect, that politics dropped out of modernism to make it more an instrument for "marking out an enclave position within bourgeois society."[6] In this chapter I focus on the Zanuck-Brown Company, which was such an "enclave" within Universal, one that Richard Zanuck and David Brown designed to insulate themselves from the bourgeois values of efficiency and profit that had come to dominate studio production. The formation of Zanuck-Brown, according to *Variety*, not only signaled "their waning satisfaction as supervisors of a large, major studio film program"—they had cut their teeth in such positions at 20th Century Fox under Richard's father,

Darryl, but then held like positions at Warner Bros.—but it signaled too the industrywide dissatisfaction with such a position. As *Variety* notes, "The latterday dilemma of that position—little specific praise for good films, but prominence in the crossfire of flops—began driving vet production heads out of office two decades ago." Zanuck and Brown preferred "indie production." In this mode they could pursue "direct, personal productions," the reporter said, "to which their entire attention can be devoted from inception to release and beyond."[7] That the studio apostates Zanuck and Brown should claim for themselves the prerogatives of independence only shows how normative such a production mode had become by then. The virtues of auteur theory, in short, were democratically available, not to directors alone but also to the producers once known for constraining them.

But what pushed Zanuck and Brown to demand respect for their "creative instinct," I believe, was the industrial pressure that television put on the film medium. When the Zanuck-Brown Company was installed at Universal, it was intended to offset television production. Television had become the reliable, rationalized product that motion pictures had been during the era of the studio system. Lew Wasserman was its herald. Having risen by way of television, and nearly displacing film production in the process, Wasserman recruited Zanuck-Brown to restore the balance that had been upset by his own successful history with MCA (MCA had bought the Universal lot in 1958, if not yet the studio, in order that Revue would have stages for television production). Zanuck-Brown brought film back, finally, by promoting Universal contract employee Steven Spielberg from the ranks of television director to feature filmmaker. For various reasons Spielberg had been desperate for his chance to make a theatrical movie. Frederick Wasser has noted George Lucas's claim that his was a "visceral generation" and that what he and Spielberg sought was "compensation for the visual deprivation of early television."[8] Spielberg's charge to heighten the "cinematic" coincided, then, with Zanuck-Brown's charge to put television's advancing industrial power in check. The ideology of modernism, Jameson would say, somewhat in passing, takes shape "only at the very beginning of the television age," in better part because television would become the object used to stigmatize "mass culture."[9] For Zanuck-Brown this would be a business ideology justifying a shift from mass production to craft techniques. There are ironies in this, as I will demonstrate, but there was a conviction too that "creative people"—as Richard Zanuck and David Brown were designated—needed an aesthetic display sufficient to ensure that within the organization, their pride of place (they supplied the media corporation with content, after all) was recognized and duly respected.

However, along the way to elaborating this argument, we should pause to ask what the cultural meaning of television was against which cinema needed to define itself. First there is the McLuhanite explanation, so popular throughout the era, that a "new scale" is "introduced into our affairs by each extension of ourselves," which for Marshall McLuhan is precisely what technologies are.[10] The scale of television is the globe, McLuhan posits, and we see variants of his "global village" in the chant at the '68 Democratic National Convention in Chicago, that "the whole world is watching" thanks to television broadcast, and the BBC program *Our World* (1967), which Lisa Parks has described as a "fantasy of global presence" thanks to satellite broadcast. The upside of this, Arthur C. Clarke notes, is that we "will be able to go anywhere and meet anyone, at any time, without stirring from our homes," but the downside, as the *Our World* narrator says, is that this "is our world as no one *on* the world can see it"—hence the technology gives rise to a paranoia that this totalizing vantage is available not to the many but the few.[11] This is the technological understanding of television, or, in McLuhan's hands, it is criticized, the technological-determinist understanding.

Second, drawn from its technological structure, there is the ontological understanding of it as a medium. For this, Stanley Cavell bears down on the idea of "presence" but suggests that in television and film, the ontology of presence is different. An actor is present to us in the movies, Cavell maintains, but we have been absent to the actor. What, then, is real about presence, and what is transfigured in the medium? He turns to André Bazin, who claims that the screen cannot put us in the presence of the actor but can only "rela[y] his presence to us, as by mirrors." This, Cavell says, is true of "live television" but not film. His sense of television is that it is a matter of "coverage": "to cover," he says curiously, "(as with a gun), [is] to keep something on view."[12] What is relayed to us by television is an "event," for Cavell, a spectacle we might call it, but nothing is revealed about it. In this Cavell helps us understand Spielberg's frustration: Goldie Hawn in *The Sugarland Express* was a spectacle, the marketing based on her being "all smiles," yet for Spielberg the movie was meant not to reveal her but the apparatus that could make her an event.[13] What Cavell says of the "comedy of remarriage" is that its actors reveal themselves in a split between their public and private identities, and to invoke this difference, the newspaper is often made to symbolize the public, whereas film symbolizes "the realm of privacy."[14] How film lays claim to privacy, I will argue, is a different operation for Spielberg than for Cavell, but in both cases film is designated a private medium because it reveals rather than relays presence. In this sense, according to Fredric Jameson, film "remain[s] an essentially *modernist* formulation," whereas television is not because it "blocks its own theorization"—it allows no self-reflection, that fundamentally modernist operation.[15]

And third, there is the industrial explanation of television, which, in the last analysis, might not have much to do with the technological and ontological (telefilm, for instance, confuses the issue) but will often take them as alibis. Here, the problem on one hand concerns the place of advertising in television programming, its puncturing of the diegesis. "Even in an institution as wholeheartedly commercial in production and distribution as the cinema," Raymond Williams says, "it had been possible, and indeed remains normal, to watch a film as a whole, in an undisturbed sequence."[16] Television, by contrast, broke into so many programmable units, with the unit of advertising equal in value. This is connected to its ontology, which is characterized by the "flow" of interchangeable units, an effect that Jameson describes as "the perpetual present of the image."[17] This seems to only redouble its power as a medium: it totalizes time in a "perpetual present," and it totalizes space in a "fantasy of global presence." On the other hand, however, because its industrial organization was nothing but the afterimage of studio-system Fordism, such television totalities seemed to be the object of managerial capitalism.[18] In his study, *Hollywood TV*, Christopher Anderson makes the case that while the studios "phased out the standardized production" of movies in the 1950s, they migrated those business practices to television production. "Supplying television programs to the networks," Anderson says, "offered a new rationale for standardized, studio-based production."[19] Escaping television, then, took on meanings at once narrow and broad: for Zanuck-Brown, it meant escaping the beat of routinized production, the thralldom to a corporate board, and the bind of being blamed for failures but forgotten amid successes. For members of the so-called youth culture, it meant escaping programming and being programmed, and for this, cinema was the antidote.

## OF MODERNISTS AND MIDDLEMEN

When they formed their own company, Zanuck and Brown sought an aesthetic program that would give body to their corporate identity, which was the congress, Zanuck would say, of an "East Coast intellectual" (Brown) and a "kid from the beach in Santa Monica" (himself). To understand how that translates aesthetically, we must consider how Zanuck-Brown reckoned with its inheritance from Darryl Zanuck and historically updated his studio style in terms of the auteur theory. "My film school was Darryl Zanuck," David Brown would say, "and so was Dick's."[20] What preoccupied Darryl Zanuck (DZ henceforth) aesthetically was the size of the screen—the shape of the support, as Clement Greenberg would say—and his preoccupation had managerial entailments that are worthwhile to adduce. Among DZ's achievements at 20th Century Fox was his ability to manage the balance of power between himself in West Coast production and Spyros Skouras in the East Coast executive offices; it was a détente that symbolically formed around their investment in wide-screen, specifically the way they could alternately interpret it in aesthetic and business terms. Skouras could control the market for wide-screen; DZ could control its meaning.[21] He specified the meaning in a piece in the *Hollywood Reporter*, "Entertainment vs. Recreation," wherein he noted the stiff competition from television but stated that more broadly, Hollywood was being faced with a rise in "recreation."[22] Golf, hunting, and gardening were several examples. In splitting the leisure market between "entertainment" and "recreation"—the former being "something that others provide for you," and the latter being "something you provide in some measure for yourself," something in which "you participate"—DZ reimagined the cinema as an active form, capable of entertaining, but with a "feeling of participation" supplied by the wide-screen process of CinemaScope. Calling cinema a participatory medium let DZ harmonize it with his own persona, rooted, as it had always been, in nearly manic activity. From his 1924–1933 tenure at Warner Bros., Thomas Schatz explains, DZ had been known as a one-man band, producing material so prolifically that "he wrote under four different names . . . to downplay the studio's dependence on his writing talents."[23] He edited and reedited movies endlessly. He prided himself on his physical vitality, often in tales of athletics. In fact, in the late '60s it was reported that DZ had suffered a stroke, but Fox claimed the article reporting it was planted to depress stock prices for a takeover; hence, a *Variety* reporter visited DZ and found him "the dynamo" and the "Zanuck of legend," whose very presence and "the breathless pace of his speech" made one rue the "managerial revolution" that was then making over the Hollywood studios.[24] In the reporter's appraisal, the managers (i.e., those with no background in filmmaking) lacked the charismatic energy that a man of pictures such as DZ had. The screen could become a dynamo in kind, could mediate his vitality, DZ thought, in the degree that the viewer was inducted into the screen's dimensions.

For their aesthetic project, then, Zanuck-Brown aligned themselves with director George Roy Hill, who, like DZ, put stress on the screen itself. For Hill, the screen was a synecdoche for the history of the medium. In the opening frame of *Butch Cassidy and the Sundance Kid* (20th Century Fox, 1969), he places a screen at an angle within an otherwise black frame, scored to the clicking flywheel of a film projector (see figs. 3.1 and 3.2). There is a frame within a frame, in other words, evoking a movie theater from the past. After the flickering leader, a title card reads "The Hole in the Wall Gang," and a silent western ensues. It irises in, and the silent film is swallowed. The next frames give Hill's version of Butch

Cassidy and the Sundance Kid, set within the film-historical perspective that is now allowed by the screen.

The film's opening is pitched to the cine-literate generation, we might say, but is nonetheless a callback to two traditions of studio experimentation that developed in answer to a problem that had arisen. The problem, put broadly, was that throughout the late '50s and early '60s, studio movies had seemed to lose their inner conviction. An individual movie might signal its place within a longer tradition but could scarcely imagine a future for the medium. The screen experiments responding to this problem are the subject of this chapter. One solution emerged at 20th Century Fox and was carried out by the likes of Frank Tashlin and

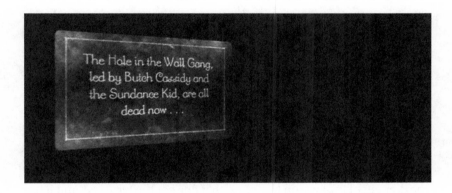

**FIGURES 3.1 AND 3.2** George Roy Hill begins *Butch Cassidy and the Sundance Kid* by casting it in relation to the long tradition of Hollywood westerns.

Richard Fleischer, and another, at Universal, was associated mainly with Ross Hunter. George Roy Hill worked in both traditions, and while his movie *The Sting* (Universal, 1973) suggested one solution for Zanuck-Brown, Steven Spielberg would suggest for them another solution altogether when he made *Jaws*. Because latter-day prejudices collapse these movies into the category of "blockbuster cinema," we perhaps overlook what radically different aesthetic solutions they pose to the same problem. That these movies set the standard for blockbuster cinema was only incidental. In their moment, rather, both movies mattered because they were quite distinct subvarieties of New Hollywood modernism.[25] I will refer to Hill's as late modernism, and Spielberg's as vernacular modernism. For now, I will limit myself to a description of Hill's late modernism. Garrett Stewart has called Hill a "pop modernist" in that he was part of the late-sixties mainstreaming of modernist devices.[26] Not only had the French New Wave made experimental form part of Hollywood's vocabulary, but universities had made High Modernism part of their curriculum.[27] Hill, for instance, began a dissertation on *Finnegan's Wake* at Trinity College.[28] That is to say, his modernism was born of institutions, and its ideological function (per Jameson) was to declare the professional training behind his technique. Hence, Ben Rogerson has called Hill a "hack professional."[29] And indeed, Stewart's sense of him as pop modernist is qualified in the same way—by then, modernism was not the domain of innovation but a sign that one got the job done, and it was a calling card of technical knowhow.

Modernism, for all that its concept has been aesthetic autonomy, was for Zanuck-Brown a claim of professional autonomy that was ready for deployment against industrial reorganization.[30] The period of reorganization at Fox is best marked by the 1962 split between DZ and Spyros Skouras, a split which signaled a diremption of the West Coast–East Coast relationship. The board at Fox wanted Skouras out, in part due to the public relations fiasco of *Cleopatra*, and DZ was not concerned with helping him. DZ was at the end of his "Paris years," time he had spent (somewhat dissolutely) in France as an independent producer after resigning from Fox in 1956. On his departure, Buddy Adler became head of production but, lacking DZ's charismatic authority, could not be a counterweight to Skouras, who, Peter Lev says, "micromanaged" him.[31] When the board later ousted Skouras, however, DZ realized that they intended to arrogate power for themselves. The activist shareholder, Judge Samuel Rosenman, filled the void left by Skouras. DZ objected. "I do not believe that stockbrokers or their attorneys are qualified to endorse or annul film proposals," he wrote in a memo, "any more than I am qualified to plead a case in court or sell stock."[32] It is fair to say that he was objecting not simply to the situation at Fox but to the situation of the film industry tout court. "As I see it today," DZ had written to his friend and screenwriter Phillip Dunne, "the boss of the Studio is actually no longer a boss—he has a title but that is all. He is the slave of agents and actors with their own corporations and insane competition from independent operators and promoters who are willing to give away 100% of the profits just as long as they get a distribution fee."[33] DZ therefore returned to Fox in 1962 to assume the presidency vacated by Skouras, not because he brought with him a new vision of Hollywood authority but because he wished to keep at bay the boardroom authority that was otherwise encroaching.

David Brown remarks that when studio employees received news of DZ's return, "there literally was dancing in the corridors of the administration building."[34] His return suggested a restored belief in Old Hollywood magic. "The pure producers such as Zanuck, David O. Selznick, Samuel Goldwyn, and Sam Spiegel," wrote Brown, "were the closest to today's auteur directors." Brown came to work for DZ in 1951, indeed, because he admired him. DZ was "the creative boss. As for the pictures he personally produced, his artistic commitment was total." Of DZ and Irving Thalberg, David Brown said, "Those men enjoyed creative autonomy." Though they answered ultimately to their bosses in New York, "they suffered no interference in their day-to-day operations."[35] But autonomy on that model would not be recovered. DZ put his son, Richard, in charge of production, and though they stabilized Fox in the mid-sixties (thanks in better part to *The Sound of Music*), they were again subject to boardroom censure by the end of the decade. A "consortium of banks" forced continued reorganization.[36] One measure was to hire the Stanford Research Institute to conduct a study of studio practices. It concluded, according to David Brown, "that our success, when we had it, depended solely on what they termed 'nonrecurring phenomena.'"[37] This, Brown might say, was only longhand for "magic." When movies were "magical," he said, "they were also casual, offhand, coming out of the commonest reality and transfiguring it." Hence, the board of directors—"who knew nothing about motion pictures, understood nothing about motion pictures, and never saw motion pictures"—"didn't understand why motion pictures couldn't be manufactured in the same orderly manner as packaged goods."[38] Yet New Hollywood financializing was insensitive to the so-called magic of Old Hollywood. Richard Zanuck's time at Fox was ruled by this. Each day when he joined his fellow executives for lunch, John Gregory Dunne reports, on his plate "was a piece of paper listing the closing price of Fox stock and the number of shares traded."[39] The stock ticker was for him a daily reminder that his company publicly traded on the unreasonable expectation that he make their "phenomena" recurrent. This was unreasonable, David Brown argued, because "a phenomenon is by definition a rare or unusual occurrence."[40] But Brown understood this to be a condition of New Hollywood, which "is a bureaucracy," he believed, "while Old Hollywood was a dictatorship, production decisions being made by a single man, the films the reflection solely of his taste."[41] How to reenchant the vision of any single person and autonomize the decision maker in turn was the task remaining for New Hollywood production.

For David Brown and Richard Zanuck, beginning a production company in 1972 was the outcome of a project to reclaim professional autonomy that they had begun in strictly aesthetic terms with the chastened return of DZ in 1962. That is, in those ten years, whatever desire they had for professional respect was sublimated in the movies they produced. The fact that they carried forth DZ's interest in screen dimensions but inflected it differently ought to be interpreted as a ripening of their managerial vision before they had the power to instantiate it. Let us begin by noting that when DZ took over Fox on July 25, 1962, his first act was to tell his son in California: "Close the studio!"[42] The only productions he allowed to go on were *Cleopatra* (the source of the studio's disaster) and the television show *The Many Loves of Dobie Gillis* (the source of the studio's revenue). It is symbolic that in DZ's effort to scale back, the Fox schedule was reduced to these two: the former a sumptuous wide-screen event designed for a roadshow presentation that had overrun its budget, and the latter a factory-tooled, small-screen product designed for living-room consumption. It is fitting, too, that DZ removed production chief Peter Levathes, who had risen from the television division, and replaced him with his son, Richard, who had cut his teeth in filmmaking.

The screen experiments to follow, predictably enough, played the media of film and television off each other. The most pronounced instance of this was Richard Fleischer's *The Boston Strangler* (20th Century Fox, 1968). Fleischer—Richard Zanuck's go-to director, who had helmed his first production, *Compulsion* (20th Century Fox, 1959), and brought to heel the roadshow musical *Doctor Dolittle*—wished to make *The Boston Strangler* a manifesto on film possibility. "We've never made use of the big screen," he said. "All we've done is take what we used to put on the small screen and make it bigger. And then pictures, all pictures, have always had the same frame."[43] In putting it this way, Fleischer is bearing the inheritance of DZ; the shape of the big screen had been put to untroubled use in Fox movies from *Gentleman's Agreement* (Kazan, 1947) to *The Man in the Gray Flannel Suit* (Johnson, 1956) but revealed the trouble of television in *Will Success Spoil Rock Hunter?* (Tashlin, 1957). There, Tashlin had satirized television by interrupting his movie. Tony Randall breaks the fourth wall and addresses "the TV fans in our audience who are accustomed to constant interruptions in the programs for messages from sponsors." The image then shrinks, Randall explains, to catch the "thrill" of the home viewer's "twenty-one-inch screens" (see fig. 3.3).

Fleischer's experiment, by contrast, forgoes the quantitative difference in screen dimensions in quest of a qualitative difference. Fleischer's movie begins with a television screen showing the parade for the astronaut heroes of Project Mercury. The screen is masked and fills only a portion of the upper-left quadrant of the frame, and the rest is blackness. The black then fades into an apartment living room (see fig. 3.4).

While at first the use of frames within the frame seems to reproduce the critique of television screen size, it soon becomes clear that the

**FIGURE 3.3** In the 20th Century Fox tradition, *Will Success Spoil Rock Hunter?* mocks the dimensions of the television screen by shrinking it within the expanse of wide-screen cinema.

**FIGURE 3.4** In *The Boston Strangler*, Richard Fleischer experiments with frames within frames.

expanse of the CinemaScope frame is being endowed with the positive function of casting frames in relation to each other. What inspired Fleischer to undertake this screen experiment was "the multi-image technique used by the films at the Montreal World's Fair," which was not only a preview of the future of screen technology (as was tradition for the World's Fair) but was also a conduit for the work of industrial designers and avant-gardists into Hollywood industry. Fleischer was likely responding to Alexander Hammid and Francis Thompson's *We Are Young!* (the pair had won an Academy Award in '64 for their short, *To Be Alive!*, and Hammid had earlier been distinguished by his collaboration with Maya Deren), but others in New Hollywood, such as Paul Schrader, had been taken with the Eameses' films such as the multiscreen experiments in the IBM Pavilion at the '64 New York World's Fair. The Montreal Expo '67, it can be said, was the tipping point, and in the Hammid-Thompson film, it linked the "expanded cinema" with youth culture.

Fleischer hoped *The Boston Strangler* would bring into the ambit of Fox's studio culture a sense that cinema was the domain of media past and future, and he made this claim (on an emergent audience, most notably) by downgrading television. In the movie, the lawyer appointed to the Strangler Bureau, John Bottomly (Henry Fonda), has not followed news of the salacious murders because he does not "look at television." His superior is surprised that he should be so out of touch. "I can't," Bottomly says of television. "It hurts my eyes. You know I actually see that electronic beam scanning the tube?" This is something of a throwaway ontological definition of television, but it seems nonetheless to situate the film's split-screen tests within an ontological distinction between the media. In its expansive frame, film can contain the television screen because it can reveal what is constitutively absent in a television frame. The television is all monitoring, we gather, but no cognition. It is a technology without a central intelligence, without a decision-making faculty. In the plot, John Bottomly becomes the figure of coordinated knowledge. "You have four police departments to absorb public criticism," he tells the attorney general. "The commonwealth can stay out of it." Bottomly suggests that the murders are compulsive, "inner motivated," and the only way to catch the perpetrator is by "fluke." This is what the fractured screens within the widescreen frame are meant to signify—the random, disconnected nature of external events. But the attorney general demurs, "There is an absolutely urgent need to coordinate the investigations," and Bottomly, who does not "look at television," has the perspective to do it.

What the movie does to bring together its moments of internalized montage, that is, its stray vantages of a crime in progress, is conclude with Bottomly's provision of a psychologizing explanation of "inner motivation." Bottomly, in short, gives a perfectly cinematic resolution to a television condition that Stanley Cavell calls "serial procedure" (in this case, serial killing, which is rather too on the nose).[44] He gets the Boston Strangler, Albert DeSalvo (Tony Curtis), to confess his psychological state in the idiom of method acting. This is why Tony Curtis wanted the role, in fact, because it culminated in a monologue that let him reveal the depth of the character. It was a serious role, and since "his career was in trouble," he hoped playing the Strangler would shore it up.[45] For Curtis's monologue, Fleischer shot largely without interruption rather than breaking the frame as he had done throughout. It is pure presence, this series of long takes; it is full revelation, Curtis disclosing for us what external appearance cannot.[46] Insofar as Fleischer had found the future of cinema, he did so by turning back to the method acting that had been pioneered in the recent past. Curtis's career was not thereby saved, it may not surprise us, and he was forced into television work shortly afterward.

## SENSIBILITY UNKNOWN

Tony Curtis ended up in television because *The Boston Strangler*, for all its novel technique, had misinterpreted its moment. Curtis turned to method acting to work through the earnest psychosis of Albert DeSalvo, whereas Warren Beatty had tapped the "New Sensibility" to put on the smirking neurosis of Clyde Barrow.[47] Zanuck and Brown, whether or not they had a good read on the New Sensibility, knew enough not to miss it. Their positions at 20th Century Fox had been imperiled, indeed, by their staking too much on an old sensibility. The failure of *Doctor Dolittle* is the story of this. Mark Harris has written that its Best Picture nomination in 1968 seemed to tokenize Old Hollywood style, with what the *Los Angeles Times* called its "armies of greybeard" technicians pitted against the rising talent of *The Graduate* and *Bonnie and Clyde*.[48] David Brown, for instance, known for his cozy relationship with New York publishers, was among the first recommending that *The Graduate* be pursued for motion-picture rights. But he was then away from Fox—this was subsequent to the lot's closure and the expulsion of personnel from all ranks—and he could only root for Larry Turman upon hearing he had made an offer.[49] Later, in an April 1970 memo to Richard Zanuck, Brown joked (perhaps anxiously) that he needed Zanuck personally to reject a script "by a 19-year-old UCLA student" so that Brown himself would not "be blamed for having kept the corporation from having another EASY RIDER." Zanuck obliged.[50] He and Zanuck consoled themselves, in fact, that while Columbia was perspicacious enough to seize the New Sensibility by making *Easy Rider*, the studio was not shrewd enough in their deals to "produce commensurate profits." Columbia, Brown said, gives away "50% or more of the profits as customary procedure."[51] Such was the bind of a New Hollywood studio. After all, Zanuck and Brown proved they could reach the youth market with *MASH*, and they had the youth-market hit *The French Connection* in the pipeline, but still they were fired.

Such that there was a New Sensibility for Zanuck and Brown, it would emerge from the crack-up of the industry and would come to rest upon its new configuration. Brown had sensed the ground shifting beneath them. "The industry generally is in a very depressed state," he wrote to his friend Herbert Mayes in late 1970, "and undoubtedly many radical changes will take place before the year is much older."[52] But Brown had roughly the same premonition in earlier moments, notably in 1962. "At this moment Hollywood is in a state of paralysis," Brown wrote to his friend Bertram Bloch in that year, and upon outlining the reasons why, he confessed to being uncertain "that the future is in Hollywood."[53] His confidence rose when Darryl Zanuck returned, but it was, of course, DZ's failure to adjust to New Hollywood culture and his indifference to the fate of his deputies that left Brown and Richard Zanuck in the lurch. Yet, in 1962, as Fox was opting to return operations to its aging mogul, Universal was setting another course. In that year, MCA would sell their talent agency, thanks to Robert Kennedy pressing a Department of Justice antitrust case against them, and Lew Wasserman, now assuming the Universal identity, pursued a version of the decentralized power of his talent agency minus the talent agency.[54] This meant, for Wasserman, contracting out the phases of studio production that he could not do himself. Revue had control of television, but if the studio were to have a serious share of the movie market, they would gain it through independent producers. Kirk Douglas's Bryna Productions was a source of movies for Wasserman, but in the early 1970s, he would turn to Richard Zanuck and David Brown for this. The New Sensibility, for Zanuck and Brown, arrived by way of "radical changes" in corporate relations. What Brown had wanted to escape in 1962, in truth, were the "internecine wars of large corporations." The motion picture industry had evolved, he thought, into "a no-fun business from the standpoint of personal relationships."[55] Brown said he might be satisfied "in a key position in a progressive organization," but Fox was not becoming that, he complained to DZ in 1969, and he and Richard Zanuck had been unable to take a "swing without being inhibited by past concepts of organization."[56]

Taking a swing, for Zanuck and Brown, meant the risk of their convictions. Forming the Zanuck-Brown Company gave legal cover to those convictions. It was a private company, not a public one, hence there was no ticker tape each morning nor a Stanford Research Institute telling them their successes were "nonrecurring phenomena." As Brown would later put it, "We relied on our guts, not focus groups, not research." Though their company was folded into a corporation that did answer to stockholders, they could behave as though it were not. "There was no committee and there were no development executives," Richard Zanuck said. "I was the committee."[57] Zanuck was the committee, it must be said, because Wasserman had designed the corporate structure of Universal this way. Wasserman's "formula," as Connie Bruck puts it, was to combine "inevitably volatile movie production with a stable and highly lucrative TV business," but because he was out of his depth in movie production, he trusted implicitly those he hired in this area.[58] One, Ned Tanen, was known as "iconoclastic, rebellious," but he was placed in an office next to Wasserman in Universal's Black Tower nonetheless. Zanuck and Brown were the others. When Zanuck pitched Wasserman their first slate of movies, including Spielberg's *The Sugarland Express*, he was met with objection. "The kid is great," Wasserman said in reference to Spielberg, "but this picture will play to empty houses." But on turning to leave, Zanuck was stopped by Wasserman, "I think you're totally wrong, but go ahead and make it. I didn't bring you over here to tell you what pictures to make." Zanuck was stunned. "I'd never seen it before and have never seen it since," he said, "where a guy in charge says, I don't believe in this but I believe in you."[59]

As an article of corporate protocol, the auteur theory was not much more than a means of distributing trust downward, in this case from Wasserman to Zanuck to Spielberg. But my point here is that there is no way of knowing whether that trust is earned without the establishment of aesthetic proof. Zanuck and Brown had tried keeping their ears to the ground, but before Spielberg, they had a fitful relationship to the New Sensibility. It had been manifest, on one hand, in their endorsement of the sexual revolution. At Fox they had made *Myra Breckinridge* (Sarne, 1970) and *Beyond the Valley of the Dolls* (Meyer, 1970) and at Warner Bros. *Portnoy's Complaint* (Lehman, 1972). On the other hand, Zanuck and Brown had relied on late-modernist screen experiments whose distinction emerged, such that it did, in their contrast with television. This is precisely the distinction Wasserman wanted from them. What Zanuck and Brown had to show, in particular, was that they brought what neither Irwin Allen nor Ross Hunter brought to cinema. Together, Allen and Hunter would create what became known as the disaster genre, which was essentially the soldering of a television ethos onto cinema's armature. In Allen's *The Poseidon Adventure* (Neame, 20th Century Fox, 1972) and Hunter's *Airport* (Seaton, Universal, 1970), the use of ensemble casts rounded out by aging movie stars recalled nothing so much as television variety programming, while the use of scale and cut-rate effects seemed nothing more than a sop to whatever monopoly the cinema had on visceral experience. Zanuck and Brown had worked with Allen at Fox, where his job was largely to supply television programming such as *Voyage to the Bottom of the Sea* (1964–1968) and *Lost in Space* (1965–1968), and they knew him to be efficient and business minded but beholden to television's low standards. In John Gregory Dunne's reportage of late-sixties production culture at Fox, he relates an incident when Allen was approached about a "Lobster Man" whose antennae were dysfunctional. He proposed a quick and dirty solution, and then preened a bit afterward. "That's what I'm sitting in the boss's chair for," he said. "You got a little problem about Lobster Man, you come to see Irwin."[60] He worked to the beat of the television schedule, which required of him a schlocky rather than artistic touch. He brought spectacle to television ("Me, if I can't blow up the world in the first ten seconds, then the show is a flop") but scaled to the small screen and produced on its Fordist timetable.[61] So when he emerged in the early '70s as the architect of disaster cinema, he made no qualitative change in his model, only a quantitative one. That is, his concept was the same, but the pictures of it got big.

But Ross Hunter is a more interesting case. It was his influence at Universal that Zanuck and Brown would position themselves against. As a producer, Hunter had a relationship of many years with Universal, and he had worked there as ardently as anyone at rival studio Fox to husband the cinematic values of wide screen and Technicolor in his collaborations with Douglas Sirk and Doris Day. In *Pillow Talk* (Gordon, 1959), for instance, the narrative device of the party line—which Brad Allen (Rock Hudson) and Jan Morrow (Doris Day) share—is occasion to solve the problem of telephony, namely its invisibility, in the space of the wide screen. In early scenes the frame breaks into three triangles, Brad on one side and his mistress on the other, with Jan wedged between them. The cinema is total visibility; offscreen space, here, is for telephones, radios, and other modes of remote connection. This aesthetic subtends the first entry in disaster cinema, Hunter's *Airport*, a movie that imagines the modernist defeat of distance not by way of the airplane but by way of the cinema screen. Disaster, in this, is just a matter of modernity, and the airplane is one of its agents. The cinema, by contrast, is posited to hold premodern powers, placing people in face-to-face contact after modernity had put them asunder. The formula is the same here as it was in *Pillow Talk*: people at a distance are placed together within a frame thanks to split screen. There are plenty of moments in *Airport*, to be sure, when the spaces drawn together in a frame are the opposite ends of a phone call, but the greater ambition of this movie is to connect the geography above and below, the cockpit and ground control. In a telling instance, the pilots above the Atlantic get a radio call from the New York airport below, and to signal that pilots Vernon Demerest (Dean Martin) and Anson Harris (Barry Nelson) are in communication with those on the ground, the two-shot of them is ruptured by an inset image of the man calling from below (see fig. 3.5).

It is the cinema that can make them present to each other, but—and this is why the wide screen is congratulating itself—it is telecommunication that effects such absence between interlocutors in the first place. Airplane communications, by some displacement, have become the figure for television broadcast. This makes the movie's reference to television more pronounced. In an early scene, we see a picket line of locals protesting the noise pollution of the airport. "They'll break it up and go home soon," the airport manager says, "after the TV cameras get a few shots." An airport commissioner balks, "TV? That's all we need." The protesters have news coverage, he realizes, which means disproportionate amplitude for their demonstration. It is easy to read this in reference to student demonstrations, and it is, in turn, easy to take *Airport* as at once a backlash against the leftist movements and a retrenchment of tradition. Critics have done just this, sometimes by making too schematic a division between "left" and "right" tendencies in Hollywood.[62] My point is only that in this operation, whatever its political inflection, a certain form of

**FIGURE 3.5** In the disaster movie's "premodern" imagination, the wide screen could be used, as it is here in *Airport*, to restore the face-to-face contact that had been lost to modern technologies.

aesthetic expression is being sought that would exonerate cinema from the distortions of subjectivity that are the by-product of the space-time reorderings of modernity. The cinema, for Ross Hunter, falls on the side of tradition; television, by contrast, is responsible for our misrecognition of the near and far, of our size and reach, and of the dynamics of our interconnectedness more generally.

Zanuck and Brown's job, as they imagined it, was the opposite. Because, while *Airport* did great business, it did very little to reconceptualize the business. In the pages of *Variety*, it was called a "handsome, often dramatically involving epitaph to a bygone brand of filmmaking." Hunter, that is, evoked what was beloved in the past but could not imagine the future. This is perhaps best indexed in his failed working relationship with Mike Nichols just before the latter broke through with *The Graduate*. In 1964, Universal had just given Hunter a lucrative seven-year contract. He was assigned a movie, *The Public Eye*, to be directed by Nichols, the wunderkind of Broadway. At the meeting between Hunter and Nichols, Mark Harris says, "The two men had absolutely nothing to say to each other." Hunter was, as Harris puts it, "probably Universal's most important in-house producer at a time when the studio didn't have much to show for itself."[63] His weakness in the moment of *Airport*, then, was that he had fit himself too neatly into the old system. "Sometimes," Hunter said in 1967, "I wish American producers could do what European producers do all the time. You know, make movies just for themselves." This is, we should note, what Mike Nichols was aiming to do. But Hunter fretted, "There is so much money involved, and so many people, that it's hard to keep on top of everything that happens."[64] Though Lew Wasserman was helped by the success of *Airport*, he did not renew Hunter's contract (his career as a producer of feature films would, in fact, more or less end with *Airport*), and while this might be explained along three lines— (1) Hunter bragged that he had saved Universal with his picture, and this angered Wasserman; (2) Hunter did not understand the kind of federalism by which Wasserman wanted to operate the studio; and (3) Wasserman wanted not only money but critical notice too—it was not explained to Zanuck and Brown but left for them to infer.

For their first slate of pictures, therefore, Zanuck and Brown pursued what was modern, new, and young, which would league them with Ned Tanen, whom Wasserman entrusted with the youth movie division, and pit them against Ross Hunter. Tanen's slate included *Diary of a Mad Housewife* (Perry, 1970), *Taking Off* (Forman, 1971), and *Minnie and Moskowitz* (Cassavetes, 1971), all of which were cheap and of distinctive character. He took a hit on *The Last Movie* (Hopper, 1971) but would rebound with *American Graffiti* (Lucas, 1973). It was in this spirit that Zanuck and Brown put together *Ssssssss* (Kowalski, 1973), a killer-snake movie made for the drive-ins, and *Willie Dynamite* (Moses, 1974), a boilerplate blaxploitation movie. Only *The Sting*, though, was able to distinguish Zanuck and Brown. With it, they delivered to Universal not just the box-office winner that year but also a set of Academy Awards. My point will be that they fell short in delivering all the studio's needs in a single movie; in that right, they left something for *Jaws* to do. But what *The Sting* did was boost the prestige of the Universal brand. This might be counted as the last of Wasserman's several stages in taking over and reconceptualizing Universal as corporate idea, but it was a last stage, I will demonstrate, that had been imperfectly completed.

In 1958 Wasserman and MCA had bought the lots and the sound stages—in short, the tangible holdings—of Universal. In 1962 they bought the studio itself, that is, its status as corporation and what Jerome Christensen notes is the barest function of the corporation, its "capitalized earning power."[65] But the final stage was carried out between the years 1962 and 1975, and it had to do with combining the land of the corporation with its indifference to land, indeed to anything concrete. This process, as described in chapter 1, goes by the name "financialization." Wasserman uniquely executed this process because while other studios such as Fox were selling their lots on the premise that a studio's value could be decoupled from its land, he was buying the land, then the studio qua brand, and then spending on "capital-improvement programs."[66] He grounded the landless value of movies, their "magic" per David Brown—or their production of charisma, as I will call it in chapter 4, which becomes their power to produce a corporate brand—on the landed, routinized production of television. He had structured the subordination of television into its relationship with cinema, but in something like *Airport*, the terms were flipped such that cinema sustained tradition against the modernizing force of television. But Wasserman wanted to modernize the studio by vouchsafing its new production model in the magic of cinema, all while underwriting it through the known outcomes of Fordist television production. In *The Sting*, I will demonstrate, Zanuck and Brown did something very close to this.

What brought *The Sting* to Zanuck-Brown was a relationship the company had developed with Julia and Michael Phillips on *Steelyard Blues* (Myerson, 1973), a movie made for Warner Bros. just before Zanuck and Brown left. The personnel behind *Steelyard Blues* were the New Hollywood young set—Donald Sutherland and Jane Fonda, freshly minted as a couple after their experience on *Klute* (Pakula, Warner Bros, 1971)—and Julia and Michael Phillips were a nexus for this young talent. Their beach house, next to Jennifer Salt and Margot Kidder's, was the social hub for the emerging "movie brats," a site of weekend parties attended by Jacob Brackman, Brian De Palma, Martin Scorsese, Steven Spielberg, Paul Williams, and the like. Julia and Michael Phillips would go on to work with these directors on *Taxi Driver* and *Close Encounters of the Third Kind* (Spielberg, Columbia, 1977), but on *The Sting* they were working in behalf of writer David Ward and pushing in their deal making for him to direct it. Part of their job, the Phillipses thought, was to put the young talent at the helm, to honor the auteurist credo, which for their cohort was the node that counterculture energy had accrued around. A share of decision making rested there, it is true, which is why when Zanuck-Brown struck the deal with the Phillipses, they brought in their director, George Roy Hill, and the writer, David Ward, was denied control. This was in part genetic to the material: it was a period piece that would require set construction, and the high budget this entailed also meant that the director would need to be a professional, not a first-timer. Zanuck and Brown believed in Hill, but Julia Phillips did not. He did not understand himself "as an auteur," she claims, "but an administrator."[67] He was a "first-class" professional, though, and Julia Phillips knew as much. Adding him also meant they would attach the project to Universal rather than MGM (and nobody wanted MGM, especially not Robert Redford).[68] Zanuck granted Hill autonomy, indeed, because he knew Hill would deliver the movie on time and within budget. "George," Zanuck ribbed him in a memo, "will you please just fuck up one shot, so I can send you a David Selznick memo explaining to you where you went all wrong. Nobody's perfect, you know." Though Hill was left alone to make the movie, he was still on the Universal lot. Zanuck joked with him on this count too: "Bill showed me a sampling of last week's work—terrific. However, as I am writing this note I can see your bungalow being towed away and I fear that the studio doesn't have as high an opinion of your work as do I."[69]

That they were all on the studio lot was not a problem, but neither was it a solution. What *The Sting* is about, in effect, is the making of movies, and so any criticism of its sound-stage artifice is refuted proleptically: *It is about movie artifice, so why criticize it for looking artificial?* But Steven Spielberg faulted it in these terms, saying it "looks like it was shot in a studio backlot," and to expect audiences to believe otherwise is to "underestimate the intelligence of the public," especially, he said, "today when pictures like *The French Connection* and *Midnight Cowboy* are shot documentary style, on location."[70] But this is because Spielberg had in mind a solution of another kind for the moving-image future. Hill was not interested, however, in compelling greater belief in the reality (or, in language applicable to Spielbergian aesthetics, the phenomenological experience) of movies. In the hands of a young director, Hill told Michael Phillips, "there would be a lot of gritty street shots, runny noses in doorways," but he wanted "to make a movie that looks like a thirties movie."[71] He wanted to cast the movie in relation to history for the modernist reason that its pleasure would be derived from one's historical awareness of the durability of its form.

On one hand, it was to be a buddy movie, and the fact that it was a reprise of the Butch Cassidy–Sundance Kid relationship made Paul Newman anxious and reluctant to sign on.[72] Hill did not share Newman's concern that they would be repeating themselves because repetition, he felt, was what one did as a matter of course. Could Newman compel belief in star power once more? That is the question that concerned Hill, and that is what the card game between Newman's Gondorff and Robert Shaw's Lonnegan is designed to stage. On the other hand, it was a movie about movies, less a buddy movie than a movie about how buddy movies elicit what they do. Fredric Jameson has characterized this moment in Hollywood in terms of nostalgia not for past history but for the bygone styles appropriate to it.[73] It would be hard to exempt Hill from criticism of this kind: he flattens history by drawing on the Depression as backdrop but scoring it to ragtime music from earlier in the century, all for the purpose, one suspects, of dressing up Newman and Redford in period style. But "nostalgia" may be the wrong word, too, as Jameson suggests. What is at stake in Hill's internal history of form is a question of another order: not simply whether styles may be consumed without cognition—without applying reason, that is, and becoming critical—but whether belief itself requires cognition. In the structure of its story, *The Sting* is a disquisition on David Brown's "magic" (but here it is called a con) that asks an audience, and the industry in turn, to decide whether it wants simply to believe in movies or to have reasons to believe in them.

In *The Sting*, there are many self-knowing moments. The opening credits with cameo introductions of the actors recalls the old 1930s practice in such movies as *The Public Enemy* (Wellman, Warner Bros., 1931). There are, too, title cards breaking down the movie into its various sequences: "The Set-Up," "The Hook," and so on. Yet the metacinema does not rest at the level of style but seeps down into story and structure. In the card game mentioned earlier, Newman's acting is thematized as he, in the character of Henry Gondorff, must act like "Mr. Shaw" (a name made up to con Doyle Lonnegan) while playing opposite the actual Mr. Shaw—the actor Robert Shaw, that is—who is in character as Doyle Lonnegan. Acting is not concealed here but staged *as acting*. We relish it or we do not, but we are not fooled by it. In another scene, Kid Twist (Harold Gould) sits in an office as though he were a casting director having a call for actors. A man named Curly Jackson comes to audition for their "big con," claiming, "Me specialty is an English man," and showing a valise that holds his various wardrobe needs. More than acting, though, the movie depicts the activity of a production crew as it transforms a location into a movie set. Kid Twist and his gangsters rent a former billiards hall with the aim of dressing it as a betting parlor. "I don't know," one of his men says. "It's kind of short notice. I'm not sure we can get it all done by Saturday." But like a producer to his doubtful production designer, another man says, "Got to. Gondorff's riding the mark down from New York on the Century." Much of the movie, indeed, is them dressing the location. And when they finally con their mark, the production wraps: everyone is all smiles, back slapping and bidding each other good luck until the next job. "Let's take this place down fast," Gondorff says, because were this studio-era Hollywood, set construction would begin immediately for the following Monday.

But it is in the structure that the movie carves out its meaning. The magic of movies is not encoded within its frame—that is, *The Sting* does not sit within the tradition of screen experiments—but is cast beyond the frame. That is the con. In Darryl Zanuck's wide screen, it was all there within the expansive frame. In Hill's earlier screen experiments, too, frames were placed within frames to call up the depth of film history. But in *The Sting*, the screen is not support enough for whatever magic the movie would vehiculate. To explain: within the arc of the con being engineered against Lonnegan, there is another complicating action introduced when the feds enter the scene and oversee the investigation into Hooker carried out by Lieutenant Snyder (Charles Durning), who is on the take himself. Snyder delivers Hooker to the feds, and they cut a deal with him to betray Gondorff. What the audience is not told in these scenes is that Hooker, Gondorff, and Kid Twist have themselves cast con artists to act as feds. Hence, the corrupt Snyder is being stung, but the ultimate sting is on the audience. There is no way an audience—no matter how astute—could know this is the plot, because it is structured outside the *syuzhet*. The audience believes that in the con, Redford will betray Newman, because the movie withholds any reason for them to believe otherwise. Its magic is a con, executed on the premise that the audience wants to believe and, moreover, that what they want to believe is that the magic lies offscreen. What lies offscreen and behind the scenes is an apparatus set to the psychic needs of an audience— call it Hollywood—which is at all times imperfect but capable nonetheless of just-in-time delivery, and in Hill's modernist deconstruction of its workings, the only thing he can depict as its power source is an absent center: that is, the audience wants to believe in movies for no other reason than that for a long time, they have believed in movies.

## THE IMMANENCE OF CINEMA

In *The Sting*, George Roy Hill reaffirms the movies by way of the movies—their history, the place of his movie within that history, and the deeper pleasure brought by a knowledge of this relationship. But the historical knowledge it asks of its audience involves the situation beyond the frame, in this case the studio lot itself. It produces a cognitive experience, not a phenomenological one. In *Jaws*, by contrast, Steven Spielberg reaffirms the movies by setting their experience off from that of television. He imagines that the different orders of experience the two media deliver are made manifest when one is nested in the other. I will analyze *Jaws* to make this point, showing that its exposé of television gawking is vital to the cinematic experience that culminates its narrative. But this must be constellated within Spielberg's early career, from his contract work in television to his autonomy in feature film, as well as the thematic recapitulation of his career stages, from *Amblin'* (Sigma III, 1968) and *The Sugarland Express* to *Close Encounters of the Third Kind* and *Poltergeist* (Hooper, MGM, 1982).

What I wish to say about Spielberg's early career is that its trajectory realized the ambition that Zanuck-Brown had set for itself in order to guard its sphere of action from corporate oversight. This entailed a display of mastery sufficient to make creative labor seem self-regulating, deserving of a site and schedule all its own. Practically, this meant on-location shooting. There, Richard Zanuck learned the lesson that Robert Altman had taught him: to escape oversight, you leave the studio. But in escaping, Spielberg knew that his job was nonetheless to reformulate the movie business in a new set of protocols. He wanted to coax from the screen the same presence it once had so automatically, not self-consciously (as Hill had tried) but innocently; in this, he would not practice late modernism but would discover instead what J. D. Connor calls Hollywood neoclassicism.[74] The latter, however, might itself be recognized as a modernism, but one of surfaces, one lending magic to vernacular experience, not one of heightened self-consciousness and a "late" relationship to tradition. Thus, in *Jaws*, Spielberg would use the defection genre as a concept map (the terrain of which, I demonstrate in chapter 2, is waning subjectivity in the media age) for a story that in other details (waxing technology, media, and all else) is what J. Hoberman identifies as a "modification" of the disaster movie.[75] The disaster movie, in this account, had sprung from the skull of technology—each technology, as Paul Virilio says, containing within itself a novel form of disaster.[76] It is useful to think of the double character of *Jaws*, then, as the twinning of *Sugarland Express*, which came from a news item the *Hollywood Citizen-News* billed as "New Bonnie 'n Clyde," with the TV movie that Spielberg had done just before it, *Duel* (Universal, 1971), which Molly Haskell characterizes as a "parable of the ordinary man, dwarfed by unknown forces."[77]

Before *The Sugarland Express* and *Duel*, however, Spielberg made *Amblin'* as something of a proof of concept. In it, he worked through some youth-culture tropes that, as he was shooting it in the summer of 1968, were just getting a foothold in Hollywood. At the heart of the story is a couple, the girl more free spirited and the boy more high strung, and the two are on the road, motivated by who knows what. Hence the movie title. In this regard they are instances of Thomas Elsaesser's "unmotivated hero." The movie is a showcase of camerawork and clever editing. It became the calling card Spielberg desired, as Chuck Silvers got the film in front of Universal executive Sid Sheinberg, who put Spielberg on a seven-year contract in the television division. Spielberg has otherwise disavowed the movie as "crass commercialism."[78] Molly Haskell says it was a "youth" movie that "the brass at Universal could understand," a purpose which Spielberg himself more or less imputes to it when he says it was intended to "prove to people who finance movies that I could certainly look like a professional moviemaker."[79] The movie, indeed, seems to be about the part played by counterculture style in dissembling career ambition. The boy carries a guitar case with him as he hitchhikes.

Throughout the short movie, the girl tries opening the case, but the boy rebuffs her. When they reach their destination, a Pacific Coast beach, the boy celebrates his arrival by diving into the surf, and the girl opens his guitar case to discover that its contents are a suit, tie, and wingtips: the accoutrements of careerism. She has been drifting without direction, she realizes, while he has been moving purposefully toward his goal. Thus, it is defection for one-half of the couple and corporate integration for the other. The very same setup will begin *Jaws*—the free-spirited girl drawing forth the college boy—but it will be violently repressed within the scheme of the disaster movie.

What *Amblin'* did was make Spielberg a television director. His cinematographer, Allen Daviau, claims Spielberg fought back "because they were trying to mold him into a Universal television director," which required that he understand workflow on the model of the assembly line. On his first episode of *Night Gallery* (1969–1973), however, he planned unusual camerawork, such as a shot through a chandelier bauble, which caused the crew to "titter," Spielberg says, because they assumed he was not long for the gig.[80] Thanks to a reputation for his "avant-garde" camera personality, in fact, Spielberg was given few television jobs after his first one. He needed to be broken, producers thought. "Television is the salt mines of the entertainment field," producer William Link said. "There is never enough money, never enough time."[81] Spielberg, for a period, domesticated his technique (just enough) and made episodes of *The Psychiatrist*, *Owen Marshall*, *Colombo*, and so on. But the medium became for him— perhaps because he experienced in it nothing but industrial constraint— the inverse of cinema. The latter was plasticity, an oscillation between scales, as Haskell notes, between an "aerial point of view" and a "humanizing close-up," while the former was a fixed shot. Formally, television looked like what it felt like professionally—immobility, unfreedom—and its studio production, Daviau said, "intended to absolutely enslave" Spielberg.[82]

What television meant to Spielberg, though, shuttled between his industrial experience and his childhood associations. In the latter respect, it was a feature of suburbia. "The anesthetic of suburbia," he said, "involves having three parents—a mother, a father, and a TV set."[83] TV, he said elsewhere, was "this big taboo piece of furniture in the living room that [he] would sneak down and watch when the babysitter was there."[84] It represented for him an incursion from outside into the domestic space. And as we see years later in *Poltergeist*, the powers it admitted into the home hailed from places unknown. In that movie, "the absence of a signal on a channel that is not receiving a broadcast" leaves the TV open to "noise" from other sources, a university expert says, including "outer space" and even "inner space." Outer space takes on a value, for Spielberg, in a paranoid hermeneutics. We do not know what is out there because it is kept from us. "The government's position on UFOs has been covert," he claimed, despite how easy it would have been for "the government to come right out and tell the public that the things you see in the night sky" were test flights of supersonic planes, say, but that is neither the "nature" nor "the structure of the U.S."[85] The operation of *Close Encounters*, then, was to transpose the paranoia abroad in '70s cinema into an open, portable key that could include extraterrestrial and spiritual experience. It was perhaps less the conspiracy that interested Spielberg than it was the structure of knowledge, particularly in a culture that, in its arrangement, spread the distance between subjects and their objects of inquiry. The TV is a function of this epistemological problem, given that the origins of the signals it fields are as good as untraceable by its users. Hence it makes sense that Spielberg would line it up with the UFO, figuring them both in the twin valences of promise and threat.

Yet Spielberg was not interested in "being the spokesman for the paranoid Seventies," he claimed, but rather in collapsing the structure that produces paranoia in the first place. Others in his cohort, such as his friend Brian De Palma, cared to intensify the mediation and to double down on the separation between spectator and event; some favored Brechtian distantiation as, for example, De Palma did in split screens in *Dionysus in 69* (Sigma III, 1970) and beyond. In *Close Encounters*, by contrast, Spielberg "bring[s] outer space down to earth for a very personal, seductive meeting of minds"; there, he denies the difference between the subject and what is alien to it, and by way of their merger (Roy Neary boards the mother ship) he hopes to bring what is transcendental into the ken of experience.[86] The transcendental, for Spielberg, first meant simply the unknown, but as he has aged, Molly Haskell shows, it increasingly meant the spiritual, and his Jewishness has been foregrounded in the process.[87] It is the cinema, again and again, that bears this faith by granting our experience such immanence. It disintermediates, so Spielberg thinks, and pulls what is unknown down into our sensory life. Its effect (for him) is to ground belief. Tellingly, when asked whether he believed in poltergeists, he said yes: "I believe in poltergeists and UFOs," and in every movie he has made, he "essentially believed in what the films were about." But, he added, as though to clarify that his conviction lay in the powers of the medium, "If I ever make a film about a fifty-foot woman, I'll believe that too."[88]

Here, it is worth drawing a bright line between Stanley Cavell and Steven Spielberg, both of whom, I have said, considered the cinema "private" because it revealed rather than relayed presence. On this point, what we might expect the television to do, ontologically, is relay to us the fact of a fifty-foot woman. We would then have to trust the findings of this public infrastructure rather than the findings of our senses. Conspiracy, we gather, is an upshot of this: what is publicly held can be rigged by private interests. But cinema would reveal to us the world in which the fifty-foot woman takes on sensuous texture. Our belief in her would be indifferent to her factual existence. The cinema is not a document of facts for either Cavell or Spielberg. For Cavell, indeed, its "magic" derives from it being a world we are absent from, and as such, its "presentness" to us is not rooted in our own mind's power to affirm it. Our selfhood is decentered in this experience, "displaced," as we are, "from our natural habitation within it."[89] A cardinal virtue of this, for Cavell, is how this places us in relation to other minds. What cinema does is reaffirm other minds despite the skepticism that comes from our subjective entrenchment. But though Spielberg might in passing pair "outer space" and "inner space," he reveals the former rather than the latter: it is outer space, the exterior surfaces and phenomena, that occupy him—not persons. This puts him at odds with many in his cohort who, on finding themselves disillusioned with Cavell's "film types," would psychologize their characters more deeply, often producing character studies rather than classical narratives.[90] For Cavell, stars are a corollary of cinema; for Spielberg, they are not. Spielberg would downgrade the star in favor of the everyman, a character that is something of an empty slot (no matter how capable the actor in the role) that the audience itself can fill. On *Jaws*, Richard Zanuck said the shark was the star, and hence they did not "need to spend a lot of money" on star actors.[91] But this felicity of production coincided with Spielberg's turn from the inner life of subjects to the rhythms and surfaces of the world enfolding them. In this he remains in touch with aspects of Cavell's ontology of film, namely that "human beings are not ontologically favored over the rest of nature" and that "objects are not props but natural allies (or enemies) of the human character."[92] In short, Spielberg draws on film ontology as Cavell understands it but deploys it not to explore its intersubjective possibilities but instead to discover its feel for the world, sustaining, in this, our "fascination with objects, with their inner and fixed lives."[93]

My concern is in the material consequence of this. Spielberg's formal interest to collapse the command structure (by removing the army as mediator of UFO secrets, say) harmonized with his professional interest in a small, privately held corporation like Zanuck-Brown. J. D. Connor has suggested that others in Spielberg's cohort, including George Lucas, were invested in the "cognitive structure of paranoid auteurism," which imputed to the studios forms of authority they never had. They imagined a studio, Connor argues, that "could plausibly be a figure of total knowledge," because only against such a totalizing figure could "individualism" as "radical as the one Lucas envisioned" be waged.[94] Spielberg had a more innocent view of the corporate studios, having found in them emotional support of a familial kind. He believed in "creating families and friendships on the set," and he considered executives such as Sid Sheinberg and Steve Ross to be father figures and cinematographer Vilmos Zsigmond to be "almost" a brother.[95] But the problem with Sheinberg's paternal attention to Spielberg was that in an enterprise as vast as Universal television production, he could not insulate his protégé from its command structure. But Zanuck-Brown could. Part of their deal was that "they had no one supervising them while shooting." Spielberg felt they gave him "total freedom, the kind of [freedom from] controls [he] never had in television." On *The Sugarland Express*,

Zanuck-Brown created the feeling that they "were doing a picture in a non-studio way," on location in Texas, using "a small, handpicked crew" that could move "like greased lightning."[96] They reproduced these conditions in a higher order on *Jaws* when they set up production on the island of Martha's Vineyard, a site that had never been used in a Hollywood production, and Richard Zanuck told Universal executives, who worried when it overran the budget, "As soon as I see a leer jet, I'm gonna tell the kid, 'Turn off the camera, we're all going back to the hotel.'" On *Jaws* they avoided shooting in tanks on a studio set, because the "documentary style" was the desideratum, but this aesthetic requirement was fit to the management ideal of isolating their labor environment. An island, so to speak, was equally the object of aesthetic and corporate design.

This is how Zanuck-Brown deployed the auteur theory, as a gate between their operation, their range of movement, and the larger corporate structure of MCA-Universal. Their company, they said, required "effective buffers" that would open a space of "protective custody" for those they hired on the basis of merit.[97] And they passed this philosophy on to Spielberg, who used it to organize the layer of employees below him on *Jaws* and, in theory, in the production company he later founded, Amblin Entertainment. This does not imply that each person had a discrete job for which he or she was hyperspecialized; Zanuck-Brown did not rationalize but generalize. They found "no area of the film too mundane for [them] to become involved in," but they did not "hover over" a director's shoulder. What subtended their generalist claim was that they, as producers, were "very creative people" with the "ability to detect a story that has both artistic and commercial appeal," and this was their license. Once it was honored, they spread it to the "directors and writers" they were able to "attract."[98] Spielberg did not come by this genetically but socially. He had begun, famously, by making amateur 8 mm films in his teens. His problem professionally was that the "more involved [he] got, the more [he] did everything." Only in television, when it became a rationalized, legal matter—when he faced "certain limitations dictated by certain unions that wouldn't let [him] run the camera, cut the film, and compose the music" on his "[Directors Guild of America] card"—did he come to think that elective affinity with a team, where each role was shading into the other, was better than an industrially circumscribed role.[99] Spielberg realized "how much other departments could do for him," Joe Alves said, and that to "rely on others gives you choices," which was "something he discovered on *Sugarland*, as opposed to television." In this capacity, Vilmos Zsigmond said, Spielberg could work "as a conductor" who calls "on the expertise of his collaborators."[100] Spielberg himself explained this version of auteur theory by recourse to "the idea." On *Jaws*, he said, "I pretty much set the camera, except when Bill comes up with terrific ideas . . . and I let him put the camera where the idea is better."[101] In this we hear a disavowal of proprietary claim— Bill Butler, the cinematographer, did not have an idea all his own but rather identified the better idea—and hence authorship in this enterprise is a game of unbinding ideas from their sources. Another way to see this, and a way whose implications it will be my duty to spell out in chapter 4, is as a matter of decharismatizing the process of idea generation. Hence Spielberg would say, in thanking his collaborators, "There is no such thing as *Auteur*."[102]

It was the new idea that Zanuck-Brown wanted on *Jaws*, and they tapped Spielberg for the sensibility he could bring, not of a narrative or generic kind but of a formal kind. What they did not want to do was make "*Moby-Dick* again."[103] This meant they did not want the "engineer" or "sure-handed" director who was apt at helming the Old Hollywood adventure, as Lew Wasserman had recommended.[104] Such "engineers" would rely on process shots to suggest the ocean as setting; in *Jaws* they wanted the ocean, its undulating vantage, to orient the spectator (in this respect, Stanley Kubrick might be the only true predecessor for this type of director, according to Annette Michelson's account of the new spectator hailed by his *2001*).[105] Hence Spielberg planned to introduce Quint (Robert Shaw) in an Amity theater watching *Moby Dick* (Huston, Warner Bros., 1956) and unnerving his fellow moviegoers by laughing throughout, most pointedly as Gregory Peck's Ahab flails with his harpoon at the great whale. In this way, Spielberg would accentuate his New Hollywood bona fides by pointing out the tacky effects of Old Hollywood. Gregory Peck denied Spielberg's request, not wanting to be the object of sport.[106] The problem with John Huston is simply that he was too much like David Brown—too literary, too given to voice-over poetics, and too much a student of the novel—and not at all like Spielberg. What Huston's *Moby Dick* did well was very much in the jurisdiction of Brown, who was the "genius" of Zanuck-Brown, the "house intellectual," whose background in the publishing world gave him a peerless sense for story.[107] But Spielberg's value lay elsewhere. The story (formerly "a good picture") had been depreciated by television, insofar as it "can be done just as effectively on television," Brown said, and "no one will go see it in the theater."[108] Brown understood his skill, that is, to be transmedial. Spielberg's skill, by contrast, was medium specific. He could give the movie "visual excitement," Zanuck believed.[109] He could make a "film" out of a "movie," so Brown claimed (in admittedly confusing vocabulary).[110] Because Brown felt that "television [was] the great adversary" at that time, the company would make *Jaws* to reestablish what was "cinematic," a value that he thought the old moguls came by very naturally, what was termed "magic" for its capacity to project the "commonest reality" and transfigure it.

In *Jaws*, Spielberg worked in a "visceral" idiom, what Paul Monaco would call the "cinema of sensation," and he did this, as Lucas would too, by dynamizing the screen space.[111] Julie Turnock notes that Lucas would do this in the opening flyover of *Star Wars* (20th Century Fox, 1977). Lucas designed this, he claims, on the model of Akira Kurosawa, whose *Hidden Fortress* (Toho, 1958) begins with two peasants being pursued by samurai who enter not from stage left or right—that is, not in the logic of the proscenium—but from behind the camera. They *emerge* into the frame. Likewise, *Star Wars* begins with a couple of rebel ships entering the frame and plunging into the "deep perspective" of space before "an imperial cruiser looms into view, filling the overhead portion of the screen."[112] The space vessel comes from above and seems to be resting its large mass on the audience. Spielberg, like Lucas, deprived the screen of a center of gravity, allowing its graphic motion to be vectorized at any point within or beyond the frame. "He must have never seen a play," a director of the older generation said of Spielberg. "He's the first one of us who doesn't think in terms of the proscenium arch. With him, there's nothing but the camera lens."[113]

The sea, of course, is the element for this—its endless variation is an alibi for camerawork that might otherwise be deemed excessive. In fact, they shot *Jaws* handheld almost exclusively, not to produce camera movement but to reduce it. Being on boats, it became clear that a fixed camera would record a constant up-and-down movement, and only by handholding the Panaflex could camera operators Bill Butler and Michael Chapman correct for the bobbing.[114] For this reason the third act of *Jaws* is often upheld as its bravura passage—as its feat of "pure cinema," as Antonia Quirke would call it—but the truth is that the conceit of ocean movement informs its camera design elsewhere in more subtle ways. For instance, in the first act, when Mayor Vaughn (Murray Hamilton) and his flunkies confront Chief Brody (Roy Scheider) about closing the beaches, the scene is staged on a ferry. Nothing requires that it be staged on a ferry, but doing so lets Spielberg put the shot in motion with a camera position that is otherwise rather stationary. The shot keeps Brody in the left foreground, and once Mayor Vaughn's car is driven onto the ferry, he and the newspaper editor and doctor join Brody. The four men huddle in medium close-up in frame left. Over the course of a long take, the scenery is rotated behind these men as they confer. They are static, but a seascape wheels behind them (see figs. 3.6 and 3.7). Moreover, rather than reframe the men for greater intimacy, Spielberg has them move toward the camera, first for a medium shot of Brody, the mayor, and the editor, and then, as conversation becomes more conspiratorial, for a still-tighter shot of Brody and the mayor. Within one fixed long take, we are put through a series of quite subtle movements that have the effect, nearly imperceptible, of shifting foci such that viewers do not linger too long on the conversation itself and whether or not it plausibly advances the story. It will, incidentally, be a weak point in the narrative that the mayor and city fathers have utter disregard for the local lives sacrificed to the tourist trade. But the story, once put in spin, once quickened phenomenologically, is not lessened by its narrative content because its details are marginalized in the gestalt of the experience.

**FIGURES 3.6 AND 3.7** In *Jaws*, when Spielberg cannot mobilize the frame by moving the camera, he mobilizes it by the sea, which is a constantly moving ground for the figures in his compositions.

The narrative content of *Jaws* is congealed in the genres overlaid on each other, namely the defection and disaster genres. The movie makes a gesture to the conspiracy thriller, of course, which had made headwinds in the recent movies *Klute*, *The Conversation*, and *Parallax View* (Pakula, Paramount, 1974), but in *Jaws*, the paranoia of this film cycle is only a coefficient of the epistemological structure that the movie invokes only to discard. That is, Mayor Vaughn embodies the moment's Nixonian conspiracy-mindedness in his engineering of a cover-up, but his cover-up only works because the real facts behind it must be mediated for an audience that is flung at a geographical remove from their happening.

The real facts are mediated for locals, of course, by the newspaper editor ("We never had that kind of trouble in these waters," he says) and the word of mouth that will challenge his official reports. But they are mediated for tourists by television. The only newscast we see from the Amity beaches is delivered in sensationalized tones. "Amity Island has long been known for its clean air, clear water, and beautiful white-sand beaches," the reporter tells us. "But in recent days a cloud has appeared on the horizon of this beautiful resort community—a cloud in the shape of a beautiful shark." This report, absurd in its rhetoric, frames the Fourth of July weekend as blood sport for those following from afar. Many have come to the island, in fact, to chase the $3,000 bounty that was placed on the shark by a bereaved mother. The fatuousness of the news report is matched to the venality of the local government. All this ends in the second act, however, and these cultural and political structures, fatuous and venal alike, get sublated in the contest between man and nature. Chief Brody had come to Amity, indeed, because he wanted to escape the social decay of New York City. "I'm telling you, the crime rate in New York will kill you," he says at one point. "There's so many problems you never feel like you're accomplishing anything." Hence, the foundational impulse in *Jaws* is defection. Brody came to Amity on the belief that, as an island, it remained a face-to-face society rather than being mediated by institutions. "But in Amity one man can make a difference," he claims. It is the defection of law and order to more manageable terrain. Even on the island, though, he is constrained to act—in the Adornian sense of "contemporary actionism," of absolutized agency—by corrupt politicians and the media apparatus.[115] Only when the three men (Brody, the oceanographer, and the salty fisherman) set out to sea do they face a situation in its immediacy.

On the waters, all else is bracketed. In *Jaws*, the "commonest reality," as David Brown calls it, is simply the water. The drama comes not from the logistical difficulty of steadying a camera at sea but from how to photograph the vessel (visually, phenomenologically) that will safely bear the protagonists on waters that will nonetheless always menace them. It amounts to a question of theater: the boat, the *Orca*, is a small floating stage that only allows for so many camera setups. Here Spielberg's "avant-garde" camera placements come into play. One solution was to film the *Orca* from the water, from a pontoon raft on which director of photography Bill Butler had rigged the camera platform to be raised and lowered and from which he had cut out a section on one side for the camera's water box (a device that generally allowed them to shoot at and below the waterline, eliminating, in the process, any "floor").[116] These devices permitted unexpected verve in the editing together of vantages. But what multiplies the vantages are shots on the *Orca* itself, for instance, a shot from within the cabin of Hooper on the bow (see fig. 3.8), of Quint perched on the prow (see fig. 3.9), of Quint edging

**FIGURE 3.8**

**FIGURE 3.9**

**FIGURE 3.10**

**FIGURE 3.11**

**FIGURES 3.8–3.12** Spielberg deploys his "avant-garde" camera techniques to add visual interest to the otherwise-confined theatrical space of the *Orca*.

along the port side (see fig. 3.10), and of Quint in the crow's nest, first from below and then from above (see figs. 3.11 and 3.12).

Our perspective on the theater of action is remarkably labile. Spielberg's stock principle of composition, the tracking shot—a kind of experiential "following around" (e.g., Chrissie running along the sand dunes in the opening sequence, or Brody walking from his bedroom the next morning)—is more or less disabled in the space of a small boat, and he substitutes a more stationary shot, inventively framed, that gets dynamized by a seascape without vertical hold, where a spectator's orientation on the object world is necessarily kinetic. It is intensely cinematic, if we define that by the rotation of the object world to ceaselessly vary our consideration of it.[117] Consider, as one instance, the first scene in which Quint detects the shark in the waters. He is framed in a tight low-angle shot, with his head seemingly perched atop the reel of the fishing rod, and behind and above him are the crisscrossing ropes and poles of the masts and sails. The reel seems like it is flush with the camera lens, pressing against our attention. It turns several clicks; Quint gives it a sidelong look. There is a sound of creaking tension, maybe from the rod. Then a cut to the line in the water. It dips just a little. There is a disturbance, known at this point only to Quint. He begins to clip himself into the harness. He puts the rod into its mount and clips the harness to the reel, and in this series of operations, each piece of his contraption begins to seem animated. His gear, so old-fashioned, holds our interest in relation to Hooper's high-tech set of tools, laid out earlier on the dock—Quint, on seeing it, called him a "half-assed astronaut." As Quint prepares for a contest with the shark, he swivels up a floorboard that he will push his feet against for leverage. There are fourteen separate shots, intercut with Brody teaching himself to tie a sailing knot, all scored to the rhythm of John Williams's taut strings. Brody cinches the knot, and then suddenly, spasmodically the reel pays out what seems to be the extent of its line. Quint yells at Brody to "wet the reel!" There is drama of a protonarrative kind here, with nothing *happening* at first but a series of subsensory disturbances, tuning us, the audience, into maritime rhythms that hint at, but wait to reveal, the nearness of the shark. It is all predicated on the shark—the gear components that lock together once activated by the tug beneath the surface—but as the production crew and later commentators have so often said, it is a mode of drama that was forced by the dumb luck of the mechanical shark not working reliably, making the stress fall on the shark as an invisible source of environmental reordering and not on the shark as an object of horror.

But the movie, for all that it plays on the sensorium, does so in a classical key. It sounds out the *Orca*'s atmospheric envelope in service of a high-seas adventure movie. Its quiet, keening attention to the clicking reel, to the air bubbles on the ocean surface, and to Quint's eco-attuned reactions, gives way in a subsequent episode to the triumphalist swashbuckling of the heroes on the march. Williams's score adapts accordingly. In part, *Jaws* marks out a classical purpose by tethering its sensuous details to the narrative template of the disaster movie. In those movies, the drama came from authority being dislodged and thrown up for grabs amid the collapse of society and the upwelling of a state of nature. In this facet, *Jaws* resembles them. But in them, what was collapsing was a figure of technological hubris such as a massive skyscraper, a cruise ship, or a jet plane.[118] *Jaws* entertains a much different relationship with technology. Technology has, at the level of appearance, seemingly been evacuated from the scene. Rather more like a defection movie, *Jaws* withdraws from the world of public institutions, from the totalizing control that these figure in their technologized monuments, and it shrinks them into an interpersonal agon between Chief Brody and the ocean. The contest is man against nature, the mise-en-scène is nature in the raw, and while the boat is motorized, in all other details it is clearly an outdated, well-loved thing more than a technological marvel. *Jaws* activates the moral schemata of the disaster genre, but it modifies the genre ethos by shunting technology offscreen, where it can never remain, because, as Walter Benjamin explains, "the equipment-free aspect of reality has here become the height of artifice, and the vision of immediate reality the Blue Flower in the land of technology."[119] This was, Benjamin tells us, the peculiar charge of cinema from the start. Spielberg, having coaxed from a mechanical shark the look of organic life, has returned us with a difference to a moment we have long known—hence the appellation "neoclassical"—but he has gotten something of Miriam Hansen's "vernacular modernism" back into cinema, not by revealing our modernity to us but by naturalizing it in the visage of our original state.[120]

Audiences clearly loved it. But my concern rests less on its box-office success, or on the transformation of release patterns (which *The Godfather* began but *Jaws* cemented); my concern is with production culture. Zanuck-Brown needed an aesthetic display that would reestablish the difference in medial experience, a difference that on the Universal lots organized the production of television and movies in their own regimes. Zanuck-Brown needed it so that they might wall off their own authority and labor practices from the corporate structure of MCA. Audience love for *Jaws* was an important datum in this regard because it suggested that Spielberg had evoked for moviegoers what was properly (if provisionally) cinematic. The late-modernist appeal to film tradition was not enough for him—its self-reflexivity hailing the knowingness of its audiences—because the experience was a cognitive one. Better this than television, perhaps, which for Spielberg was a structure of knowledge in which it was not apparent who did the knowing. But the cinema was a procedure in which knowledge was drawn into the body; it was an encounter with the phenomenal world that did not need explaining. Delivering the new cinema to Wasserman certainly gained Zanuck-Brown and Spielberg their professional autonomy. So long as the cinematic quotient was their possession, they were beholden to no one. As Richard Zanuck said, "I didn't like going to board of directors' meetings, and having to make speeches at stockholders' meetings. Meeting with bankers, with moneymen. That's not my *shtick*." Instead he claimed, "I'm a filmmaker. That's what I like to do. That's what I'm doing now."[121] Zanuck got his self-determination by entering into what Jean-François Lyotard called the new culture of the "temporary contract."[122] Zanuck-Brown got to do what they do, in short, but the qualification was that the magic of *Jaws* had no timetable for recurring. Free of rationalized, Fordist labor, they were now to make an industrial precedent for irrational, post-Fordist creation. This happens, we will see, when art leads the economy.

# 4

# THE ETHOS OF INCORPORATION

## BBS and the Law of Unnatural Persons

*Schneider was an outlaw with connections, family ties.*

Patrick McGilligan, *Jack's Life*

BS Productions opened its final, Columbia-authorized movie, *The King of Marvin Gardens* (Rafelson, 1972), on a scene of Jack Nicholson's face, in tight close-up, swallowed in darkness. Photographed in full face, in half-moon shadow for much of it, Nicholson is all we see for more than five minutes. Only in the last thirty seconds or so do we see a flashing red light as a second source of illumination added to the key light trained on Nicholson. The red light, we soon realize, is from the producer's booth, and Nicholson is in the studio of a radio station. In that moment, audiences would be ready for this concentrated attention on Nicholson. Several years earlier he had been the breakout star, albeit in a supporting role, in BBS's epochal *Easy Rider*, and on the heels of that, he was the lead in the company's next big success, *Five Easy Pieces*. Hence, the bright light on Nicholson in tight close-up seems to tailor his charisma for audience consumption; it seems a demonstration, indeed, that his person can bear the limelight because it carries within it the powers of stardom.

The producer Bert Schneider had invited Michael and Julia Phillips (producers of *The Sting*) to an advance screening of *Marvin Gardens*, and Julia Phillips reports that while watching the first five minutes, she thought she was about to see "the greatest movie ever made." She changed her opinion drastically enough that in an elevator ride with Schneider afterward, pressed for her opinion, she admitted, "Oooh, I didn't like it." But Schneider said, "I don't care, I love this movie."[1] They were both right: the movie did poorly at the box office, so Julia Phillips was speaking for the audience, but it was the self-narration of Schneider's company, BBS, which at the time preoccupied him more centrally than audiences did. Phillips was reveling, as an audience would, in Nicholson's star power; Schneider was interested in how his corporation had helped construct it. The red light interrupting Nicholson in the movie's opening scene, indeed, has the force to direct our attention away from his image and toward the apparatus supporting it. Its focus on the producer's booth is a baring of the mechanics of star power, which sets the movie up to experiment with how readily different persons can be swapped in and out of this machinery. Though Nicholson was the signature BBS star, he plays the "down vibe" character and trades off his usual "up vibe" persona to Bruce Dern.[2]

One way to look at this is as a means for Nicholson to deepen what Barry King has called the theatrical skill of "impersonation," with the actor showing he can play a restrained wallflower, too. But unlike his peers in the emergent generation of Hollywood actors—such as Dustin Hoffman and Robert Duvall—Nicholson had not started on the New York stage, nor would he ever look to its skill set to legitimate his own screen stardom. His stardom was cut to the measure of the cinema. Another way to look at it, then, is as a test in the other art that King has called "personification," a test that would have Dern personify BBS as Nicholson had done previously. What it means to personify, in King's argument, has to do with the morphology of bodies—what they are constrained to signify in their physical attributes—in a given historical moment. An actor's "hair color, body shape, repertoire of gestures, registers of speech, accent, dialect and so on," King says, "always presignif[y]."[3] In this historical moment, the morphological set that marked off New Hollywood actors (Dustin Hoffman, Robert Duvall, Gene Hackman, Al Pacino, et al.) was something like a rebuke to the actors of studio-era Hollywood (Cary Grant, Gary Cooper, and so on). The difference in the younger actors at the level of bodies—short stature, ethnic features, nasal voice—came to personify Hollywood counterculture, and BBS was in the business of converting this yield into corporate style.

How a body could bear the values of BBS, a corporation, was in the end a matter of charisma. Richard Dyer has posited that charisma—the "little something extra" of stardom—is the "condensation" of transpersonal values, of "some *very central* feature of man's existence," into a person's being.[4] BBS in this moment was concerned with how the charisma of the corporation (an institution "*very central*" to economic existence) was made intelligible and indeed could be celebrated when condensed in a person. And there was no better display of this operation than in the cinema, the machinery of which, Nico Baumbach suggests, has the power to anthropomorphize nonhuman actors just as it "cosmomorphizes" (in Edgar Morin's coinage) its human actors. It calls its objects, both human and nonhuman, into other orders of being; such are its animating powers.[5] Jean Epstein tried staking out these ineffable powers when he theorized the "photogénie," noting how the camera could charm whatever fell in its line of sight. "A close-up of a revolver is no longer a revolver," he says, but "is the revolver-character."[6] In the '60s Andy Warhol paid these effects forward, experimenting with the promiscuity of the camera's star-making capacity. As he notes in *The Philosophy of Andy Warhol*, the Empire State Building was his "first Superstar," and his screen tests were an arch exercise in the egalitarian sharing of stardom with whoever arrived at his parties.[7] BBS learned from him, as I will discuss in this chapter. Hence, while *Marvin Gardens* narrates a business partnership between the Staebler brothers, mirroring the partnership at the heart of BBS between Schneider and Bob Rafelson, at the same time it is a meditation on the cinema, beginning as it does on the star-making close-up of Nicholson and ending on images of the Staebler brothers that are thrown onto a door by a 16 mm projector (see fig. 4.1).

Why the powers of cinema might be recruited into the projects of the corporation, Jerome Christensen argues, is explained by the place that

**FIGURE 4.1** The opening shot of *The King of Marvin Gardens* is a self-conscious display of Jack Nicholson's star power.

Thurman Arnold's New Deal–era notion of "capitalized earning power" might assume in understandings of corporate value. Arnold's notion is meant to describe how a corporation, independent of its assets, can still hold value; the idea is that something like a personality, generative in itself, lies behind and organizes the assets in the first place. Christensen argues that the personality behind a corporation—what Arnold says we might call its "goodwill," which "confers value on a corporation above and beyond the market value of its material property"—is "nothing other than star power."[8] For Christensen, we can therefore look at MGM if we want a concrete understanding of corporate personality. What is interesting about BBS, though, is that this immaterial or "extra-economic" root of the corporation made it seem compelling, for Bert Schneider at least, as a political device more than as a commercial one.[9] This makes perfect sense since, as Scott Bowman demonstrates, there is no fine distinction to be made between the corporation's economic and political power.[10] The trajectory of BBS, assessed crudely, took them from commercializing youth culture with *The Monkees* (1966–1968) to politicizing mainstream culture with *Hearts and Minds* (Davis, Warner Bros.,

1974).[11] My job in what follows is to nuance this trajectory, but the crude version of it is useful nonetheless. In the moment of the '60s, as the corporation refurbished itself, the better to accommodate the emergent class of knowledge workers, the BBS movement from Jack Nicholson and the counterculture to Huey Newton and Black Power suggested that the firm was more versatile and multipurpose than its caricature as a soulless machine of profit. The latter had been the C. Wright Mills critique of it, but it became so conventional an image of the firm throughout the '50s that variations on Mills's critique were being produced by the ideologists of corporate capital everywhere from *Fortune* to the *New York Times*.[12] But if the corporation could be understood in new terms, it might be used as a device supple enough to organize value in even the most recalcitrant territories, and it could do so (in this new understanding) by drafting into its charismatic community all that might seem—according to the workings of capitalism—to remain outside it. It could bring the outside inside.

The BBS self-understanding of this process was imperfect—the company's principals felt guilty, at times, about their relation as insiders to the world of outsiders. Schneider, in particular, joked that if the revolution were to wait until "after his death," he might then "hang onto his sauna, pool, and Porsche."[13] He felt guilty, but unlike, say, Jane Fonda, he did not think the relation could be dissimulated.[14] In the words of his critics, this was "radical chic."[15] But this was also, it is worth noting, the role of the firm: the act of internalizing and stabilizing what is unwieldy when outside of it—i.e., the price mechanism—is its reason for being.[16] Whereas the firm had learned to strike this balance in rational terms (such was the technocrat's appeal at least), its innovation of the '60s was to deploy charisma as the quality that would mediate the relation between inside and out. The firm would be "hyperpersonal" not "extrapersonal," embodied not abstract, and in turn inspiring not stultifying.[17] BBS was here in the vanguard. How it achieved this, I contend, is by way of a star system that was on loan not from the theater, as had been the case in the Hollywood studios, but from the art world.[18] At BBS the auteur theory was the instrument for modifying Hollywood stardom as well as the conduit for importing art-world charisma into its management culture.

In this chapter I consider *Marvin Gardens* as a moment in the firm's self-understanding, one that BBS had evolved for itself but was purveying generally for a labor force that had been reconstituted under the sign of creativity—which, as Dennis Hopper understood it, meant "doing something that is *yours*."[19]

## LOCK THEM IN THEIR IRON CAGES

BBS Productions came into being, was christened as such at any rate, when the producing team of Bert Schneider and Bob Rafelson moved from television into cinema. They added Steve Blauner to help them with distribution issues they did not entrust to their parent company, Columbia. Schneider and Rafelson had met at Columbia's television arm, Screen Gems, and it was there that their trajectories were joined. As a partnership in television, formed on creating the British Invasion knock-off, *The Monkees*, they called themselves Raybert (RAY-felson and BERT Schneider); as a movie production company, they called themselves BBS (Bob, Bert, and Steve). On one hand, it is good to remember that both Bert Schneider and Bob Rafelson enjoyed privileges at Screen Gems, owing to the Schneiders at the top of Columbia's executive charts—Bert's dad, Abe, going from president to chairman of the board and his brother Stanley assuming the presidency under their father. This insulated whatever antiauthority streak Bert and his partner, Bob Rafelson, had from what otherwise would have been its institutional repercussions. They had a "fuck-all" attitude, Rafelson claimed, and in consequence, he "never held a job for more than eight months before [he] started working for [himself] and Bert Schneider."[20] On the other hand, it is worth believing that no matter how privileged their tenure at Screen Gems, it was still television production, which meant for them, as it had for Spielberg, their subordination to rationalized, Fordist labor. Jay Boyer remarks that Rafelson was "poorly suited for the regimentation and rigors of network-television."[21] It became the BBS credo that one could not meaningfully work for someone else, and while part of my argument is that this became for them a management style, the stronger claim I want to make is that they—and they were not alone in this, but rather kept company with corporate insurgents of the '60s—effected a world-historical restoration of agency within capitalist economy, which might be put this way: if a corporation is purchasing labor power as a commodity, then there is practically no way to think of the bearer of this labor power as having agency, but if one identifies with the personality of the corporation, then the agency of the firm redounds to that person. That is, at BBS you were not a commodity but a corporate person; such was the attraction. The attraction is prolonged, Christopher Newfield says, in the contemporary moment, wherein "individualist fulfillment" remains possible "only within the borders of the firm."[22]

BBS exhibited many of the traits that characterize my other case studies—Bryna, Lion's Gate, and Zanuck-Brown—chiefly in what I am deeming their post-Fordist inflections. They were small and could work swiftly and cheaply, very much on the model of the guerrilla unit—Schneider had a picture of himself and Fidel Castro hanging in his office, and Peter Bogdanovich describes the approach he and others brought from the Roger Corman "guerrilla university."[23] They were committed to location shooting as a means to escape both the studios and the Hollywood unions. "Our philosophy is to shoot everything outdoors," BBS said, "without going into a studio."[24] The escape from the studio lot, as we saw for Robert Altman and Steven Spielberg alike, was an escape from oversight. Dennis Hopper would approvingly quote Jean-Luc Godard's call to "lock them in their studios" and "shoot in the street"—which is at once managerial and aesthetic, granting filmmakers release from studio hierarchy while also charging them with finding the resources for filmmaking in the streets.[25] Lock the managers, in Max Weber's phrase, in their "iron cages"; let the artists hit the paving stones. But also, BBS was regularly in the crosshairs of Hollywood unions for recruiting nonunion crews on location. They had refused to sign the Writers Guild's basic agreement, had resisted the Publicists' Guild, and were in general "at odds with the Coast unions, maintaining (with other indie producers) that various guilds make inordinate demands that complicate low-budget, adventurous filmmaking."[26] In a revealing instance, the International Alliance of Theatrical Stage Employees, IATSE Local 659, came after BBS when they tried to hire Nestor Almendros as cinematographer for Jim McBride's *Gone Beaver*, a film that was ultimately canceled. The union charged that BBS was guilty of a pattern in "indie production" wherein a small company was set up on "a pic-by-pic basis" so that the larger Columbia could "avoid their obligations under existing agreements."[27] BBS had reason to object, for in their perspective, the small corporation was not a ruse of Columbia's but a shield from the larger company. Location shooting for BBS was a way to safeguard their autonomy. This ramified in the legal regime, to be sure, but its primary function for the small company was that location shooting made for close relations within a production unit. The relationships of control internal to the firm could, in this way, be passed off as familial or friendly. As Bob Rafelson would put it, they were a "disoriented family" working together on film after film, subtract a member here and add a member there.[28] Jack Nicholson put it still more cynically: "If I hire my friends, the people I work with will be willing to do anything for me."[29] Hence, the legal character of these relations could be rendered unnecessary—what was compulsory could suddenly look volitional.

But, of course, there is a legal character imposed from above, whether acknowledged or not, and it is derived from property rights. The questions besetting BBS were old ones, addressed by business historians in terms of the "top-down" or "concession" theories of the firm versus the "bottom-up" or "aggregate" theories, but their ways of dealing with them were novel.[30] Though Jack Nicholson associated with Schneider and Rafelson freely, lending his ideas and writing skills and personal charm to their venture, he was conscious of the qualitative difference between them and him. "He was without portfolio in Raybert, a nonpartner," as Patrick McGilligan notes of Nicholson's contributions early on. Even upon emerging as a star, he was not party to key BBS decisions and would object, McGilligan says, by asking whether he was nothing but another Monkee.[31] Such anxiety was fended off, though, in the BBS practice of shifting personnel in and out of their roles. If the limit on Hollywood actors had historically been that they were employees, not owners—the "powerless elite," as Francesco Alberoni put it—then it makes sense that few at BBS identified as mere actors.[32] Everyone was in the process of becoming a director. Nicholson, once minted as a star, began directing *Drive, He Said* (Columbia, 1971). Henry Jaglom, Nicholson's friend from method-acting workshops and Schneider's friend from childhood, began directing *A Safe Place* (Columbia, 1971).

On one hand this was an outcome of auteur theory. Nicholson's visit to Paris in 1966 had an effect on him, and he returned stateside, as McGilligan claims, intent on "becoming what the French admired most, an *auteur*."[33] On the other hand this was BBS's oppositional ethos to scientific management. They encouraged, Teresa Grimes reported, "a great deal of collective participation in each other's ideas," what Jaglom described as a "tremendous overlapping" of roles."[34] In this effort the auteur theory was less a lever for raising the director above the fray and more a key for reclassifying the director as a "filmmaker."[35] No longer constrained by a hyperspecialized status, the filmmakers "scripted, directed, edited and acted in the films they were involved in making."[36] This policy of cycling in and out of roles was fundamental to the BBS corporate identity. Schneider joked that his role shuttled between "manager, coach, doctor, psychiatrist, cheerleader, manipulator, guide," but if the policy is assessed in earnest, its function was to keep the power of charisma free floating and make it seem as though the transference of charisma were the basic operation of their company. In their early days, indeed, Schneider and Rafelson seemed as much the movie stars as Nicholson, if not more. Candice Bergen, who dated Schneider in this period, called him "the romantic lead of the company."[37] It was suggested in *Variety* that BBS's choice of directors was an anointment of sorts: when Peter Bogdanovich's *The Last Picture Show* "broke through to excellent notices" and "smash boxoffice returns," their "Midas touch seemed affirmed," and "their decision to back McBride caused many to think that they might once again be on the verge of launching a directorial talent."[38] They had a claim on stardom, in other words, and they could extend it in whichever direction they pleased.

But their claim, when it put them at odds with Hollywood unions, confronted a claim of another kind. In BBS's effort to hire Nestor Almendros as cinematographer for *Gone Beaver*, an IATSE representative asked why an "American company has to import so-called artists" when "there is such high unemployment" and "the American worker is as competent as anyone in the world."[39] Disputing the terms of the debate, for the union, was crucial. If it is a cinematographer, a director, or what have you, it is a "worker" and therefore within their legal jurisdiction. But if the technician is renamed an "artist," they are right to worry that the rationality underpinning the legal system is being swapped out for something more indefinite. The case was decided by the Justice Department, and while there are ways to decide whether someone is an artist—it is, in fact, a question of being "so-called" by experts in the field, other artists and critics—BBS may not have pressed their case too vigorously, and the union won the decision.[40]

My purpose is not to dwell on this specific case, but on the principle at its heart. Calling Almendros an artist was not only a strategy for getting a work visa and union exemptions; it was simply the name given, for example, to Robert Towne (an actor in *Drive, He Said*, but a screenwriter more often, and later a director), Polly Platt (a screenwriter, a production designer, and later a producer), and others as they floated from one activity to another. As Dennis Hopper put it, "I think you work with the same instrument, and just apply it to different disciplines. . . . I really thought acting, painting, music, writing were all part of being an artist."[41] Artists could shape shift, rather than be fixed to a task, and it was the charisma written into the designation—the "little something extra"— that let BBS unsettle the division of labor. Howard Becker, in his study *Art Worlds*, notes that a historical aspect of art worlds is that the "core activities . . . necessary to make the work art rather than (in the case of objects) an industrial product, a craft item, or a natural object" are subject to change in status.[42] Putting these "core activities" in play was central in what I am calling Hollywood's post-Fordist transformation, but the challenge was being put to an artist's essential activity more forcefully and dramatically in the art world, and my point here is that BBS was responsible for porting these art-world polemics into the film industry. Hopper was the main conduit between these two worlds: though an actor originally, working alongside James Dean in *Rebel Without a Cause* (Ray, Warner Bros., 1955) and *Giant* (Stevens, Warner Bros., 1956) in his late-teenage years, he was blackballed from film work after a famous clash with Henry Hathaway, and from there he moved into the art world. Hopper took up photography, and he hung out at the Ferus Gallery on La Cienega, which became a hub of the Los Angeles art scene, and he befriended gallery owners Walter Hopps, Ed Kienholz, and Irving Blum. He was friends, too, with the artists, namely Ed Ruscha and Andy Warhol. Hopper and the principals at BBS—Schneider, Rafelson, and Nicholson—would overlay art-world values on Hollywood so that the informal practice organizing the former could penetrate the latter.

It was Andy Warhol's Factory, in particular, that modeled fluid work relations and a coy sharing of stardom. When Warhol famously said he thought "somebody should be able to do all my paintings for me," he radically unsettled which "core activities" made one an artist and therefore recast the relations between artist and what Howard Becker calls "support personnel."[43] This was, for Warhol, a way to thematize managerial relations while in the same motion liberating in the Factory's bacchanal the energies that were otherwise pent up in the industrial labor force.[44] The assembly line and the after-hours party were ironized in the Factory. Scrambling labor conditions in this way, Helen Molesworth argues, was the art-world response to a shift in the postwar economy "from manufacturing to service."[45] But Caroline Jones notes that Warhol's Factory did not so much foretell practices of a "new economy" as it recalled factories of old, "before time-motion studies, division of labor, and line production." In it, there were "no fixed workstations or functions."[46] As BBS was becoming BBS, they drew on this model to decouple themselves—and their creation, the Monkees—from the assembly-line Fordism of television production. Their first movie, *Head* (Rafelson, Columbia, 1968), is full of art-world references. At points we see Warhol's *Silver Clouds* (see fig. 4.2) and Ed Kienholz's *Back Seat Dodge '38*.

*Head* also depicts two kinds of factories. The first is an industrial factory, seemingly involved in the manufacture of television sets. As the four Monkees are being led on a tour of it by the plant manager, we see an assembly line bearing cardboard boxes with an image on the box exterior of a "black box" (see fig. 4.3).

But their ambition seems much greater than the manufacture of hardware, based on the manager's remarks that "to the degree that we are

**FIGURE 4.2** *Head* uses solarized photography to depict Monkee Michael Nesmith moving among Andy Warhol's *Silver Clouds*.

**FIGURE 4.3** The "Prefab Four" being led through a television manufacturing plant.

capable of understanding these mechanical-electrical devices as simple extensions of our brains . . . we are capable of using these machines productively." The thesis of the whole movie has been that television is complicit with the Vietnam War. In the opening sequences of the movie, the frame turns into a wall of televisions, equally spaced, with each screen depicting a genre of adventure that the Monkees will be run through (a western, a boxing movie, a musical, etc.), and in the final screen is the recent gruesome footage of the point-blank execution of a Viet Cong officer (see fig. 4.4).

A "theme song" song plays over these screens: "Hey, hey, we are the Monkees / You know we love to please / A manufactured image with no philosophies." In contrast to this factory, there is another, one more clearly modeled on Warhol's Factory, in particular on the Exploding Plastic Inevitable mixed-media shows that traveled from New York and recently had great impact at Bill Graham's Fillmore in San Francisco. It is a psychedelic party, with a rock band, complete with a Nico lookalike (see fig. 4.5). Milling through the crowd is director Bob Rafelson with a movie camera, as though to expose his part in the spectacle being produced. Evident in this self-exposure is a sense that baring the mechanism and showing how implicated one is in it might exculpate one from its workings. The movie is run through with such moments, such as one in the Columbia commissary in which walking through the set are not only Rafelson but Hopper, in his *Easy Rider* getup, and Nicholson as well. Being hip to the con— their theory went—ought to secure one a critical space from which to

**FIGURE 4.4** Rows of television screens culminating in the execution of a Viet Cong officer.

**FIGURE 4.5** A figure resembling Nico signals that the psychedelic party is meant to evoke Andy Warhol's Factory.

comment on it. "The money's in / We're made of tin," say the lyrics. "We're here to give you more."

But if Rafelson and Schneider were "here to give you more" (such as their upcoming *Easy Rider*), they would offer it in another mode. Though *Head* was a movie, it was a movie rooted in the themes, sites, and industrial organization of television. It was necessarily haunted by the problems associated therein. The artificial stardom of the Monkees was not easy to purge, because doing so would benefit Rafelson and Schneider but damage the actors in the "Prefab Four." One of the Monkees, Michael Nesmith, explained it: "I don't think we were victimized any more than people on the Old Hollywood contract system—we were just a product of the machine."[47] Astute as this insight is, BBS did not want to reproduce the Old Hollywood system, neither its star-making formula nor its labor relations. BBS did not want the ownership-labor split to keep their company riven, and hence, what *Head* did was expel the rationalized economy, which still organized television as it had Old Hollywood, and replace it with the rather underground network that configured the art world. They might not have wanted the movie to tank at the box office, but they considered it their right after they had made Columbia so much money. The advertising campaign, both the one-sheet and the lone TV ad, featured a headshot of John Brockman, who was not in the movie but was connected to Warhol's Factory and some of the media experiments that were then prevalent in New York. Nothing in the ad suggested the movie was connected to the Monkees; instead, it was a pun on Andy Warhol's film *Blow Job* (1964), which wittily focused only on the subject's face. By calling their first movie *Head*, BBS was preparing to advertise their future movies with the tagline: "From the people who gave you head." This misdirection likely sealed the commercial fate of *Head*, but it anchored the corporate identity of BBS.

## "RECEIPTS IS THE RULE FOR EVERYBODY": BBS AND THE MARKETPLACE

Between *Head* and *The King of Marvin Gardens*, a four-year run, BBS had achieved a lucid self-understanding. They had made themselves a legitimate movie company with *Easy Rider* and had changed the movie industry while doing so. Their subsequent movies—*Five Easy Pieces*; *Drive, He Said*; *A Safe Place*; and *The Last Picture Show*—seemed to hang together well enough that, for some, BBS had established a "corporate style." Mitchell S. Cohen, for instance, notes that all the company's movies are about "the concept of disintegration"—of private plans and the American Dream, of small towns and industrial cities, and of families and the country at large.[48] This is true enough, but given that Cohen is rooting this in the zeitgeist, all BBS movies being, he says, "products of the first Nixon administration," the claim is sufficiently broad to apply to many contemporaneous movies besides. Perhaps BBS made more direct contact with the zeitgeist than other movie producers did. But my claim is much narrower. I feel thoroughly justified saying *The King of Marvin Gardens* is their most personal movie, provided we understand this with reference to a corporate person. This is not to say that it did not resonate with youth-culture themes or Nixon-era disaffection but that it routed all this through the circuit of corporate belonging. This is not too surprising: short of outright defection (a theme which, as chapter 2 demonstrates, had legs) one had to link one's projects to capitalized joint ventures if one wanted a livelihood, at least, or a social purpose at best. This much is acknowledged in *Marvin Gardens*: "I wish you didn't think I was part of all this," one character says. "Aren't you?" Nicholson's character presses. "Of course I am," she says. "We all are." These are the realities of corporate capitalism. But BBS has not typically been valorized in terms of their hardheaded negotiation with these realities but rather their maverick refusal of them. My reading of *Marvin Gardens* tries to square this circle.

For starters, in *Marvin Gardens* the uncompromising individualism of *Five Easy Pieces* is eschewed in favor of partnership. The partnership, in fact, resembles the one between Rafelson and Schneider. The movie's two brothers, David (Jack Nicholson) and Jason Staebler (Bruce Dern), align with Rafelson and Schneider respectively. David Staebler does radio monologues, for instance, as Rafelson did during his military service.[49] And while David is putatively left to do the creative work, Jason is in charge of business details, as Schneider was at BBS. There are more personal details. The screenwriter Jacob Brackman—part of Michael and Julia Phillips's beach crowd and former Harvard dorm mate of Terrence Malick—had grown up in Atlantic City and thus knew the city intimately. A buried detail is that in the early Philadelphia subway scenes, the name H. D. Stanton is scrawled on a column. Harry Dean Stanton had been Nicholson's roommate, and it was in their house that Nicholson and Rafelson had written the screenplay for *Head*. So while it might be true to say that the diegetic partnership between David and Jason has a real-life referent, it is perhaps less a one-to-one correspondence with any actual person than it is with a dynamic process. That is, the partnership might include Rafelson, Schneider, Brackman, Nicholson, Stanton, and whichever members of a rotating group of friends, but the more decisive facts were where the partnership derived its value and where it secured capital. For BBS these facts might have appeared settled: they derived value from their connection to the youth market (as manifest in both the profits of *The Monkees* and *Easy Rider* and the discovery of next-generation stars such as Nicholson), and they secured capital from Columbia. They did not want their value reducible to profits, but they were satisfied defining it in terms of talent scouting and star making. "There is so much talent here in the U.S. but little talent for recognizing it," Rafelson said. "I thought together we could do this."[50] The question was how long Columbia would extend them capital if they did not continuously monetize their ability to recognize talent.

One way of seeing *Marvin Gardens*—the most instrumental way, I might say—is as a pitch made to Columbia to measure success in nonpecuniary terms. But if *Marvin Gardens* allegorizes the relationship that BBS had to Columbia, it does so by involution. The Staebler brothers are financed by an African American crime boss, Lewis (Scatman Crothers), and his identity—his blackness—hardly maps onto Hollywood power. Instead we might understand Atlantic City itself, its spectacle as a resort town in decline, as the displaced image of the studio system in ruins. David Staebler suggests that this is both literally and existentially true of Atlantic City: "Have you ever had the feeling that you were uncertain," he muses to himself, "that you were where you sensed yourself to be, that you were in a set, and all of the things were props?" To reinforce this "feeling," the movie employs the tropology of the Monopoly game, which took Atlantic City for a model and redeployed its place-names in a game of business enterprise. The abstraction of business, this suggests, has a reifying effect, which makes "things" into so many "props"; hence, Hollywood is another iteration of this model, but one that renders this make-believe—what I will here call "social purpose"—an occasion to give figure, both sentimentally and symbolically. It is, if you will, a mise-en-scène of economy. I will address this more fully in what follows. But the important last note is that both Atlantic City and Hollywood are monopolies of the industrial era, and in tatters as they are, the movie posits the black crime syndicate (i.e., the specter of Black Power) as a source of value in a postindustrial age, one figured at once as market expansion and financialization.

These considerations gather their urgency in retrospect. In 1973 Columbia would shake up their executive ranks and purge themselves of all the Schneiders. BBS got the axe, too, despite their independent status. David Cook writes, "The new management seized BBS royalties on previous films, took back their 16 mm rights, and tried to cancel the rest of the six-picture deal."[51] But in late 1971, as cast and crew began *Marvin Gardens*, Patrick McGilligan notes, "Nobody realized that it was destined to be one of the company's last productions."[52] Yet, within Columbia, the annual bookkeeping showed that 1971 was the worst year in studio history, recording losses of more than $28 million. This led to David Begelman replacing Stanley Schneider as president in July 1973. What followed were successes and scandals alike, but my point is to lift BBS above the short-term focus on balance sheets that constrained studio thinking in the moment and to reflect on the long-term traction that the BBS model had. Part of what their model offered is what theorist Peter Drucker had claimed was needed in industrial society, namely legitimacy, and as its central institution, the corporation had a responsibility to supply it. What Scott Bowman says this is, in effect, is a political theory of the corporation, a way to justify why such power accrues to it that is essentially inaccessible to state controls.[53] Because the postwar society that Drucker had been theorizing was transforming into a postindustrial society, his main claim was only heightened: amid such radical social change, an institution at the heart of society would need to give "social purpose" to its citizens or else risk upheavals on the order of the two World Wars. It might sound like a category error to say that BBS produced a political theory of the corporation—it is hard to say that this was their job, after all—but if *Marvin Gardens* is an inquiry into the social purpose of the knowledge worker emerging in a society designed for industrial workers, then I will argue that it takes the form of political theory, albeit in an aesthetic key.[54]

Indeed, at points it elaborates a political theory much like Drucker's own. His great equivocation lay with the place profit had in business enterprise. "For profit is not a cause," he claims.[55] Why, then, start a business? In a curious scene in *Marvin Gardens*, David and Jason watch a series of auctioneers try out their styles. It seems to be a job interview, yet the proprietor of the store questions why he is hosting their audition: "Nobody hires an auctioneer in the depths of winter," he upbraids Jason. The scene is curious because it is not clear who authorized Jason to hire an auctioneer. He is doing it in another man's store, and the other man objects. Even in a movie as loose-limbed as this, one often criticized for being nothing more than a sequence of set pieces, this scene is hard to explain. It is possible that Jason is setting up this auction for Lewis, the don of the city, and that the proprietor is a fence for Lewis's plunder. Nothing much indicates this. The proprietor does say, "If Lewis came here, wanted to play Santa Claus—" But Jason cuts him short. In a way, this is the emblematic scene, because throughout the movie, the mystery is where Jason gets his authority. He is a con man, it seems, but he has some backing from Lewis. The question is how much. His authority, we are left to infer, is largely self-arrogated. The scene seems to be a demonstration of charisma. When a group of older women amble before the storefront, Jason races out and snatches one of their purses. He lures them into the store before returning it and then proceeds to sell them goods at cut rates. It is a hustle. "I love all the hustle around here," Jason had earlier said. "It's out in the open." Jason believes the women do not care what goods they are being sold so much as they care about the manner in which they are being sold. David gives them a blender and toaster, no charge, and then shoos them along the boardwalk. The frustrated store owner asks, "What about my merchandise?" But David pushes back, "Why be so shortsighted? Why don't you think of the goodwill that it bought you?" Here, we are in the ambit of Drucker's theory: the activity of business is not to produce a profit, he says, but "*to create a customer.*"[56] Absorb the cost of a blender on the premise that you will, in turn, create a market for blenders. This is a conventional way to understand promotional giveaways. But Jason assures the store owner that "these grandmas are coming back with half the widows of South Jersey, and not because they got a handout for nothin', but because merchandise was presented to them with style." That is, it is not the product but the personnel. This is Drucker's managerial view of the world, which Jerome Christensen describes as "marketing all the way down."[57] In the movie, the store owner is not at all convinced—"Receipts is the rule for everybody." Spoken like a studio exec.

The scene makes sense, then, of the relationship between BBS and Columbia. Some BBS movies were money makers, some were not. Bert

Schneider said—on seeing the answer print of Henry Jaglom's *A Safe Place*—"I'm not going to try to make it into a commercial success." He knew it was not that kind of movie. "I made a poem for a studio," Jaglom would say, "and I was allowed to make it."⁵⁸ In this light, what bears remarking on in the above scene is that David, a downcast, disengaged character, joins with his brother and participates for the first time. Though Rafelson had cast Nicholson against type in this role, here his kineticism comes out. It is brought out by Jason's promise to utilize it, to augment it by harnessing it to an enterprise with economic and political power and cure him of his social alienation in the process. Lewis is depicted as a figure with resources of this kind, though just how one taps into his organization is not socially available knowledge. Jason is the nexus. Entering a partnership with Jason is a way to channel those resources outward and into society. It is a chance for David to apply his style in a socially meaningful project. But the project ought to be understood in terms of the social instrumentality of the partnership—the corporation, we could call it—not its economic instrumentality. This was the nub of contention between Peter Drucker and Milton Friedman.

In 1970 Friedman published his famous article, "The Social Responsibility of Business Is to Increase Its Profits," in the *New York Times Magazine*, an article more or less reiterating the thesis of "Monopoly and the Social Responsibility of Business and Labor" from his 1962 book, *Capitalism and Freedom*. In both he pushed against ideas that Drucker had been advocating in response to the thesis of Adolph Berle and Gardiner Means's *The Modern Corporation and Private Property*, namely that there was a separation between control and ownership in modern corporations. Friedman pushed toward a shareholder-value theory of the firm, according to a critique by latter-day management theorist Steve Denning.⁵⁹ The trajectory that follows from this, the Drucker-Friedman agon, is complicated, and one of its upshots (flowing from shareholder value) is financialization as the last hope against secular decline. But Drucker was making a point about social harmony that fell well outside Friedman's purview. Drucker understood that on the basis of the corporation's great economic power, it held great social and political power too. The fact that *Marvin Gardens* thematizes monopoly shows that its concerns also lie with the dimensions of power that unfold from the scale of an organization. For Drucker, it was key, Nils Gilman explains, "*to conceive of the corporation as a social entity and to analyze its social function in political terms.*"[60] To the extent that the assembly line stole skill from workers and alienated them from the product of their labor, Drucker argued, it was producing social problems that its economic yield could not tamp down. He offered a "conservative" solution insofar as it repudiated the "planners" and "technocrats" that engineered the regnant Keynesian economy.[61] Drucker posits the power of the corporation as a power that it is entitled to but is also responsible for. It discharges this responsibility, he argues in *Concept of the Corporation*, not only when it "organizes individuals for a community effort" but when it "organizes man for his moral victory over himself." It must "induce" from its "members an intellectual and moral growth beyond a man's original capacities," and it must encourage them "to take initiative, give them a chance to show what they can do, and a scope within which to grow."[62] My point is that in *Marvin Gardens*, this is the social purpose that Jason is trying to lend David. But David is wary of this utopian scheme: "Jason, you're asking me to believe in another dream."

The dream, in the movie, is Staebleravia, the name Jason and David will give the island of Tiki, which is located only "seven miles off the coast of Honolulu" but yet available for acquisition. It has been the object of enterprise already, Jason explains, but Donald Dimbleby invested $6 million building a resort on the island before being denied a gambling license. "A casino is the name of the game," Jason says. It is a prescient feature of *Marvin Gardens* that in depicting Atlantic City in 1971–72, several years before the city would legalize gambling, the movie would set itself in its midst only to imagine a resort built on casinos elsewhere. Perhaps BBS had a fine sense of the economic winds and could extrapolate the developing relationship between the deindustrializing city and financialization. Lawrence Webb has called this a "magic bullet" approach to urban renewal, one that has been dubbed "casino capitalism."[63] But the quick money is only part of the dream. They require financial backing, of course, but Jason plans to "parcel out ten-acre packages" for "vacation villas" to "amortize" their investment. It is his "pal Lewis's front money.

He owes [Jason] favors." David worries that he does not "know too much about real estate," but the plan seems designed to insulate him from the investment structure.

The important part of the dream is that it is an island. "It's really gonna be good to talk island again," Jason says. "You know we haven't talked island in years." The dream is to self-define far from the reach of oversight. What this means is that Lewis's money is offscreen, and must be, and the movie must work to shield it from view amid its effort to stage what seem like spectacles of performance art (a Salvation Army Band welcome party, a mock Miss America Pageant)—hence its effect of being a sequence of set pieces. There only needs to be a conduit between Jason and Lewis, we understand, as at BBS there was between Bert Schneider and Columbia. Once this much is established, the rest is play and invention. Hiding the money, so to speak, is a means of suppressing the hierarchy that ownership produces. This again evinces Drucker's ideal for "devolving authority" within the corporation "into smaller, functionally complete and separate divisions."[64] Schneider did this routinely, making each production its own integral unit, and he did it under the auspices of auteur theory. Every director to work for him attests to it, from Henry Jaglom to Peter Bogdanovich. To take one instance, Peter Fonda claims that on *Easy Rider*, "We had full liberty from the day Schneider gave us bread."[65] This is mirrored in *Marvin Gardens*. On the island, David will be free to do his radio show, only now it can have the full force of corporate infrastructure behind it. "We package your show," Jason tells him. "We can syndicate you to the whole goddamn English-speaking world."

This is making a poem for a studio, as Jaglom put it, with the rational trappings of the firm wished away. The work of management, Drucker says, "cannot be a bureaucratic" or "an administrative" task. It "must be a creative rather than an adaptive task."[66] Hence, *Marvin Gardens* is persistently confusing the roles of artist and businessman. On its face one might think the movie is about Jason, the businessman (coded as con artist), trying to draw forth his brother, David, the artist (coded as moody, withdrawn). But the movie makes a point of denying such an easy taxonomy. When David bypasses his brother and attempts to resolve a mix-up with Lewis directly, the latter identifies David as the businessman. "You I can talk to," Lewis says, but Jason is "no businessman." Despite the fact that Jason has a record of business deals with Lewis and thinks he is owed something in return, Lewis says, "I think he's an artist." In this, one can isolate the promiscuity of roles— the destabilizing of job descriptions—that BBS had raised to a corporate ethos, lifted originally from the art world in accord with its underground codes of behavior but transposed here to the underworld of crime. That Jason is called an artist means that he has charisma and might act on his own without orders from above. David understands this to be the natural order: "You send Jason down there, of course he's got ideas of his own." The idea of his own, it turns out, is to pursue Tiki for himself irrespective of Lewis's plans. But "what do you expect?" David asks Lewis. "That's what you like about him. . . . That's the way you got started." Lewis, we might say, is constrained by the rules of monopoly. He imagines that Jason's charisma diminishes his own authority. The suggestion implicit in this scene, and in the movie as a whole, is that one might radicalize the relations of production—letting charisma float free in this sphere in order to grant each producer, each artist, a space to discharge his unique skills—by way of the marketplace. Jason, as David points out, "opened up some territories" for Lewis. There is no reason to assume, in other words, that mass markets require the techniques of mass production. Jason and David, in fact, joked that the decline of Atlantic City ("It was full-out class until about 1930," Jason says) was rooted in its cheap, tacky products. The lesson for their own venture is "no Pokerino, no frozen custard, no salt-water taffy." Customers gave these up once they were no longer limited to them, that is, once they "could hop a plane to Bermuda for the weekend."

This is BBS talking to themselves, I believe, but even in such a private work, they seem to push up against limits they know to be public. There is a sleight of hand, after all, in Drucker's utopian appeal to the corporation. Though management ought to create "economic conditions," not adapt to them, it "ultimately" is a "rational activity." So it must seek "what is desirable of attainment" not "(as the maximization-of-profit theorem implies) aim at accommodation to the possible," but in the last instance the question should "be raised what concessions to the possible have to be made."[67] The pragmatic turn in his thought takes on unexpected shades of Marx's dictum that "men make their own history" but not "as they please"—they make it, rather, "under circumstances existing already."[68] BBS was guarded, too. They conceived the corporation as the agent of charismatic community, and they deployed its legal sanction to that end, but they were wary of its economic self-definition.

We can now return to the scene of Jack Nicholson playing late-night DJ in the radio booth, which both begins and ends the movie. He is, we ought to note, isolated in his stardom. Despite a plot dedicated to partnership, he begins and ends alone in close-up, in what seems to be a comment on the characteristic operation of the star-making apparatus—its aptitude, that is, for selecting out, for individuating. In what follows I will suggest that understanding the precise nature of this operation, for good and bad, formed the ethos of BBS. There was something cynical, I believe, in their exploitation of it. But here I want to observe how attuned they were to its pathos. In the opening scene, as noted, David Staebler's monologue is broken up by a red flashing light, signaling the intrusion of his producer. There is necessary infrastructure, this signifies, supporting his self-examination. He laments in another scene that he has been "deprived" his "literary right" (because "no one reads anymore") and that he "crave[s] an audience." He is granted an audience on radio, but the cost is that its mediation is still more modern and highly capitalized. When David leaves the radio station, indeed, he is plunged into infrastructure: he walks on city sidewalks, passes the Industrial Valley Bank (he is poetic even in the names of banks he walks past), and then stops in an all-night café before descending into the Philadelphia subway system. In a subtle irony, David is shown in the foreground of the café, hunched over his coffee, while in the background a group of people communicate in sign language around a table, suggesting they are deaf. He is a radio artist, yet the only people nearby would not even be able to listen to his show. In another irony, he had delivered a monologue narrating the lifelong connection that he and his brother forged when they helped along the death of their grandfather. Their partnership, that is, was predicated on the overthrow of the patriarch. But when David arrives home after his commute, his grandfather (still alive) is the person to greet him. Hence, the plot that we watch phantasmagorically unfold—in which David "authors his life"—only takes shape as it does if an infrastructure of connectedness (agents to principals, artists to finance, sons to patriarchal dispensation) is suppressed.


## THE POLITICAL FORCE OF UNNATURAL PERSONS

One assessment of *Marvin Gardens*, then, is that while it outlines a business philosophy, it is less than optimistic about its practicability. This might register the fact that BBS was pulling apart internally. They would only make one more movie, *Hearts and Minds*, and even that was abandoned by Columbia and released by other means. But it registers, too, the precarious nature of what they were doing: on the equipoise between corporate agency and commodification, they were apt to pitch toward the latter. Paul Schrader understood it this way when dismissing *Easy Rider*: Were they, too, not just Hollywood liberals "exploiting" every "youth truth" right down to its "paranoia"?[69] Bert Schneider was mindful of this critique, even if he had a countervailing theory. His beliefs about the corporation (the kind of enclave it builds, the legal agency it confers) required connections to spaces that he considered to be nonmarket. In Andrew Schroeder's perspicacious analysis of BBS, he notes that the very groups externalized by the regular activity of capitalism, such as the "young, the *lumpenproletariat*, some cultural avant-gardes, and many of the Third World revolutionary movements," became the source of political values that were not shot through with economic values.[70] My analysis of *Marvin Gardens* ultimately turns on a claim that Schneider, if he understood the economic and political power of the corporation to be forever bound together, needed the black community in the form of the Black Panthers to purify the political force of the corporation. It is important, I think, that in *Marvin Gardens* the power structure has been racialized. Lewis, the neighborhood don, is African American, and from the moment of David's arrival in Atlantic City, he is shadowed by a black man (see figs. 4.6 and 4.7).

**FIGURE 4.6**  Jason meets the neighborhood don, Lewis.

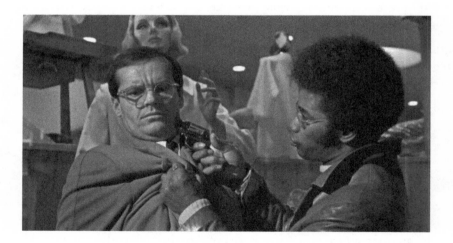

**FIGURE 4.7**  Jason has been followed throughout the movie by figures of "black power," and here, he is confronted.

To the extent that the movie allegorizes the BBS relationship to Hollywood, it seems an inversion to imagine that the Staebler brothers would rely on a black organization for financing. Hollywood, both in matters of production and representation, had operated on the exclusion of black America. But in part, the BBS critique was that Hollywood had exhausted its market, and wringing further value from it made capitalism seem like a sclerotic system. Value in a postindustrial landscape was figured in the form of the marginalized groups that inhabited it. This holds true, I suggest, for the friendship between Schneider and Black Panther cofounder Huey Newton as well as for *Marvin Gardens*. Though it was their last Columbia movie, the enterprises that BBS had in the offing (narrative movies, documentaries, and even political projects) were rooted in colonies of the capitalist system. This was Huey Newton's language—the "Black colony," he called black America—but the concept was homologous with Schneider's version of the corporation. Indeed, from the perspective of BBS, their fortunes were coarticulated with Newton's and the Black Panther Party's alike. This is so because their money had flowed to Newton and the Panthers, but so too were their projects designed around them. On August 25, 1971, for instance, just as *Marvin Gardens* was going into production, Schneider sent Newton a letter saying, "Enclosed are two checks each in the amount of $2,000.00, one from myself and one from Bob Rafelson." And when Rafelson finished *Marvin Gardens*, he sent Newton an update on its reception, noting that it had been understood in "the same way" in France and England, but it had not in the United States.[71] The other deals BBS had lined up, according to their contracts and communications, were an Alan Myerson movie about an "insurrection" in Harlem that Schneider says was "in effect an anti-war film," and a movie involving Newton that would be based on his memoir, *Revolutionary Suicide*, which Steve Blauner told Newton was "fantastic" and which he encouraged Schneider to adapt as a movie, but the latter project fell apart.[72] I will further discuss the *Revolutionary Suicide* project, but for now, I want to address what seems to be incompatible about BBS and the Panthers, namely their legal and economic statuses, because only through an odd interpretation of Maoism did the two organizations work together in a symbiosis that has been too little explored.

Schneider felt compromised by his bourgeois background, like fellow Hollywood radical Jane Fonda, and Newton turned this screw rhetorically by calling their ilk "mother-country radicals."[73] Whereas Fonda was often resented on sets for her to-the-manor-born radicalism, as in the case of *Steelyard Blues*, when she would declare, "There are no stars here," while calling her daughter's nanny a "member of the collective," Schneider was committed to stardom of a kind and did not deny himself luxuries. "I get high on the contradictions," he said. In fact, he spread these luxuries to Newton. Schneider believed that Huey Newton was a star, "the most charismatic and special figure" that he had met, and this belief, I surmise, had much to do with the political strategies they both endorsed.[74] A key distinction between Fonda and Schneider was that she walked onto a set with individual prerogatives that, her declarations notwithstanding, were not enjoyed democratically, but he had the power to arrange the relations of production within his corporate enclave. The BBS offices at 933 La Brea Avenue were an expression of this scaled revolution in the workplace. Schneider's office was roughly "forty by fifty, complete with a white Tiffany chandelier, a billiards table, and an antique nickelodeon."[75] There was a "50-seat private theater" where they screened their own movies (*Marvin Gardens* for Julia and Michael Phillips, *A Safe Place* for Anaïs Nin) and other counterculture movies such as Alejandro Jodorowsky's *El Topo* (ABKCO Films, 1970). In Peter Biskind's account, their building "became a hangout for a rag-tag band of filmmakers and radicals of various stripes." While Huey Newton, Abbie Hoffman, and Timothy Leary were part of the ambience—part of the intellectual culture—the filmmakers were, Henry Jaglom said, "working at scale, everybody participating." If you were "eccentric and strange enough," according to Jaglom, "people said, 'Okay, what do you want to do?' And it all came out of a sensibility that nobody was supposed to exploit anybody else, were all supposed to be sharing, working collectively."[76]

This leveling of hierarchy and emancipation from below comes partly from the French uptake of Maoism. Tellingly, in the BBS reception room, there were "French posters from the student riots of 1968."[77] It is the case, too, that the Black Panthers had pushed Maoism into the counterculture earlier in 1967 when Huey Newton, Bobby Seale, and Bobby Hutton sold Mao Tse-tung's *Little Red Book* on the Berkeley campus in their efforts to arm the Panthers.[78] But what influenced BBS markedly was a French iteration of Maoism, which had steered its doctrines away from Red Guard discipline and toward May '68 jouissance. In Daniel Cohn-Bendit's analysis, the May protests were a repudiation of a "chain of command," in politics and beyond, and any popular action thus required not "leadership" or "organization with a capital O, but a host of insurrectionary cells, be they ideological groups, study groups—we can even use street gangs."[79] This Maoist version of spontaneous self-organization dovetailed with a sense that a corporation derived political power from its "access to the productive organization," which, because productivity set the terms of a person's "social effectiveness," had a determinant effect—Peter Drucker would say—on his "very citizenship." [80] From this perspective, what the Panthers were doing in Oakland could look to Bert Schneider like what he was doing in BBS, except the Panthers were doing it in a "colony"—in a nonmarket society, if you will—and thus they had less need for the corporation to carve out their own juridical space. For the Panthers, the productive organization, such as it was, seemed political (because it was not commercial) in the first instance.

Not everyone on the Left accepted Schneider's view of things. For instance, filmmaker Emile de Antonio articulated an antiliberal complaint, specifically about *Hearts and Minds*, but one that no doubt applied to the BBS oeuvre. "It's a contemptible work," he said. "It has no politics, no structure," and to him this seemed a product of the "CBS–Beverly Hills" mindset of the Hollywood liberal.[81] In discussion with Schneider, film journalist Mitch Tuchman prosecuted this point. *Hearts and Minds* was a case of "political filmmaking," he accused Schneider, "but not political film distributing." His counterexample was Emile de Antonio's *In the Year of the Pig* (1968). But Schneider did not accept the distinction. "All filmmaking is political," he claimed, "in the Maoist sense that all art is either revolutionary or bourgeois." Even if the art "reflects a bourgeois point of view," Schneider insisted, "it's political." To make his case, he defended *Introduction to the Enemy* (Wexler, IPC Films, 1974), the documentary that Jane Fonda and Tom Hayden had made in North and South Vietnam. "If you read Tom Hayden's pamphlet 'Indochina Peace Campaign,'" he argued, "you realize that that film is exactly a film version of his pamphlet, that film was made specifically as an embodiment of their politics."[82] Their film is political not because of its distribution, according to Schneider, nor even because it accompanied Hayden's rise into electoral politics (he ran against Senator John Tunney in the 1976 primaries), but because the film embodied their ideological struggle. And it was this film, not coincidentally, that marked the founding of Fonda's production company, IPC Films (IPC for Indochina Peace Campaign), which went on to make *Coming Home* and *The China Syndrome* (Bridges, Columbia, 1979) among other movies. Fonda embodied ideological struggle in film, that is, in the same step that she incorporated. In *Introduction to the Enemy* she personified IPC, too, just as Jack Nicholson (and perhaps Bruce Dern in his turn) did BBS, and for this she was denounced—by conservatives, who would call her Hanoi Jane, and famously by Jean-Luc Godard and Jean-Pierre Gorin, who in the grips of their antiauteur Dziga Vertov Group experiment, dressed down Fonda in *Letter to Jane* (1972) for her part in a star system—but in doing so, she could shield the work done in her company by means of her personality while channeling capital to it. Though I will not comment on IPC Films in detail, I want to note only that for both Fonda and Schneider, remarkably, their work in politics led them to a corporate philosophy.

For Schneider, too, his politics were embodied in film and corporation alike by way of the technology of stardom, and this depended on the legal alienation that produced the corporate person. When IATSE representatives came after BBS, as noted above, part of their complaint was that BBS had created a shell company, NB, to contract Nelson Almendros.[83] It was true that they had created such a company, but it was also entirely consistent with their business practice and that of other small production companies.[84] When the BBS relationship with Columbia fell apart, for instance, Henry Jaglom formed Rainbow Productions with Howard Zucker, bought back the rights of *Hearts and Minds* from them, and made a deal to distribute it through Warner Bros.[85] Schneider, indeed, prolifically incorporated. This was for tax and legal reasons, but also because, as Thurman Arnold put it, the requirement that we personify "great industrial enterprise" had devolved the corporation's rights to even the slightest individual transaction, which meant that business as such was constantly triangulated through these artificial persons.[86] Significant, here, is that Schneider spread these practices to Huey Newton, who would incorporate under the name Stronghold, which subdivided into Stronghold Consolidated Productions, Inc., and

Stronghold Link. Newton liked the name, Elaine Brown says, because to him it described what he was establishing "within the walls of the citadel of capitalism."[87] At first blush, one sees irony in this, the fact that Newton would deploy a main device of capital in a project to weaken capitalism. My point has been, however, that on one hand the irony lies in the jurisprudence of the corporation, which is, Scott Bowman says, a legal tradition squaring liberalism with corporate rule, but on the other hand Bert Schneider's politics had, in both theory and practice, already ironized the architecture of the corporation. If what the corporation needed for its legitimacy were nonpecuniary measures, then it needed nonmarket conditions such as the counterculture, the Black Panthers, and so on. But Schneider's purpose was to make political actors of these nonmarket forces precisely by formalizing their energies in corporate form, i.e., in the form designed to open markets. Now, one can say that they (the counterculture, the Black Panthers) were always already markets. But they nonetheless gave the look of market resistance. However, they were forever embedded in what they resisted once they tapped the market logic of the corporation.

I do not want to dwell on this irony or catch out this or that person as a hypocrite, because it seems to me the irony was woven into the historical situation. That is, many people will look like hypocrites simply because they availed themselves of the tools that history left them. What I want to dwell on is that Newton incorporated when he began to mediate his personality in books such as *To Die for the People* and *Revolutionary Suicide* and in his various unrealized movie projects. Stronghold, to the extent that it was rooted in private property, was *a media company.* In the early '70s, after his prison stint, Newton hatched all sorts of media projects. Many were with Schneider.[88] He had sold *Revolutionary Suicide* via Stronghold to Schneider's Audjeff (a corporation Schneider formed, whose name was a portmanteau of his children's names, Audrey and Jeff). Steve Blauner, as noted, had urged that it be adapted into a movie. But other projects had no relation to Newton's personal story. Some concerned the Panther mythos. The Panthers at large had strong responses to the blaxploitation cinema that had been targeting the African American demographic. The general suspicion was that these movies were yet again exploiting the black community despite being ostensibly pitched to that community. But both Huey Newton and Bobby Seale had been fascinated by *Sweet Sweetback's Baadasssss Song* (Van Peebles, Cinemation Industries, 1971), and Newton had written an in-depth analysis of it in the party newspaper, the *Black Panther*, which highly regarded the "effective use" Van Peebles had made "of one of the most popular forms of communication, the movie," and he had done so in "revolutionary terms."[89] Newton and Seale had planned their own movie based on a *Newsweek* story about "a black man from a Midwestern city" whom local police had deemed "some sort of gangster" but the "local black community" saw as a "kind of antihero figure." Newton "decreed that Bert Schneider could produce" it.[90] Though it never happened, it is important to note that whether they controlled their own image or not, the Panthers were media stars from the beginning. When they entered the Sacramento capitol bearing arms, Seale had cameras following him the whole time. Later, they would construct the party image very conscientiously ("a centralized symbol of the leadership," Seale put it) in the photograph of Newton sitting in the wicker chair with a shotgun in one hand, a spear in the other. He wears the Panther uniform of leather jacket and beret, and Eldridge Cleaver dressed the scene further with African shields. What Newton qua image was meant to symbolize, Seale says, was "a shield for black people against all the imperialism, the decadence, the aggression, and the racism in this country."[91] In her study *Spectacular Blackness*, Amy Abugo Ongiri suggests that the "visual iconography" by which the Panthers became world famous left them vulnerable to co-optation by the "same commodity forces" that they critiqued. Hence, the importance of Newton's Stronghold as an organizing device for the party's "economic interests," Ongiri says, is an examination "yet to be undertaken."[92]

Neither the Panthers nor the counterculture ever existed outside the marketplace, to be sure, and it is fair to argue that they could have assumed their form only in the stage of corporate capitalism in which mass media was so highly developed. What mattered to BBS was that they gave the appearance of nonmarket origins. Yet the problem for

Newton in the early '70s was that his leadership seemed to separate him from the rank and file. Bert Schneider paid for him to live in a penthouse apartment on Lake Merritt, which caused Candice Bergen to observe wryly, "Maybe the Revolution wouldn't be so bad."[93] His political power could be confused by some for mere celebrity. But the role that the secondary, artificial personhood that Stronghold seemed to foist on him—he was, in the last instance, its personification—became for him a political and legal liability locally and beyond. For instance, Stronghold inherited all that George Jackson had possessed "in capitalist terms," as he put it, when he willed it the rights to *Soledad Brother* and *Blood in my Eye*, which started rumors about Newton but created no formal problems; the disbursement of royalties from *Revolutionary Suicide* led ghost cowriter J. Herman Blake to bring suit against Stronghold; and in general, its economic instrumentality put Newton at a remove from party members.[94] Newton also spun off Oakland & the World Entertainment as a corporation that would enter "the potentially lucrative business of concert promotion," and its leasing of a York Street theater led to a contretemps with management and ultimately to arson at the theater. Newton had leased a restaurant and bar, too—the Lamp Post—but had done so under market value against the lessor's will. In short, he was becoming a neighborhood don, though he was doing so on the premise, lifted from E. Franklin Frazier's *Black Bourgeoisie*, that black proprietors who had separated themselves as a class from the black community "had a duty" to lend assistance in turn.[95] And because the Panthers held that the "colony" was prepolitical (because its inhabitants were not represented by the state, only terrorized by its agents) and nonmarket (because the price mechanism did not coordinate the activity of rights-bearing agents), such a "duty" could not be codified. Elaine Brown claims, in this respect, that they were properly "outlaws," but of course their money went into a creature of law, the corporation.[96] Stronghold Link had been used throughout to buy properties from its publishing proceeds, Hugh Pearson demonstrates, and the properties had been posted for bail when Panther leaders were arrested. But because bail had been jumped often, corporate assets were largely diminished by the later '70s.[97] By then, whatever the symbolic shield had been—Newton's body against the black community or the corporation against Newton's body—it had largely lost its function.

If we wheel back to *Marvin Gardens* now, we can see its thematics in light of the social history that ensues. Part of Huey Newton's downfall was that stardom stuck to him to the point that in his later years he felt he could not "do it anymore, but [he felt] this pressure from people." Likewise, part of the pathos in *Marvin Gardens* comes from the possibility that stardom might not be easily transferred between Jack Nicholson and Bruce Dern, and that one of them might hoard it instead. In chapter 2 I argued that Thomas Elsaesser's "pathos of failure" comes from an unwillingness to reckon with the corporation as the effective unit of agency and that movies of the "unmotivated hero" wished away the corporation's transpersonal agency in favor of a bygone romance of the individual, but *Marvin Gardens* does the opposite. And still it derives pathos from a flaw in the corporation's version of agency, namely that its personhood might forever lodge in a single individual. This leads to the so-called Superstar CEO (Lee Iacocca, Jack Welch, Steve Jobs, et al.).[98] Consider that *Marvin Gardens*, as noted, bookends its story of partnership with long takes of Jack Nicholson in close-up. For all that it imagines the collectivized framework supporting its stardom, what we get is Julia Phillips's response that the Jack Nicholson scenes are great and the rest is not. The audience is riveted by star power, and its bearers are seduced by the scale of the audience. Peter Bogdanovich has suggested that the auteur theory had this baleful effect. "What happened was that we all fucked up," he said. "What happened was that the director became the superstar."[99]

But BBS's intent in relying on the auteur theory was to distribute autonomy down the ranks and permit people to do their work. "The only philosophy we had," Schneider said, "was backing particular people."[100] The check on a particular person's authority becoming tyrannical was the BBS policy of circulating people through various roles. As Henry Jaglom explained, "The original idea of BBS is that we were all hyphenates. We were all writers, directors, and actors, and we would work on each other's movies."[101] Jaglom and Nicholson, for instance, cut Dennis

Hopper's *Easy Rider* together. Indeed, Schneider would regret that Nicholson settled into the job of actor so exclusively. "I still feel it is unfortunate that his acting career has been so successful," he said, "as to shut him out of directing." One might suppose this to be a danger of charisma: its specialness, when perceived as property of a person, isolates him in a role. BBS tried to run on charisma without letting it harden them in their roles. Hence Schneider was uncomfortable with analyses of his company that imputed to it an ideology. "I've read a couple of very long articles on the corporate ideology of BBS—long analyses of the threads running through all the films," he said. "I won't deny their existence, but there was nothing premeditated about it. There was no corporate ideology."[102] There was to be no top-down governance, nothing on the order of an ideology; it was to be a dynamic space of movement, not a reified space of stasis.

When I think of *Marvin Gardens*, in fact, my attention always falls on its final scene. The final scene is not actually Jack Nicholson's close-up. Though his radio monologues bookend the plot, the final scene is his character's return home. He walks into the darkened corridor, hears his grandfather in the next room, and opens the door. His grandfather has been projecting 16 mm film of David and Jason playing on the beach as young children. There is a way in which the beach is the prototype for the island that the Staebler brothers had planned to acquire. The two of them, kneeling in the sand building castles, rhymes with an earlier scene of the two brothers huddled on the floor over a map of Tiki (see figs. 4.8 and 4.9). Their dream had been to professionalize their early experience of play. But the important detail is that this is projected in 16 mm. This format of film, after all, was preferred by amateurs, and it provided the idiom of avant-garde experiments. In *Head*, Rafelson had called back to Stan Brakhage, Kenneth Anger, and Norman McLaren, the filmmakers from the underground and the art world who had earlier inspired him. But these filmmakers, by and large, had not professionalized the informal energies they drew on.[103] BBS had.

Once they professionalized, they had to politicize. The power that BBS had arrogated to itself in virtue of economic success (i.e., monetizing the counterculture) was a form of political power separate from state power,

**FIGURE 4.8** The adulthood postures of David and Jason Staebler, hunched over a map of the island Tiki.

**FIGURE 4.9** The childhood postures of the brothers, hunched over sandcastles, projected on 16 mm film.

yet unlike the power of a revolutionary enclave of another kind—the Panthers' power in Oakland—their power was never seriously threatened by the state. The FBI had a large file on Bert Schneider, true, but because, in Drucker's rationale for corporate power, "the successful functioning of the enterprise required that the state respect corporate autonomy," Schneider was entirely free to politically organize within the ambit of his corporation.[104] The disappointment of the counterculture, namely that it could be neutralized in commodity form, was assuaged for Schneider in his turn to radical politics.

The story of *Hearts and Minds* is the story of Schneider discovering a sweet spot between consumer culture and electoral politics. When Schneider had become involved in the 1969 Moratorium to End the War in Vietnam, he visited the headquarters in Washington, D.C., and thanks to his roughly $50,000 contribution, he was hooked in with many of the main players—Sam Brown, Allard Lowenstein, and Abbie Hoffman. Alan Myerson said this exposure left a deep impression on Schneider. "Bert's art is manipulation—people, events, ideas. He is extremely skillful at it," Myerson said. "These people were involved in manipulation on a scale he had never thought of, in areas he had never explored."[105] Scale mattered, for Schneider, in two ways. When he brought Peter Davis from CBS to Hollywood to make *Hearts and Minds*, he was insistent that Davis make the documentary cinematic. "Now, remember," he counseled Davis, who had made many CBS documentaries by then, "this isn't a TV show, this is a movie." Davis's images needed to be scaled to the size of the movie screen, Schneider told him; this would not be simply the parade of talking heads one would put on CBS.[106] But the scale of the audience mattered to Schneider, too. Unlike Emile de Antonio, Schneider had ambition that was political, but his politics did not shunt his work into small-scale distribution. Schneider believed in a mass audience, even if he did not believe in mass-production techniques. He was an "aesthetic and intellectual" elitist, Peter Davis claimed, but his goal for *Hearts and Minds* was to have "lines around the block."[107] This, I would say, is the hallmark of post-Fordism: to utilize the techniques of craft production for a mass market, though it might be broken down into niche markets—they would, these market segments, be delivered by the apparatus of mass distribution.

But it was, no doubt, Schneider's talent for manipulation that let him reach his customer by way of his firm in what seemed, nonetheless, a resolutely political appeal. In the 1975 Academy Awards ceremony, when Davis and Schneider were awarded the Oscar for Best Documentary, Schneider read a wire from Dinh Ba Thi, chief of the Provisional Revolutionary Government's delegation to Paris, in which the Vietnamese people sent viewers of the Oscars their "greetings of friendship." The ceremony's emcee, Bob Hope, raged backstage and had Frank Sinatra disavow Schneider's statement: "The academy is saying we are not responsible for any political utterances on this program." Warren Beatty dismissed Sinatra, "You old Republican." Francis Ford Coppola maintained that Sinatra and Hope were "too old to understand a message like that."[108] Schneider had wanted to send the message precisely because it would be received by "65 million Americans."[109] Sinatra and Hope did not understand that in this gesture Schneider was creating a customer—in Drucker's phrasing—on seemingly nonpecuniary grounds, that indeed his brand appealed to that market segment made of those who wanted to imagine themselves in nonmarket terms, as something more than

**FIGURE 4.10** The BBS logo overlaid on Uncle Sam.

a market, that is, but less than a nation-state. Schneider was creating customers as a political cohort. Interesting, on this note, is the fact that the BBS logo is deployed a final time in the last frame of *Hearts and Minds*, when a patriotic street parade is passing by the camera operator and a person dressed as Uncle Sam, looking strangely devilish because his face is painted red, hails bystanders to "Be Happy" and "Smile." Overlaid on him, the figure of nationhood, is the logo of BBS, the figure of personhood (see fig. 4.10). How unnatural both constructions are, and how unsettled the contest between nation-state and corporation still is.

## THE ESTABLISHMENT

The Academy Awards ceremony was in April 1975, and *Jaws* was released that June. New Hollywood histories are often structured around *Jaws*, but not around *Hearts and Minds*. This is perfectly understandable, given that *Jaws* broke box-office records and consolidated the distribution model of the saturation release. I would suggest, though, that we think of *Hearts and Minds* and *Jaws* as concatenated events that established the New Hollywood. *Jaws* deployed the distribution model used by *The Godfather*, after all, but by doing it in summer months, it transformed Hollywood's release calendar. That is to say, the New Hollywood had been in formation for years, but in that year its operations were patented. It became the establishment. The Academy Awards dramatized this: Bob Hope and Frank Sinatra faced the past; Francis Ford Coppola (*The Godfather, Part II* won the Best Picture) and Bert Schneider faced the future. On that night Coppola and Schneider helped recruit a young generation into the New Hollywood style. If *Jaws* is often isolated as the epochal movie ringing in a new industrial model, it is because it lends a neatness to our periodizing. *Jaws* is a monument, to be sure, but the pernicious effect of our monumentalizing it is that we pluck it from the historical moment. Hollywood needed a product it could reproduce, and *Jaws* became its aspirational object, but before that it needed producers.

Our historiography can still be better attuned to how the labor process is reproduced. Lew Wasserman needed *Jaws* to be rapturously received by audiences, but first he needed a corporate form that would attract the producers of this *Jaws* and the next. Hence, I lay stress on these small production companies, whether BBS or Zanuck-Brown, because they helped renew the labor process. The product would flow from there. But BBS deserves pride of place in this analysis, I think, because in correcting for the flaw in Fordism, namely that people craved meaning in their work, they understood that such could be gotten by casting work in political terms. Bert Schneider had a flare for dramatizing this. And perhaps this explains why it remains the case that the Academy Awards is the venue for celebrating Hollywood as if it were a political institution and not the economic one it so surely is.

I have wanted to single out the corporation for special attention. If the counterculture and the Black Panthers needed to consider themselves external to the market, the corporation needed to reconceive itself in the face of this. To revitalize itself, the corporation had to reckon with what it externalized, with whatever became recalcitrant in relation to it. This is the constant behind capitalism, this need to expand markets by subsuming whatever it is not, and this is its claim on being a permanent revolution. Hence Joseph Schumpeter's "creative destruction" has become its celebrated byword; it became clear in the moment when every tradition was rejected that capitalism's tendency to overthrow systems and processes had better be associated with innovation and with the arts, whose institutions had consecrated breaking from tradition as their defining activity. It had better be made attractive and hip if it was not going to be stabilizing and comforting. The corporation would be the site of this, as only it had the power to be, and its interior would be renovated for those whose tenure would coincide with the waxing phase of their creativity. What unfolds from this, it seems today, is a history of struggle between the corporation's prerogatives and the social programs that are the legacy of the welfare state that was designed to offset them.

# AFTERWORD

## Auteurs, Amateurs, Animators

*The creative process is an expensive undertaking.*

Ed Catmull, *Creativity, Inc.*

What became of the hegemony of the artist in the industrial arrangements of post-Fordist economy? Did the authority that artists gathered by 1975 remain theirs in the years to come, or did authority return to its expected place? If we hew to the standard history, then we are to believe that the artist's Waterloo was Michael Cimino's *Heaven's Gate* (United Artists, 1980) and executive prerogative quickly snapped back into place in response. Jon Lewis describes the "corporate era" as what displaced the New Hollywood of auteurs, periodizing the auteur cinema as a blip between two eras of monopoly.[1] One reason it is easy to see it this way is that grownup themes seemed to be replaced by childhood ones in the 1980s: the decade's high-earners such as *E. T.* (Spielberg, Universal, 1982), *Ghostbusters* (Reitman, Columbia, 1984), *Back to the Future* (Zemeckis, Universal, 1985), the Indiana Jones series (Spielberg, Paramount, 1981, '84, '89), and the Star Wars series (Kershner and Marquand, 20th Century Fox, 1980, '83) all seemed to be pitched to a young audience and buttressed by merchandising. No more art-cinema ambiguity here, only "Reaganite entertainment" and a flush bottom line.[2] While this is true, it is also true that *E. T.* and *Back to the Future* came out of Spielberg's small production company, Amblin, and the Indiana Jones and Star Wars movies came out of George Lucas's small production company, Lucasfilm. And *Ghostbusters* was part of a clutch of movies from *Saturday Night Live* alumni Dan Akroyd, Bill Murray, et al., and as I argue elsewhere, their television show is a site of the institutionalized professionalism of the counterculture.[3] In these perspectives, it is easy to see the continuity between the '80s and the corporate projects of the '60s and '70s that are the heart of my study. It is also the case that the "auteur cinema" was dropped into a lower order of financing in what emerged as the "independent cinema" of the '80s.[4] Spike Lee, Jim Jarmusch, and Joel and Ethan Coen came into this moment professionalized by film school. They followed the industrial model of the New American Cinema of the early '60s, wherein filmmakers such as John Cassavetes and Shirley Clarke scraped together financing to make the kinds of movies that Hollywood would never make, but Lee, Jarmusch, and the Coens recast the amateurism of those filmmakers in the professional credentials of auteurism. This, it seems to me, is the curious blend of the often-antagonistic viewpoints modeled by Jonas Mekas and Andrew Sarris at *Film Culture* and the *Village Voice* in the '50s and '60s. In the '80s it became independent cinema, underpinned institutionally by the Sundance Institute, and in the '90s it hardened into "indie" (borne by an ensemble of small production companies such as Good Machine and October), which was formalized as "Indiewood" when the Hollywood majors once again drew them, and Miramax and New Line, into their conglomerate armature.[5]

But to demonstrate the continuity in its strongest lines—that is, to show how a discourse of creative economy durably reconfigured Hollywood industry—I will make a brief case study of Pixar Animation Studios. Today Pixar sits within Disney's conglomerate structure, alongside Marvel and Lucasfilm (and at the time of writing, it seems 21st Century Fox will be added to the fold) in a perfect image of Lew Wasserman's New Hollywood. Wasserman's 1962 rearticulation of corporate structure was one moment in the New Hollywood, but Francis Ford

Coppola and George Lucas were responsible for another. When they chose San Francisco as the site for their company, American Zoetrope, the reasons were its distance from Hollywood, its bohemian culture, and its technology community. Coppola attests that Xerox PARC had a strong influence on his company, and of course, as Stephen Prince has said, both Coppola and Lucas were instigators of the technological evolution of Hollywood cinema.[6] Julie Turnock has shown, too, how central Lucas's Industrial Light & Magic has been to the maturation of the special-effects industry.[7] American Zoetrope, in short, coarticulated Hollywood and Silicon Valley just as Wasserman had coarticulated television and Hollywood. A managerial culture has circulated among these industries, and Pixar, in certain obvious ways, is the nexus between them. Most obviously, its two benefactors were George Lucas and Steve Jobs. Lucas had employed Ed Catmull and Alvy Ray Smith in the computer-graphics division at Lucasfilm, and they hired John Lasseter as animator after his tenure at Disney was up. The group began producing computer-generated shorts, such as *The Adventures of André and Wally B* (Smith, 1984), but the ambition of their work was "staggeringly expensive," requiring unusual amounts of computer power, and their official charge within the company was research and development of hardware and software products. Steve Jobs bought the Pixar unit (named after their Pixar Image Computer), and it was spun from Lucasfilm into an independent firm. Jobs was chairman of the board, and Catmull and Smith the cofounding executives. They opted to form their own corporation simply because they believed in the nature of the firm, as Ronald Coase had theorized it. That is, they believed that the cost of internalizing contracts was offset by the benefit of keeping together a greatly talented staff. Catmull understood that in the '80s and '90s his philosophy was "the antithesis of the free-agency practices that prevail[ed] in the movie industry."[8] Richard Neupert has explained that "for animators" in particular in the '80s, and "to say nothing of the industry model since," the norm was "temporary, limited-time contracts," but whatever the expense, Catmull and Smith "were determined to maintain a dedicated crew within a sustainable, innovative work environment."[9]

The firm, even if it was a skeleton crew, was the means for insulating a creative culture, and the Disney "merger" tested whether these means could withstand their installation within a larger conglomerate structure. "We knew," Catmull says, "that the prospect of our little studio being absorbed into a much larger entity would worry many [employees]."[10] In 2006 Disney acquired Pixar, in effect, but the deal was referred to as a merger despite the organizational asymmetry—the capital leverage was all on Disney's side.[11] It has proved the case in the years since that Pixar's culture has had enough of a transformative effect on Disney that the language of their combination was justified. The two companies had originally partnered for a three-picture deal before the making of *Toy Story* (Lasseter, Buena Vista, 1995), a deal that was renegotiated following that movie's success thanks to Steve Jobs's shrewdness. In the partnership, ultimately, they acted as coequals. But the merger was struck for different reasons. Steve Jobs argued that Pixar was "a yacht" but that the merger would "put us on a giant ocean liner, where big waves and poor weather won't affect us as much."[12] Although this was the same premise motivating, say, Zanuck-Brown's deal with Universal, Pixar was taking it a step further when they merged with the larger Disney but still hoped to retain their unit integrity. But again Jobs negotiated safeguards into the deal that would ensure the autonomy of Pixar's culture. He stipulated that Catmull be appointed president of both Pixar and Disney Animation and John Lasseter chief creative officer of both. This way, Pixar's "traditions [would not] get overtaken by those of the much larger corporation, the Walt Disney Company."[13] In this way, too, Catmull and Lasseter would have a chance to see whether their "theories about how to manage creative people," which had been derived in their "smaller shop," obtained in a large setting.[14] But the centerpiece of the deal was the "Five Year Social Compact," a "seven-page, single-spaced list" spelling out the features of the Pixar culture that were sacrosanct and must remain untouched by Disney. Its egalitarian ethos was foremost: "No assigned parking for any employee, including executives. All spaces are first come, first served." Its parties, too, were protected. And, most significantly, a main "tenet" of Pixar culture was that "people should work there because they want to, not because a contract requires them to, and as a result, no one at Pixar was under contract." Bob Iger told the gathered employees of Pixar on the day of the sale, "I promise you that the culture of Pixar will be protected."[15] Culture assumed its hallowed part in this deal, Jerome Christensen argues, because it was being regarded as one of the proprietary technologies, "a creative technology," that Pixar brought to Disney. The "agent of a corporate principal," Christensen specifies with respect to the Disney-Pixar merger, may be its culture. And the culture of Pixar, I will demonstrate, stems from the codification of auteur theory as management doctrine. Whether traceable to George Lucas or whether New Hollywood imparted this management doctrine to Silicon Valley—the so-called California Ideology—and its reemergence in Hollywood is traceable to Steve Jobs, I will not try sorting out here.[16] I only want to demonstrate that in one of the most unerringly successful production companies in new-millennium Hollywood, the management culture animated by the auteur theory remains intact.

In a *Harvard Business Review* article, Ed Catmull professes his company's belief that the "creative vision propelling each movie comes from one or two people and not from either corporate executives or a development department." They are, he says, "filmmaker led." Sounds enough like the auteur theory. Yet it was imperative, he would add in another breath, that "creativity must be present at every level of every artistic and technical part of the organization." That is, autonomy in a creative organization must be distributed downward. The director, whose authority is walled off from executive interference, "must set people up for success by giving them all the information they need to do the job right without telling them how to do it," Catmull says, and "each person on a film should be given creative ownership of even the smallest task." A director, too, must "appreciate all contributions, regardless of where or from whom they originate, and use the best ones."[17] Sounds a lot like the auteur theory in the form of management theory. Sounds like Altman, for instance, and Spielberg too.

How Pixar provided for this, though, was to structure it into their physical architecture. The company moved their headquarters from Point Richmond to Emeryville at the turn of the millennium, in part, as Steve Jobs planned, to structure a space that maximized "inadvertent encounters." The former tenant of the Emeryville site was Del Monte Foods, and architect Bohlin Cywinski Jackson designed Pixar's main building to evoke its industrial past. But it is a strictly postindustrial space, a "campus" in the style of other tech companies such as Google. Anthony Lane has called it the "fun factory," which captures the fault line between the Fordist and post-Fordist modes of production.[18] There are rooftop bars on the Brooklyn building, soccer fields and volleyball courts, and a cereal bar. Diversion is designed into the workplace. "It helps [employees]," says Adrienne Ranft, "to do their job and get away from their job."[19] But the main building's atrium, because it houses meeting rooms, a cafeteria, bathrooms, and mailboxes, induces productive encounters between people, no matter their rank or department. Productivity, in other words, pours into these liminal moments.

The historic feat of the post-Fordist labor regime, after all, has been to blend into a single experience the time of labor and leisure that Fordism itself had carefully held apart. In Fordism, the workday was ineluctably dull: so many repetitive tasks, made simple and efficient precisely so that one could compress the time of labor and create time for leisure afterward. But Pixar has been dedicated to the work-as-fun ethos. Like much of Silicon Valley, Pixar employees are known for sleeping under their desks in the peak of a project, and projects tend to peak one after the other. John Lasseter was famous for living his life at work. Sharon Calahan, the director of photography (which, for computer animation, means the simulation of lighting design), was known to "only go home to do her laundry."[20] Ed Catmull admits that because their credo is "one quality bar for every film we produce," they at times ask their "crew to work inhumane hours, and lots of people suffe[r] repetitive stress injuries." They can "rejec[t] mediocrity at great pain and personal sacrifice," he says, only by giving their employees "enormous leeway and support."[21] The "leeway" is simply the self-governing work that had made Peter Drucker observe that knowledge workers cannot be managed. When allowed to work of their own accord, such workers perceive their activity as play. It "looked like a playground," an employee said of the Pixar studio. "It was loose, it was free, it was rough, it was like two hundred people sharing a college dorm room."[22] John Lasseter so rarely stopped working between their early movies that once *A Bug's Life* (Lasseter, Buena Vista, 1998) premiered, his wife demanded that he take a vacation with his family. But production of *Toy Story 2* (Lasseter, Buena Vista, 1999) was troubled, and Lasseter was called in to save it. No vacation for him. "The people at Pixar are my best friends," he would later say. "Not only do I want to see them every day—I can't wait to see them every day—but, when my wife, Nancy, and I make a list of whom we are going to take on vacation, the top group is Pixar." A vacation was the workday relocated. Lasseter hatched the idea for *Cars* (Lasseter, Buena Vista, 2006), indeed, when taking a road-trip vacation with his family.

If it is easy to trace Pixar's mode of operation within the New Hollywood regime of self-organizing small firms, why, then, does its textuality not seem rooted in the pessimism, paranoia, and ambiguity that were the ground tones of New Hollywood art cinema? Why, to put it differently, does Pixar's cinema not seem ideologically transgressive? A main point of my study has been that one of the defining ideological contests of New Hollywood was waged in the name of professional autonomy. What might be said of Pixar is that they took from George Lucas his radical redefinition of the youth market—"If you can tune in to the fantasy life of an 11-year-old girl," Lucas said, "you can make a fortune in this business"—and vouched their autonomy in it. Inventing a new medium, as they were doing in computer animation, required a stabilized market, and for this, a metaphysicalized notion of childhood would do. "When planning a picture, we don't think of grownups, and we don't think of children," Walt Disney once said, "but just of that fine, clean, unspoiled spot down deep in every one of us that maybe the world has made us forget, and maybe our pictures can help recall." This much describes Lasseter, and it is therefore ironic that when he brought the first *Toy Story* to Disney, Michael Eisner insisted he "make it edgy, make it for adults." Pixar was told they absolutely could not have "Toy" in the title "because no teenager or young adult will see it."[23]

Yet *Toy Story*, in its finished form, would be a defense not strictly of Walt Disney's "unspoiled spot" of raptured innocence but of the value the toy gathered when subordinated to it. In its opening scenes, this case is made in rather canny terms. The owner of the toys, Andy, is enacting a stick-up of a bank, when his favorite toy, Sheriff Woody, steps in to defend the scared townspeople from One-Eyed Bart. Andy's imagination has been informed by the Hollywood western. In choosing this most inveterate Hollywood genre, Pixar is paying deference to the traditions of the cinema it is poised to disrupt. The value of any of these traditions (i.e., toys), Pixar is affirming, lies not in the vicissitudes of their reception (i.e., how often they are played with), but in the audience (i.e., Andy). "No one's getting replaced," Woody assures his fellow toys. "This is Andy we're talking about. It doesn't matter how much we're played with; what matters is that we're here for Andy when he needs us." The constancy of audience needs is taken for granted here as a way to flatter the absolute value of the cinema vis-à-vis the relative value of its tools. It is clear, though, that Pixar is anxious about its own art receiving the cinema's imprimatur. Hence, *Toy Story* introduces the new toy, Buzz Lightyear, to show that the cinema is capacious enough for high-tech toys and old-fashioned ones as well. Digital images fall within the tradition of cinema as easily as photochemical images do. This can be so because Andy, the audience, feels endless fascination for them.

More significant than Pixar's effort to ease the way for digital cinema, however, is its use of self-reflexive storytelling. In Andy's bedroom, after all, his bookshelf is filled with titles from Pixar's filmography of shorts— *The Adventures of André and Wally B, Red's Dream* (Lasseter, 1987), *Tin Toy* (Lasseter, 1988), and so on (see fig. 5.1).

Pixar is comfortable with allegory. It is a feature of the creative economy, I have already suggested, to inscribe one's marketplace authority in the very product of one's labor—so typical of creative personnel, John Caldwell says, is this "tendency to narrate one's career in public."[24] Pixar, in this gesture, is narratively conjuring a prehistory to their company. It is a way for them to assert their staying power: *Toy Story* is not a flash in the pan but is part of a catalogue of titles. It has a before and an after. In the trailer for *WALL-E* (Stanton, Disney, 2008), they built on this sense that a catalogue had platonically attended their incorporation. "In the summer of 1994 there was a lunch," begins Andrew Stanton. "Me, John Lasseter, Pete Docter, the late John Ranft all sat down . . . at that lunch we knocked around a bunch of ideas that eventually became *A Bug's Life,*

**FIGURE 5.1** In *Toy Story*, Andy's shelf is filled with the library of Pixar short films.

*Monsters Incorporated, Finding Nemo. . . .* The last one we talked about that day was the story of a robot named *WALL-E*." In a spare hour, they tell us, in what for many is leisure downtime, the Pixar team bandied back and forth ideas that would become billions of dollars at the box office. This is a trailer, of course, a genre forthrightly geared to advertise, but the movie advertised therein is a self-mythologizing pitch no less. *WALL-E*, Paul Flaig has argued, imagines Pixar's ideal worker in robot form: "a creative laborer in the mode of the precarious, self-sculpting and flexible 'knowledge-worker.'"[25] This figure of boutique production, moreover, saves humanity from its thralldom to corporations of mass production. In a similar move, Angela Allan has read *Cars 3* (Fee, Disney, 2017) as commentary on the lack of diversity in the Silicon Valley labor force, with the "confidence gap" modeled by Lightning McQueen and his mentee, Cruz Ramirez.[26] This is just to acknowledge that the company's penchant for self-narrating is well known. So well known, in fact, that their movies are subject to online searches for "Easter eggs," which is a tech-world term originating in gaming for hidden messages and inside jokes planted throughout a work. WALL-E, for instance, builds a sculpture, the right arm of which is a Luxo, Jr., desk lamp (see fig. 5.2)—the icon of Pixar—and every movie bears the number A113 somewhere in its mise-en-scène as a tribute to the California Institute of Arts classroom for graphic design and character animation.

Such self-narration might seem strange, even ostentatious, a sign that its authors expect rapt study of their movies. It is also a mark of anxiety, however, if we think of it as the movie's effort to self-justify. Ed Catmull has pegged his management strategy to an ongoing fear of complacency. "Observing the rise and fall of computer companies," he said, had deeply affected him. "If we are ever successful," he once wondered, "will we be equally blind?" In part, the Pixar movie—aside from entertaining an audience—is an occasion for the "organization to analyze itself," which, he admits, is an uncomfortable activity and hard to do objectively.[27] Hollywood movies, Jerome Christensen has argued, assume their peculiar textuality by saturating entertainment with corporate strategy. For Pixar, it is perhaps the case that the tension most fundamentally at play in their identity is between their reputation for original stories and the risk management of sequels. "Around the time of the merger," Catmull says, "we were evaluating how to strike a balance between original films and sequels." Though they required the "constant churn of new ideas" that original films excited, it was "riskier" to make them. And sequels, because they "were likely to do well at the box office, gave us more leeway to take those risks."

**FIGURE 5.2** In *WALL-E*, the robot builds a protagonist using Pixar's icon, Luxo, Jr., for its arm.

The proposed solution—that they blend "an original film each year and a sequel every other year"—is one they negotiated in the form of *Ratatouille* (Bird, Buena Vista, 2007).[28] That movie sounds the notes of a manifesto. The rat at the center of the story, Remy, is a scavenger like his successor WALL-E. He sifts the detritus of Parisian food culture then recombines the best of its leftovers into unexpected high art. "Not everyone can be a great artist," the movie intones, "but a great artist can come from anywhere" (even cartoons). That this figure of low culture is the source of next-generation high culture is another spin on Pixar's insurgent message. The rat qua art emblem is a callback to Disney's mouse, no doubt, but in *Ratatouille*, Pixar stages its difference from what was becoming its parent company. In it, the old figure of haute cuisine, Chef Gusteau, has died, and the name he lent his five-star restaurant is now being spun off by the restaurant's current head, Skinner, as the brand name of a line of frozen dinners (Gusteau's BBQ Dip 'N Ribs, Chopsocky Pockets, and so on). Skinner's money grab is depicted as meretricious, and the obvious inference we are to make is that the depreciation of Gusteau's brand—which began when it lost one of its five stars "after a scathing review by France's top food critic Anton Ego" and was compounded when Gusteau's death cost it another star—will be completed by Skinner. In these lines, the story parallels the Pixar-Disney merger. The Disney brand had struggled after Walt Disney's death in 1966 and his brother Roy's death in 1971, but Michael Eisner revived the brand in the '80s, and the animation studio had a run of success with *The Little Mermaid* (Clements and Musker, Buena Vista, 1989), *Beauty and the Beast* (Trousdale and Wise, Buena Vista, 1991), *Aladdin* (Clements and Musker, Buena Vista, 1992), and *The Lion King* (Allers and Minkoff, Buena Vista, 1994). From there, the Disney brand dropped in prestige. Eisner was a businessman, but in Pixar's perspective, not an artist. He had such low regard for quality, in their eyes, that Steve Jobs killed the first merger talks. Indeed, what Disney planned to do with the Pixar titles it owned, thanks to their distribution deal, was make sequels to them through the new division, Circle 7, without input from the original makers. Catmull remarked that he had seen such "subversion" before in this or that failed company, "when efficiency or consistency of workflow are not balanced by other equally strong countervailing forces," and "emphasis is placed on doing safer projects that mimic proven money-makers."[29] Circle 7 was the line of Gusteau frozen dinners.

Pixar did not consent to the merger on Eisner's terms. Only when Bob Iger replaced Eisner was the merger effected. Iger was the legitimate heir to the Disney legacy; he was the Alfredo Linguini to Eisner's Skinner. Iger, as noted already, let Pixar pull the strings, preserving their culture and allowing Pixar to reform Disney's. What *Ratatouille* suggests is that this happened as it did because Pixar propounded a philosophical outlook on sequels that would keep it financially solvent in perpetuity yet leave its integrity intact. In the movie's final scenes, the critic Anton Ego, who had dealt the fatal blow to Chef Gusteau, is returning to Gusteau's after having written it off. The buzz around its new head chef makes him curious. As Ego awaits his dinner, Linguini streaks across the dining room on roller skates waiting tables. The restaurant is crowded with highbrows who may have acquired their tastes by passion but blunted them, it seems, through a regimen of effete overpractice (see fig. 5.3).

When the critic Ego is served ratatouille—a "peasant dish"—he seems unimpressed, but his first bite rushes him vertiginously into his childhood, when his love of food was formed in combination with the shelter of his mother's love. After so much art, he now rediscovers why he first loved it. What had taken on the character of deadening

**FIGURE 5.3** In *Ratatouille*, the haute cuisine diners have dined too long to retain their elemental love of food.

familiarity has been redeemed. This, we are asked to believe, is a solution to the sequel in a philosophical key: originality is simply the thrill of virgin experience when one has no fixed ideas but only sensory aliveness. Whatever returns us to experience in this form, whether an original or a sequel, earns the name of art. Pixar, it might be said, had to believe this; indeed, they had to formulate a metaphysics of childhood if they were to vouch the purity of creativity in a durable market (childhood is not an age range but an "unspoiled spot down deep in every one of us," says Walt Disney), and they had to do this if they were to trade their precarious "yacht" for an all-weather "ocean liner." Pixar learned this reorientation on the youth market from Lucas, it bears remembering, who had desired professional status (autonomy, remuneration) for his amateur passion, and whose Lucasfilm now sits alongside Pixar within the Disney Corporation.

# NOTES

## INTRODUCTION

Epigraph: David Newman and Robert Benton, "The New Sentimentality," *Esquire*, July 1964, 25.

1. Jon Lewis, *Whom God Wishes to Destroy* (Durham, NC: Duke University Press, 1995), 16.
2. Peter Bart, "Three's 'Company,'" *Variety*, December/January 2005.
3. Lewis, *Whom God Wishes to Destroy*.
4. Bart, "Three's 'Company.'"
5. The term "independent" (vis-à-vis Hollywood production) has been much debated, and while I recognize that there are some cases of pure independence, much independent production is qualified by its reliance on studio distribution. Debate over how to periodize independence within the mode of production was informatively carried out by Janet Staiger and Matthew Bernstein in a back-and-forth in *Cinema Journal* (Spring 1993 and Winter 1994). In my own scholarship, I have retained Staiger's periodization because I am persuaded by her nuanced sense of residual and emergent practices. For my own terms of analysis, though, I am less concerned with how independence is *defined* in relation to larger, hegemonic corporate enterprises than with how it is *shielded* by corporate structure and the scaling of autonomous units within a supply chain that is inevitably regulated by the oligopoly of large corporations. In other words, I care about independence not as an external matter within the market but as an internal matter within the firm.
6. For the state of postwar higher education, see John R. Thelin, "Gilt by Association: Higher Education's 'Golden Age,'" in *A History of American Higher Education* (Baltimore, MD: Johns Hopkins University Press, 2004); Clark Kerr, *The Uses of the University: The Godkin Lectures on the Essentials of Free Government and the Duties*

*of the Citizen* (Cambridge, MA: Harvard University Press, 1995). For discussion of "knowledge workers," see Peter Drucker, *Post-Capitalist Society* (New York: Harper-Collins, 1993). For discussion of the "creative class," see Richard Florida, *The Rise of the Creative Class* (New York: Basic, 2002).

7.   See Barbara and John Ehrenreich's canonical essays on the class formation, "The Professional-Managerial Class," *Radical America* 11, no. 2 (March–April 1977): 7–31; Ehrenreich and Ehrenreich, "The New Left: A Case Study in Professional-Managerial Class Radicalism," *Radical America* 11, no. 3 (May–June 1977): 7–22.

8.   Tom Gunning, "'Loved Him, Hated It': An Interview with Andrew Sarris," in *To Free the Cinema*, ed. David E. James (Princeton, NJ: Princeton University Press, 1992), 74. Gunning conducted this interview with Sarris in 1990.

9.   See Christian Keathley, *Cinephilia and History, or the Wind in the Trees* (Bloomington: Indiana University Press, 2005); Nico Baumbach, "All That Heaven Allows: What Is, or Was, Cinephilia," *Film Comment*, March 12, 2012.

10.  Fred Turner, *From Counterculture to Cyberculture* (Chicago: University of Chicago Press, 2006), 12.

11.  "Confrontation: The Old Left and the New," *American Scholar* 36 (Autumn 1967): 581.

12.  Paul Goodman, "The New Reformation," in *Beyond the New Left*, ed. Irving Howe (New York: Horizon, 1970), 85–86.

13.  Joseph Dorman, *Arguing the World* (Chicago: University of Chicago Press, 2000), 133. More evidence of the power of Mills's influence is that Richard Flacks, Tom Hayden's closest collaborator in drafting "The Port Huron Statement," named his son C. Wright Flacks.

14.  C. Wright Mills, *White Collar* (Oxford: Oxford University Press, 1951), 112, 159, 157.

15.  Gore Vidal, "Who Makes the Movies?," in *Auteurs and Authorship*, ed. Barry Keith Grant (Malden, MA: Blackwell, 2008), 149, 155. This piece originally appeared in the *New York Review of Books*, November 25, 1967, a good deal after Vidal's late-fifties tenure as a Hollywood screenwriter.

16.  Andrew Sarris, "Notes on the Auteur Theory in 1962," in *Film Culture Reader*, ed. P. Adams Sitney (New York: Cooper Square, 2000), 133.

17.  Douglas McGregor, *The Human Side of Enterprise* (New York: McGraw-Hill, 2006), 94.

18.  Luc Boltanski and Eve Chiapello, *The New Spirit of Capitalism*, trans. Gregory Elliott (London: Verso, 2005), 170.

19.  Drucker, *Post-Capitalist Society*, 65.

20.  Louise Sweeney, "The Movie Business Is Alive and Well and Living in San Francisco," *Show* 1 (April 1970): 35.

21.  William Murray, "*Playboy* Interview: Francis Ford Coppola," in *Francis Ford Coppola Interviews*, ed. Gene D. Phillips and Rodney Hill (Jackson: University Press of Mississippi, 2004), 37–38.

22.  Susan Royal, "Steven Spielberg in His Adventures on Earth," in *Steven Spielberg Interviews*, ed. Lester Friedman and Brent Notbohm (Jackson: University Press of Mississippi, 2000), 95.

23. For a history of business schools and management qua academic discipline, see Rakesh Khurana, *From Higher Aims to Hired Hands* (Princeton, NJ: Princeton University Press, 2007).

24. See Wyatt Wells, *American Capitalism, 1945–2000* (Chicago: Ivan R. Dee, 2003), 69–76.

25. David Halberstam, *The Best and the Brightest* (New York: Ballantine, 1993). In JFK's Yale commencement address of June 11, 1962—a speech drafted by favorite technocrats Mac Bundy, John Kenneth Galbraith, Ted Sorensen, et al.—he made the case for "practical management of a modern economy." The economy posed "subtle challenges for which technical answers, not political answers, must be provided." See "Address at Yale University, 11 June 1962," John F. Kennedy Presidential Library and Museum, https://www.jfklibrary.org/Asset-Viewer/Archives/JFKPOF-039-001.aspx.

26. Tom Hayden, *The Port Huron Statement: The Visionary Call of the 1960s Revolution* (New York: Thunder's Mouth, 2005), 71, 81, 85, 84.

27. Jacob Brackman, "The Graduate," *New Yorker*, July 27, 1968, 37.

28. Hayden, *The Port Huron Statement*, 84.

29. Hayden, 72, 52, 54.

30. Andrew Sarris, *The American Cinema: Directors and Directions, 1929–1968* (New York: Dutton, 1968), 37.

31. Sarris, "Notes on the Auteur Theory," 133.

32. Pauline Kael, "Circles and Squares," in *Auteurs and Authorship*, ed. Barry Keith Grant (Malden, MA: Blackwell, 2008), 51.

33. Though it was an aporia for Sarris, it is one that he seemed to be aware of. He tried solving it by substituting terms, using the term "cultist" instead of "careerist" to confer dignity on his own work. "The main difference between a cultist and a careerist," he says, "is that the cultist does not require the justification of a career to pursue his passion, and a careerist does." He dismisses out of hand "the journalistic reviewers who would be equally happy in the Real Estate departments of their publications." For them, "passion is too strong a word." If one is paid for these passions, Sarris seems to be saying, all to the good, but the motivation for them exists in advance of them being commercialized. See Andrew Sarris, *Confessions of a Cultist* (New York: Simon & Schuster, 1970), 14.

34. Sarris, 52.

35. Sarris.

36. Gunning, "'Loved Him, Hated It,'" 71–73.

37. Sarris, *The American Cinema*, 28.

38. "Pauline Kael's attack on me was very difficult," Sarris told Tom Gunning in an interview. "And also I was very provincial, very unsophisticated, very vulnerable," he went on to say. "And she had a kind of Berkeley hard edge." See Gunning, "'Loved Him, Hated It,'" 77.

39. Nils Gilman, "The Prophet of Post-Fordism: Peter Drucker," in *American Capitalism*, ed. Nelson Lichtenstein (Philadelphia: University of Pennsylvania Press, 2006), 117.

40. Peter Drucker, *The New Society* (New Brunswick, NJ: Transaction, 1993), 5.

41. Peter Drucker, *Concept of the Corporation* (New York: John Day, 1946), 16–18.

42.  In "Notes on the Auteur Theory in 1962," Sarris rather dutifully acknowledges Bazin's remark on "a disharmony between the subjective inspiration of the director and the objective evolution of the medium," which is Bazin's critique of the auteurist notion that the trajectory of a director's greatness lies simply in the chronology of the director's biography rather than in the situation of the industry. But he dismisses it in this line: "If directors and other artists cannot be wrenched from their historical environments, aesthetics is reduced to a subordinate branch of ethnography" (128). In *The American Cinema* he again broaches it only to diminish its significance: "George Stevens has testified," he writes, "when the movie industry was young, the film-maker was its core and the man who handled the business details his partner," but in time, "the film-maker became the employee and the man who had the time to attend to the business details became the head of the studio." He concedes this point to the "forest critics," who are interested in the history of the "so-called system." But he can only hear this criticism as their attempt to discount the individuality of the directors. "The problem with these examples," he writes, "is that in most instances the forest critics repudiated the afflicted directors long before the industry curtailed their careers" (21).

43.  William H. Whyte, *The Organization Man* (Philadelphia: University of Pennsylvania Press, 2002), 12.

44.  Gilman, "The Prophet of Post-Fordism," 121.

45.  Drucker, *The New Society*, 172–73.

46.  See Edward Hoffman, *The Right to Be Human* (New York: McGraw-Hill, 1999).

47.  Douglas McGregor, "The Human Side of Enterprise," *Management Review*, November 1957, 41, 43.

48.  Jeff Mauzy and Richard Harriman, *Creativity, Inc.* (Boston: Harvard Business Review Press, 2003).

49.  Thomas Frank, *The Conquest of Cool* (Chicago: University of Chicago Press, 1998), 22.

50.  Shyon Baumann, *Hollywood Highbrow* (Princeton, NJ: Princeton University Press, 2007), 60–61.

51.  Peter Drucker, *The Practice of Management* (New York: Harper & Row, 1954), 36.

52.  McGregor, "The Human Side of Enterprise," 10.

53.  Peter Cowie, *Coppola* (New York: Da Capo, 1990), 57, 10.

54.  Pauline Kael, *Raising Kane* (London: Methuen, 2002), 131.

55.  Kael, 132.

56.  Drucker, *Concept of the Corporation*, 46.

57.  John Micklethwait and Adrian Wooldridge, *The Witch Doctors* (New York: Times, 1996), 69.

58.  Drucker, *Concept of the Corporation*, 35.

59.  Peter Lev, *Twentieth Century-Fox: The Zanuck-Skouras Years* (Austin: University of Texas Press, 2013), 183–84.

60.  Aubrey Solomon, *Twentieth Century-Fox* (Lanham, MD: Scarecrow, 2002), 146. Janet Staiger outlines the modes of production culminating in the "package-unit system" in David Bordwell, Janet Staiger, and Kristin Thompson, *Classical Hollywood Cinema* (New York: Columbia University Press, 1985), 330–38.

61. Thomas Schatz, *The Genius of the System* (Minneapolis: University of Minnesota Press, 2010), 463, 478.

62. Mark Harris, *Pictures at a Revolution* (New York: Penguin, 2007), 4.

63. Stephanie Frank, "Why a Studio Without a Backlot Isn't Like a Ten-Story Building Without an Elevator: Land Planning in the Posfordist Film Industry," *Journal of Planning History* 15, no. 2 (2016): 131.

64. Frank, 130.

65. Lawrence Webb, *The Cinema of Urban Crisis* (Amsterdam: Amsterdam University Press, 2015).

66. See David A. Cook, *Lost Illusions: American Cinema in the Shadow of Watergate and Vietnam, 1970–1979* (Berkeley: University of California Press, 2000), 302–5. In the chapter "Orders of Magnitude I," Cook gives a rundown of the various fates of the major studios—which ones were bought, which ones were not—at the beginning of the 1970s.

67. These tendencies were channeled early on—in the late '50s and early '60s—through the transformation of exhibition wrought by suburbanization and the hollowing out of the urban core, which led to art-house, grind-house, and drive-in theaters. In these sites movies from abroad and from the so-called exploitation sector flourished. For scholarship on these historical developments, see Thomas Doherty, *Teenagers and Teenpics* (Philadelphia: Temple University Press, 2002); Barbara Wilinsky, *Sure Seaters* (Minneapolis: University of Minneapolis Press, 2001); Austin Fisher and Johnny Walker, eds., *Grindhouse* (New York: Bloomsbury Academic, 2016).

68. Harris, *Pictures at a Revolution*, 3.

69. Derek Nystrom rehearses the critical accounts in "The New Hollywood," in *The Wiley-Blackwell History of American Film, Volume III, 1946–1975*, ed. Cynthia Lucia, Roy Grundmann, and Art Simon (Malden, MA: Wiley-Blackwell, 2012), 408–12. Nystrom describes the period from 1967 to 1976—the so-called Hollywood Renaissance—as New Hollywood I, and the period from *Jaws* and *Star Wars* and beyond as New Hollywood II. He then goes on to discuss why New Hollywood I "takes such precedence over other New Hollywoods in the critical and popular imagination," citing in particular the notion of "historical rupture" and the cover that gives to those who would self-define as "mavericks," whose practices can be assessed against the ones dominant in Hollywood (411).

70. See Thomas Schatz, "The New Hollywood," in *Film Theory Goes to the Movies*, ed. Jim Collins, Hillary Radner, and Ava Preacher Collins (New York: Routledge, 1993). There he alludes to the problem in writing history from the foreshortened perspective of reception, noting that though the "exploitation and art cinema movements" of the late '50s and early '60s "produced a few commercial hits—Hitchcock's *Psycho* and Fellini's *La Dolce Vita* in 1960, for instance—the box office was dominated well into the 1960s by much the same blockbuster mentality as in previous decades" (14).

71. David A. Cook tries to nuance what is too schematic in this account by breaking the industry personnel into the overlapping classes of "Major Independents from the 1960s" (Arthur Penn, Stanley Kubrick, Robert Altman); "Auteurs Manqué and

Maudit" (Mike Nichols, Peter Bogdanovich, William Friedkin); "Film Generation Auteurs, or Hollywood Brats" (Francis Ford Coppola, George Lucas, Steven Spielberg, et al.); and so on. Cook, *Lost Illusions*, 67–157.

72. Denise Mann, *Hollywood Independents* (Minneapolis: University of Minnesota Press, 2008). Another project that I think will help scholars to periodize the New Hollywood is Peter Labuza's dissertation, "When a Handshake Meant Something: The Emergence of Entertainment Law and the Constitution of Hollywood Art, 1944–1967" (PhD diss., University of Southern California, forthcoming 2019).

73. Giovanni Arrighi, *The Long Twentieth Century* (London: Verso, 2010), 4–6.

74. See Irving Bernstein, *Hollywood at the Crossroads* (Los Angeles: Hollywood AFL Film Council, 1957); Susan Christopherson and Michael Storper, "The City as Studio, the World as Backlot," *Environment and Planning: Society and Space* 4 (1989): 305–20; Eric Hoyt, "Hollywood and the Income Tax, 1929–1955," *Film History* 22, no.1 (2010): 5–21.

75. David Harvey, *The Condition of Postmodernity* (Cambridge, MA: Blackwell, 1990), 142, 155, 152, 157, 150.

76. Harvey, 152, 158.

77. Michael Piore and Charles Sabel, *The Second Industrial Divide* (New York: Basic, 1984), chaps. 3 and 4.

78. See Janet Wasko, *Movies and Money* (Norwood, NJ: ABLEX, 1982), chap. 1; Susan Christopherson and Michael Storper, "The Effects of Flexible Specialization on Industrial Politics and the Labor Market," *Industrial and Labor Relations Review* 42, no. 3 (April 1989): 331–47. "Partly as a result of unionization," Christopherson and Storper note, "work in the motion picture industry was well paid and reasonably stable by the 1930s" (333).

79. Christopherson and Storper, 334.

80. Allen J. Scott, *On Hollywood: The Place, the Industry* (Princeton, NJ: Princeton University Press), 2005.

81. Harvey, *The Condition of Postmodernity*, 142, 155, 152, 157, 150.

82. Christopher Newfield, "Corporate Pleasures for a Corporate Planet," *Social Text* 44 (Autumn–Winter 1995): 31.

83. See Peter Drucker, "Henry Ford: Success and Failure," *Harper's Magazine*, July 1947, 1–8; Mills, *White Collar*, 235–38.

84. Thomas Frank, *The Conquest of Cool*, 81.

85. See Tino Balio, *United Artists, Vol. 2, 1951–1978* (Madison: University of Wisconsin Press, 2009).

86. See Diane Jacobs, *Hollywood Renaissance* (South Brunswick, NJ: Barnes, 1977).

87. McGregor, *The Human Side of Enterprise*, 30.

88. Thomas Elsaesser, "American Auteur Cinema," in *The Last Great American Picture Show*, ed. Thomas Elsaesser, Alexander Horwath, and Noel King (Amsterdam: Amsterdam University Press, 2004), 53–56.

89. Elsaesser, 49.

90. Beverly Walker, "Go West, Young Man," *Sight and Sound* 41, no. 4 (Winter 1971–72): 25, 22.

91. A. D. Murphy, "Hollywood's Wave of the '70s," *Daily Variety*, 42nd Anniversary Issue, 1975, 10.

92. Derek Nystrom, "Hard Hats and Movie Brats: Auteurism and the Class Politics of New Hollywood," *Cinema Journal* 43, no. 4 (Spring 2004): 18, 21.

93. See Florida, *The Rise of the Creative Class*, in particular the section entitled "Building the Creative Community," in which he makes recommendations for ordering cities in support of "creativity" ("the 'hip' urban lifestyle") that mayors in turn implemented. Sam Wetherell has read Florida's new book *The New Urban Crisis* as a mea culpa, which accepts that the "rise of the creative class in places like New York, London, and San Francisco created economic growth only for the already rich, displacing the poor and working classes." See Sam Wetherell, "Richard Florida Is Sorry," *Jacobin*, August 19, 2017, https://www.jacobinmag.com/2017/08/new-urban-crisis-review-richard-florida.

94. Angela McRobbie, *Be Creative: Making a Living in the New Culture Industries* (Cambridge: Polity, 2016), 7, 6.

95. Sarah Brouillette, "Academic Labor, the Aesthetics of Management, and the Promise of Autonomous Work," *Nonsite*, May 1, 2013, http://nonsite.org/article/academic-labor-the-aesthetics-of-management-and-the-promise-of-autonomous-work.

96. Stefano Harney, "Creative Industries Debate," *Cultural Studies* 24, no. 3 (May 2010): 434.

97. Boltanski and Chiapello, *The New Spirit of Capitalism*, 65.

98. Michel Aglietta, *A Theory of Capitalist Regulation*, trans. David Fernbach (London: Verso, 2000), 19.

99. Alain Lipietz, "New Tendencies in the International Division of Labor: Regimes of Accumulation and Modes of Regulation," in *Production, Work, Territory*, ed. Allen J. Scott and Michael Storper (Boston: Allen & Unwin, 1986) 19.

100. Aglietta, *A Theory of Capitalist Regulation*.

101. John Clarke, Stuart Hall, Tony Jefferson, and Brian Roberts, "Subcultures, Cultures and Class," in *Resistance through Rituals: Youth Subcultures in Post-War Britain*, ed. Stuart Hall and Tony Jefferson (London: Routledge, 2006), 45–48.

102. Paolo Virno, *A Grammar of the Multitude*, trans. Isabella Bertoletti, James Cascaito, and Andrea Casson (Los Angeles: Semiotext(e), 2004), 41, 56.

103. John Caldwell, *Production Culture* (Durham, NC: Duke University Press, 2008), 2, 47.

104. J. D. Connor, *The Studios After the Studios: Neoclassical Hollywood, 1970–2010* (Stanford, CA: Stanford University Press, 2015), 50.

105. Press Kit for *The Fury*, Kirk Douglas Papers, 1945–1978, box 5, folder 7, Wisconsin Center for Film and Theater Research, Madison.

106. Press Kit for *The Fury*.

107. For readings of De Palma's cinema as an ongoing allegorization of his career, see Chris Dumas, *Un-American Psycho* (Chicago: Intellect, 2012).

108. Julie Turnock, *Plastic Reality: Special Effects, Technology, and the Emergence of 1970s Blockbuster Aesthetics* (New York: Columbia University Press, 2014), 106, 111.

109. Turnock, 49–50, 105–12.

110. Tom Sito, *Moving Innovation* (Cambridge, MA: MIT Press, 2013), 179.

## 1. POST (HENRY AND JOHN) FORDISM

Epigraph: John Caldwell, *Production Culture* (Durham: Duke University Press, 2008), 144.

1.   See Michel Foucault, *Discipline and Punish*, trans. Alan Sheridan (New York: Vintage, 1997), 297, 299; Gilles Deleuze, "Postscript on the Societies of Control," *October* 59 (Winter 1992): 5.

2.   Douglas had, in fact, originally accepted the role after he and Ted Kotcheff agreed on certain script revisions, but when he arrived on set, he realized that Kotcheff "did not have artistic control over the picture"; Sylvester Stallone did, and hence the unmodified script was retained, and Douglas quit the role. See his discussion of it in Kirk Douglas, *The Ragman's Son* (New York: Simon & Schuster, 1988), 417–18.

3.   Douglas, 309.

4.   Press release, Kirk Douglas Papers, 1945–1978, box 2, folder 6, Wisconsin Center for Film and Theater Research, Madison.

5.   The idea of "industrial reflexivity" has been attended to more meticulously in recent years. John Caldwell's *Production Culture* (Durham, NC: Duke University Press, 2008) was among the first to theorize self-reflection in the film/video community by way of rigorous ethnographic method. This methodology was developed and modified in Jerome Christensen, *America's Corporate Art: The Studio Authorship of Hollywood Motion Pictures* (Stanford, CA: Stanford University Press, 2012); J. D. Connor, *The Studios After the Studios: Neoclassical Hollywood, 1970–2010* (Stanford, CA: Stanford University Press, 2015). Connor thoroughly elaborates the idea elsewhere in "The Biggest Independent Pictures Ever Made: Industrial Reflexivity Today," in *The Wiley-Blackwell History of American Film, Vol. 4*, ed. Cynthia Lucia, Roy Grundmann, and Art Simon (Malden, MA: Wiley-Blackwell, 2011).

6.   Despite the fact that *Lonely Are the Brave* was indeed a Bryna property, it was ultimately produced by a company that Douglas spun off from it, Joel Productions. In this chapter, I make no distinction between the two companies: Bryna was named after Douglas's mother, Joel was named after his son, and they are only different names under which he carried out his corporate operations. In chapter 4, I make more of the multiplication of shell corporations that seems to follow inevitably upon the formation of a corporation and, moreover, the tendency to name these shell corporations after family members in effort to make it seem a "family" of corporations. The reason for Joel Productions, however, was simply that Douglas's law firm, Irell & Manella, decided that for tax purposes, Douglas should form Joel and have it buy *Lonely Are the Brave* from Bryna and then "independently make an employment agreement with Kirk Douglas as an actor." See letter from Irell & Manella to Milton Shapiro, February 3, 1961, Kirk Douglas Papers, box 40, folder 27.

7.   See Will Wright, *Six Guns and Society* (Berkeley: University of California Press, 1975), for figures on Hollywood westerns. See Christopher Anderson, *Hollywood TV* (Austin: University of Texas Press, 1994), for figures on television westerns.

8.   André Bazin, "The Evolution of the Western," in *What Is Cinema, Vol. II*, trans. Hugh Gray (Berkeley: University of California Press, 2005), 149.

9.  Bazin, 150.
10. Bazin, 151.
11. Bazin, 153.
12. See Scott Simmon, *"My Darling Clementine* and the Fight with Film Noir," in *The Invention of the Western Film* (Cambridge: Cambridge University Press, 2003).
13. See Mark Harris, *Five Came Back* (New York: Penguin, 2014).
14. Harris, 418.
15. Harris, 419.
16. Harris, 241.
17. Harris, 271.
18. Harris, 248.
19. Bazin, "The Evolution of the Western," 151.
20. See Robert Pippin, *Hollywood Westerns and American Myth* (New Haven, CT: Yale University Press, 2010), 1–11, for an excellent discussion about *Stagecoach,* the chance at community, and the "aspiration toward a form of politically meaningful equality" (5).
21. Jacques Rancière, *Film Fables,* trans. Emiliano Battista (Oxford: Berg, 2006), 74.
22. Bazin, "The Evolution of the Western," 155.
23. Jeanine Basinger, *Anthony Mann* (Boston: Twayne, 1979), 84.
24. Hannah Arendt, *The Origins of Totalitarianism* (San Diego, CA: Harcourt, 1976), 244.
25. For various accounts of this deal, see Dennis McDougal, *The Last Mogul* (New York: Crown, 1998), 154–56; Denise Mann, *Hollywood Independents* (Minneapolis: University of Minnesota Press, 2008), 49–51; Thomas Schatz, *The Genius of the System* (Minneapolis: University of Minnesota Press, 2010), 470–71; Bernard Dick, *City of Dreams* (Lexington: University Press of Kentucky, 1997), 155–56.
26. Douglas, *The Ragman's Son,* 124.
27. See Schatz, *The Genius of the System.* Schatz notes that "Stewart was by no means a Universal 'house' star at the time. He had a nonexclusive agreement with the studio, and some of his best work in the mid-1950s was done with Alfred Hitchcock at Paramount—through an elaborate deal also arranged by Lew Wasserman. What's more, Wasserman persuaded Universal to let Stewart take Anthony Mann with him to do a few of their distinctive westerns for other studios: *The Naked Spur* for MGM in 1952 and *The Man from Laramie* for Columbia in 1955" (471–72).
28. See McDougal, *The Last Mogul,* 243–45.
29. McDougal, 244.
30. Aida Hozic, *Hollyworld* (Ithaca, NY: Cornell University Press, 2001), 88.
31. I do not see a great distinction between Hozic's "merchant economy" and my preferred "financialization," but the latter marks a phase in a longer capitalist process, which Giovanni Arrighi marks out, and hence I take up this term to stress that my analysis is of a phase of development.
32. See Eric Hoyt's study, *Hollywood Vault* (Berkeley: University of California Press, 2014).
33. See Peter Drucker, *Concept of the Corporation* (New York: John Day, 1946).
34. Drucker, 12–13.

35. Hozic, *Hollyworld*, 99; Paolo Virno, *A Grammar of the Multitude*, trans. Isabella Bertoletti, James Cascaito, and Andrea Casson (Los Angeles: Semiotext(e), 2004), 70.
36. Hozic, 93.
37. Hozic, 93–94.
38. Douglas, *The Ragman's Son*, 259.
39. Giovanni Arrighi, *The Long Twentieth Century* (London: Verso, 2010), 1.
40. Arrighi designates this cycle, from commodity to money form, by the Marxian formula M-C-M'. For a fuller elaboration of this, see the introduction. See also Arrighi, 5–8.
41. Timothy R. White, "Life After Divorce: The Corporate Strategy of Paramount Pictures Corporation in the 1950s," *Film History* 2, no. 2 (June–July 1988): 99–119.
42. White, 103.
43. White, 103.
44. White, 102.
45. Arrighi, *The Long Twentieth Century*, xi, 5.
46. Arendt, *The Origins of Totalitarianism*, 275, 282.
47. Arendt, 275.
48. Douglas, *The Ragman's Son*, 117.
49. Alla Gadassik, presentation from her forthcoming work on the Disney move from Hyperion to Burbank, "Fantasyland: Walt Disney Studio at Burbank," Society for Cinema and Media Studies Conference, Toronto, Ontario, 2018.
50. Douglas, *The Ragman's Son*, 278.
51. Stan Margulies to Kirk Douglas, May 16, 1960, Kirk Douglas Papers, box 6, folder 3.
52. Douglas, *The Ragman's Son*, 305.
53. Memo, October 28, 1958, Kirk Douglas Papers, box 6, folder 6.
54. See Eric Hoyt, "Hollywood and the Income Tax, 1929–1955," *Film History* 22, no. 1 (2010): 15.
55. Stan Margulies to Pete Martin, March 30, 1955, Kirk Douglas Papers, box 2, folder 6.
56. Margulies to Martin, March 30, 1955.
57. Ray Stark to Kirk Douglas, August 21, 1953, Kirk Douglas Papers, box 2, folder 1.
58. Ray Stark to Budd Schulberg, September 20, 1954, Kirk Douglas Papers, box 2, folder 3.
59. Ray Stark to Kirk Douglas, December 29, 1954, Kirk Douglas Papers, box 2, folder 5.
60. Mann, *Hollywood Independents*, 46.
61. Correspondence between Kirk Douglas and Stan Margulies, July 1958, Kirk Douglas Papers, box 2, folder 3.
62. The studios notoriously tended the images of their contract players. See, for instance, Janine Basinger, *The Star Machine* (New York: Vintage, 2009).
63. Stan Margulies to Pete Martin, March 30, 1955, Kirk Douglas Papers, box 2, folder 6.
64. Pete Martin, "I Was Always Hungry," *Saturday Evening Post*, June 29, 1957, 98.
65. Douglas, *The Ragman's Son*, 129.
66. Memo, October 28, 1958, Kirk Douglas Papers, box 6, folder 6.
67. Sam Norton to Kirk Douglas, August 21, 1957, Kirk Douglas Papers, box 6, folder 4.
68. Ben Nathanson to Bryna Productions, Kirk Douglas Papers, box 6, folder 6.

69.  Jerry Bresler to Sam Norton, August 21, 1957, Kirk Douglas Papers, box 6, folder 6.

70.  See Derek Nystrom, "Hard Hats and Movies Brats: Auteurism and the Class Politics of the New Hollywood," *Cinema Journal* 43, no. 3 (Spring 2004): 18–41.

71.  Memo, October 28, 1958, Kirk Douglas Papers, box 6, folder 6.

72.  Max Boot, *Invisible Armies* (New York: Norton, 2013), 398.

73.  See Robert Taber, *War of the Flea* (Dulles, VA: Potomac, 2002), 20.

74.  Kirk Douglas to Arthur Krim, June 20, 1960, Kirk Douglas Papers, box 6, folder 3.

75.  See Jon Lewis, "Money Matters," in *New American Cinema*, ed. Jon Lewis (Durham, NC: Duke University Press, 1998). Lewis notes that the roughly coincident events of the Paramount decree and the House Un-American Activities Committee hearings precipitating the blacklist gave the studios, which understood that the studio system was over, a means of policing the "post–Paramount decision workforce and as a result [they] effectively stripped the various industry guilds and unions of their bargaining power" (89).

76.  See Kirk Douglas, *I Am Spartacus* (New York: Open Road, 2012), for Douglas's account of Howard Fast's failure to adapt his novel for the screen.

77.  Lewis, "Money Matters."

78.  Richard Slotkin, *Gunfighter Nation* (New York: Atheneum, 1992), 410.

79.  See Noël Carroll, "The Professional Western," in *Engaging the Moving Image* (New Haven, CT: Yale University Press, 2003).

80.  Michael Coyne, *The Crowded Prairie* (London: Tauris, 1997), 106.

81.  Taber, *War of the Flea*, 6, 5; italics original.

82.  Norman Mailer, *The Armies of the Night* (New York: Plume, 1994), 87.

83.  Taber, *War of the Flea*, 6; italics original.

84.  A teeming body of literature on how guerrilla warfare can be implemented in business has evolved over the years. See, for example, I. C. MacMillan, "How Business Strategists Can Use Guerrilla Warfare Tactics," *Journal of Business* 1, no. 2 (1980): 63–85; William C. Finnie, "The Basics of Business Warfare," *Journal of Business* 3, nos. 3–4 (1981): 10–15; Fred Gibbons, "The Secrets of Guerrilla Management," *Inc.*, February 1, 1987; Ramya Priyanka Guthena, "The Guerrilla Warfare Techniques with the New Age Startups and Managements Methods: A Comparative Study," *International Journal of Advance Research, Ideas, and Innovations in Technology* 3, no. 6 (2017): 620–22.

85.  See Theodor Adorno, "Marginalia to Theory and Praxis," in *Critical Models: Interventions and Catchwords*, trans. Henry W. Pickford (New York: Columbia University Press, 1998).

86.  Douglas, *The Ragman's Son*, 416.

87.  See Deak Nabers, "The Martial Imagination: World War II and American Culture," *American Literary History* 25, no. 1 (Spring 2013): 115–29.

88.  See Stanley Corkin, *Cowboys as Cold Warriors* (Philadelphia: Temple University Press, 2004); Carroll, "The Professional Western."

89.  I take the phrase "expertise-based culture" from Alan Liu's historical discussion of the knowledge worker in *The Laws of Cool: Knowledge Work and the Culture of Information* (Chicago: University of Chicago Press, 2004), 35.

90.  Peter Drucker, *The Effective Executive* (New York: HarperCollins, 2006), 3.

91.  Edward Abbey to David Miller, March 17, 1961, Kirk Douglas Papers, box 40, folder 26.

92.  Abbey to Miller, March 17, 1961.

93.  Memo carbon copy to Paul Price at Columbia, November 10, 1959, Kirk Douglas Papers, box 6, folder 1.

94.  Pete Martin, "The Actor in Me," *Saturday Evening Post*, June 22, 1957, 45.

95.  C. Wright Mills, *White Collar* (Oxford: Oxford University Press, 2002), 182.

96.  Martin, "The Actor in Me."

97.  Mills, *White Collar*, 142–43, 149.

98.  Virno, *A Grammar of the Multitude*, 41.

99.  Virno, 55.

100.  Virno, 58–59.

101.  Liu, *The Laws of Cool*, 33.

102.  Liu, 3.

103.  Douglas, *The Ragman's Son*, 243.

104.  Stanley Corkin, *Starring New York* (Oxford: Oxford University Press, 2011), 165.

105.  Liu, *The Laws of Cool*, 28.

106.  Martin, "The Actor in Me," 50.

107.  Douglas, *The Ragman's Son*, 32.

108.  Virno, *A Grammar of the Multitude*, 33.

109.  Between 1962 and 1967, Douglas and producer Edward Lewis continued to petition Universal and Lew Wasserman to rerelease the movie. Letters from Kirk Douglas to Lew Wasserman dated August 6, 1962; December 13, 1962; and January 19, 1967, suggest that it was an ongoing discussion between Douglas, Lewis, and Wasserman, or at least that Douglas tried to keep such discussion going.

110.  Dick Guttman of Rogers & Cowan, Inc., to Kirk Douglas, June 14, 1962, Kirk Douglas Papers, box 40, folder 27.

111.  Kirk Douglas to Dick Lemon at *Newsweek*, May 7, 1962, Kirk Douglas Papers, box 40, folder 27.

112.  Edward Lewis to Milton Rackmil, June 13, 1962, Kirk Douglas Papers, box 40, folder 27.

113.  Lewis to Rackmil, June 13, 1962.

114.  Clipping, *Chicago Daily News*, January 1963, Kirk Douglas Papers, box 47, folder 7.

115.  Memo, n.d., Kirk Douglas Papers, box 40, folder 27.

116.  Curtis Harrington to Kirk Douglas, July 2, 1962, Kirk Douglas Papers, box 40, folder 25.

117.  Memo, n.d., Kirk Douglas Papers, box 40, folder 25.

118.  Memo, n.d., Kirk Douglas Papers, box 40, folder 25; the London returns are published in a 1962 press release from Universal International Films, Inc. Douglas's concerns about how to reach U.S. audiences is from the above undated memo.

119.  Memo, n.d., Kirk Douglas Papers, box 40, folder 25.

120.  David Newman and Robert Benton, "The Movies Will Save Themselves," *Esquire*, October 1968, 69.

121.  Newman and Benton, 70.

122. Nico Baumbach, "All That Heaven Allows: What Is, or Was, Cinephilia?," *Film Comment*, March 12, 2012.

123. Baumbach.

124. Miriam Bratu Hansen, "The Mass Production of the Senses: Classical Cinema as Vernacular Modernism," *Modernism/Modernity* 6, no. 2 (1999): 62.

125. Hansen, 61.

126. Bryna publicist Fred Banker to Robert Eckhouse, May 8, 1962, Kirk Douglas Papers, box 47, folder 25.

127. Kirk Douglas to Lew Wasserman, January 19, 1967, Kirk Douglas Papers, box 47, folder 25.

128. Newman and Benton, "The Movies Will Save Themselves," 72; italics original.

129. Jacques Rancière, *The Emancipated Spectator*, trans. Gregory Elliott (London: Verso, 2009), 12.

130. Kirk Douglas to David Newman and Robert Benton, April 11, 1969, Kirk Douglas Papers, box 47, folder 6.

## 2. THE CINEMA OF DEFECTION

Epigraph: Joseph Gelmis, *The Film Director as Superstar* (Garden City, NY: Doubleday, 1970), 196. Penn says this with reference to the community depicted in *Alice's Restaurant* (United Artists, 1969).

1. Robin Wood, *Hollywood from Vietnam to Reagan* (New York: Columbia University Press, 1986), 53.

2. It is also worth recognizing *Weekend* (Godard, Athos, 1967) as the first movie to make this explicit warning. "We blacks are at war with America and its friends," a voice-over says, "but can't actually fight them because we haven't enough arms or the knowledge to use them. Furthermore, we are fewer in number. We have chosen guerrilla warfare perforce. It is an advantageous tactic and easy to conduct. . . . It is not by accident that Viet Cong guerrilla warfare impresses us. Our black brothers fighting in Vietnam for white America are gaining priceless lessons in modern guerrilla techniques. They'll be useful when they come back to our midst." Godard was not a New Hollywood filmmaker, of course, but he had a huge influence on those who were, including Scorsese and De Palma. As Todd Gitlin notes in *The Whole World Is Watching* (Berkeley: University of California Press, 1980), the *New York Times* ran a story on May 7, 1967, that quotes Gregory Calvert: "We are working to build a guerrilla force in an urban environment" (183). In other words, the rhetoric of internalized guerrilla warfare was circulating in the news media before it took form in New Hollywood movies.

3. See Fredric Jameson, "Immanence and Nominalism in Postmodern Theoretical Discourse," in *Postmodernism, or the Cultural Logic of Late Capitalism* (Durham, NC: Duke University Press, 1991), 216. In this chapter Jameson engages closely with Walter Benn Michaels's argument in *The Gold Standard and the Logic of Naturalism* (Berkeley: University of California Press, 1987).

4.  Michael Harrington, "We Few, We Happy Few, We Bohemians," *Esquire*, August 1972, 102.

5.  Harrington, 103, 102, 99.

6.  Neal Gabler, "Ältmän Mediätized," *Cinegram* 2, no. 1 (1977): 2.

7.  Terry Curtis Fox, "Talking with Robert Altman," *Real Paper*, April 16, 1977, 13.

8.  Thomas Elsaesser, "The Pathos of Failure: American Films in the 1970s," in *The Last Great American Picture Show*, ed. Alexander Horwath, Thomas Elsaesser, and Noel King (Amsterdam: Amsterdam University Press, 2004), 279.

9.  David Bordwell, "The Classical Hollywood Style, 1917–1960," in *The Classical Hollywood Cinema*, ed. David Bordwell, Janet Staiger, and Kristin Thompson (New York: Columbia University Press, 1985), 13.

10. David Bordwell, "Classical Hollywood Cinema: Narrational Principles and Procedures," in *Narrative, Apparatus, Ideology*, ed. Philip Rosen (New York: Columbia University Press, 1986), 18.

11. Elsaesser, "The Pathos of Failure," 281.

12. See Murray Smith, "Theses on the Philosophy of Hollywood History," in *Contemporary Hollywood Cinema*, ed. Steve Neal and Murray Smith (London: Routledge, 1998), 3–19; Todd Berliner, *Hollywood Incoherent* (Austin: University of Texas Press, 2011).

13. Richard Maltby, *Hollywood Cinema* (Cambridge, MA: Blackwell, 1996).

14. Elsaesser, "The Pathos of Failure," 280.

15. Todd Gitlin would say that *Bonnie and Clyde* "launched not only new fashions but a hero cult." See Gitlin, *The Whole World Is Watching*, 197.

16. Arthur Penn, when working on his next movie, *Alice's Restaurant*, would say this about the level of self-understanding he found in the youth culture: "The intellectual level of the group was quite high, I would say. But they were feeling somehow that their own thing was being overlooked, whatever that need was, that their personal need was not being dealt with by society." See Gelmis, *The Film Director as Superstar*, 196.

17. Eric Orts, *Business Persons: A Legal Theory of the Firm* (Oxford: Oxford University Press, 2013), 12. There were many commentators on the postwar corporation. For instance, Adolf Berle Jr. remarked that in the Progressive Era, one could oppose the social force of the corporation by assigning it to "individual people"—Carnegie and Rockefeller, say, who were "vastly richer and personally more powerful"—but in the postwar era the interpersonal agon had faded as corporate wealth was divided among "millions of American shareholders" rather than "a tiny, dictatorial oligarchy." See Adolf A. Berle Jr., "Bigness: Curse or Opportunity?," in *The Corporation in the American Economy*, ed. Harry M. Trebing (Chicago: Quadrangle, 1970), 186.

18. Paul Monaco, *The Sixties: History of the American Cinema, Vol. 8* (Berkeley: University of California Press, 2001), 182. Mark Harris makes a study of this year, specifically the year's Best Picture nominees, in his book *Pictures at a Revolution* (New York: Penguin, 2007).

19. Theodore Roszak, *The Making of a Counter Culture: Reflections on the Technocratic Society and Its Youthful Opposition* (Berkeley: University of California Press, 1995), 30, 34.

20. See Nicola Chiaromonte, *The Worm of Consciousness and Other Essays* (New York: Harcourt Brace, 1976), 62–65; Herbert Marcuse, *One-Dimensional Man* (Boston: Beacon, 1991), 63–70.

21. Stanley Cavell, *Pursuits of Happiness* (Cambridge, MA: Harvard University Press, 1981), 28.

22. Cavell, 28. While each movie that I include here as being in the genre might count as a member for a slightly different reason, or rather might ask us to understand the genre in a slightly different way, it is nonetheless true that each of the movies selected makes a straightforward case for genre membership. In fact, it might be more instructive to assess a borderline case, a movie bearing a resemblance to other genre members that, for whatever reason, repudiates a condition that makes the genre what it is. The movie *The Getaway* (Peckinpah, National General Pictures, 1972) is a case study for throwing into relief what constitutes the genre as I will outline it. In it, a fugitive couple mortgages their future in order to chase their freedom. Yet the narrative ends in a way that secures closure. Though branded as lifelong criminals by dint of their crime spree, the two create a future for themselves by escaping U.S. jurisdiction and fleeing into Mexico, which, in the film's imaginary, stands as an order free from positive law. Once they cross into Mexico, their driver—an aging man representing the other side of the generation gap—conspicuously counsels them on their reproductive status. "You know, if I was you kids, what I'd do," he offers, "I'd quit this running around the country, you know, get a little bit of money together and buy a place and settle down and raise a family." The respect and gratitude the couple expresses to their driver leaves the audience believing that they might repay him by acting out his advice, that is, by producing a society that is consonant with his understanding of social life. One might argue that *The Getaway* belongs to the genre because, while it denies the generic requirement of nonreproductivity, it wages this denial by way of canceling out the U.S. juridical order and replacing it with a suggested return to an order of natural law. This is all to say that the edges of a genre are a site of negotiation, of adding to and subtracting from the genre in ways that may or may not transform its charge, and at the edges, the status of a genre is left to argument.

23. Wood, *Hollywood from Vietnam to Reagan*, 47.

24. Bordwell, "Classical Hollywood Cinema," 21.

25. In Laura Mulvey's famous essay, "Visual Pleasure and Narrative Cinema," *Screen* 16, no. 3 (Autumn 1975): 6–18, she notes a trend of eliminating the woman from the narrative altogether, and she cites Molly Haskell's account of the emergent "buddy movie."

26. Leo Marx, *The Machine in the Garden* (New York: Oxford University Press, 1964), 3.

27. Marx, 31, 28.

28. Northrop Frye, *Anatomy of Criticism* (New York: Atheneum, 1968), 46.

29. Frye, 39.

30. Marx, *The Machine in the Garden*, 23.

31. Tom Hayden, *The Port Huron Statement: The Visionary Call of the 1960s Revolution* (New York: Thunder's Mouth, 2005), 65.

32.    See David Riesman's essay "Individualism Reconsidered," in *Individualism Reconsidered and Other Essays* (Glencoe, IL: Free, 1954); C. Wright Mills, *White Collar: The American Middle Classes* (Oxford: Oxford University Press, 1951); William H. Whyte, *The Organization Man* (Philadelphia: University of Pennsylvania Press, 2002).

33.    Hayden, *The Port Huron Statement*, 82–83.

34.    Hayden, 51. For the substitution of symbolic for practical politics, see Michael Szalay and Sean McCann, "Do You Believe in Magic? Literary Thinking After the New Left," *Yale Journal of Criticism* 18, no. 2 (2005); Mark Garrett Cooper and John Marx, *Mass Media U.: How the Need to Win Audiences Has Shaped Higher Education* (New York: Columbia University Press, 2018).

35.    In the next section I will turn to and elaborate the argument in Michael Fried, "Art and Objecthood," in *Art and Objecthood* (Chicago: University of Chicago Press, 1998), 148–71.

36.    Douglas McGregor, *The Human Side of Enterprise* (New York: McGraw-Hill, 1960), 25.

37.    Peter Drucker, *Concept of the Corporation* (New York: Transaction, 1993), 46.

38.    Marcuse, *One-Dimensional Man*, 10.

39.    The first quotation ("$40,000-a-year anthropologists") is from Elinor Langer, "Notes for Next Time," in *Toward a History of the New Left* (Brooklyn, NY: Carlson, 1989), 65. Langer notes that a main spur for student radicalization was the revelation that professors were being funded by the state. The second quotation ("They expected more from the university") is from Kirkpatrick Sale, *SDS* (New York: Random House, 1973), 165.

40.    See Clark Kerr, *The Uses of the University: The Godkin Lectures on the Essentials of Free Government and the Duties of the Citizen*, 4th ed. (Cambridge, MA: Harvard University Press, 1995), 111. Kerr refers to himself as a "kept-apologist," in the perspective of the Free Speech Movement, in a chapter added to the original Godkin Lectures delivered at Harvard in 1963.

41.    Kerr, 65, 67, 93.

42.    Todd Gitlin, *The Sixties: Years of Hope, Days of Rage* (New York: Bantam, 1993), 20.

43.    Marcuse, *One-Dimensional Man*, xlii.

44.    Ronald Aronson, "Dear Herbert," in *The Revival of American Socialism*, ed. George Fischer (New York: Oxford University Press, 1971), 268.

45.    Harris, *Pictures at a Revolution*, 385.

46.    Gelmis, *The Film Director as Superstar*, 284.

47.    Gelmis, 274.

48.    Harris, *Pictures at a Revolution*, 121.

49.    Commentary track, *The Graduate*, 40th Anniversary Edition (Beverly Hills, CA: 20th Century Film Corporation, 2007).

50.    André Bazin, "Theater and Cinema—Part Two," in *What Is Cinema?*, trans. Hugh Gray (Berkeley: University of California Press, 2005), 106.

51.    Commentary track, *The Graduate*.

52.    See Pap A. Ndiaye, *Nylon and Bombs*, trans. Elborg Forster (Baltimore, MD: Johns Hopkins University Press, 2006); Arthur Holly Compton's insider memoir, *Atomic*

*Quest* (New York: Oxford University Press, 1956), 132–34, 162–67, wherein Compton discusses asking and contracting DuPont for plutonium.

53. Mario Savio, "An End to History," in *The Times They Were a Changin'*, ed. Irwin Under and Debi Unger (New York: Broadway, 1998), 75.

54. Savio, 75.

55. Savio, 75, 77.

56. Harris, *Pictures at a Revolution*, 397.

57. Gitlin, *The Whole World Is Watching*, 197; Savio, "An End to History," 78.

58. See Harris, *Pictures at a Revolution*, 338–44.

59. Pauline Kael, "Bonnie and Clyde," *New Yorker*, October 21, 1967. For discussion of Kael's "put-on," see Jerome Christensen, *America's Corporate Art* (Stanford, CA: Stanford University Press, 2012), 20.

60. Joseph Morgenstern, "The Thin Red Line," *Newsweek*, August 28, 1967.

61. C. Wright Mills, "The Cultural Apparatus," in *Power, Politics & People*, ed. Irving Louis Horowitz (London: Oxford University Press, 1967), 409.

62. Irwin Unger, *The Movement* (New York: Harper & Row, 1974), 13, 14.

63. The quote from Irving Howe and a more general portrait of select Old Leftists can be found in Joseph Dorman's documentary *Arguing the World* (1998; New York: First Run Features, 2005).

64. While class self-understanding in leftist discourses would typically refer to the proletariat or working class, for Dwight Macdonald it actually seemed to refer to the bourgeoisie and in particular its specialized intellectuals.

65. The quote from Dwight Macdonald comes from "Confrontation: The Old and New Left," *American Scholar* (Autumn 1967): 575.

66. "Confrontation," 571.

67. "Confrontation," 570.

68. See Mills, "The Cultural Apparatus."

69. "Confrontation," 572.

70. "Confrontation," 574.

71. Sale, *SDS*, 158–59.

72. "Confrontation," 581.

73. Gitlin, *The Whole World Is Watching*, 167–69.

74. C. Wright Mills, "Letter to the New Left," *New Left Review* 5 (September–October 1960): 22.

75. Gitlin, *The Whole World Is Watching*, 3; italics original.

76. Gitlin, 154, 148.

77. Herbert Marcuse, "On the Affirmative Character of Culture," in *Negations*, trans. Jeremy J. Shapiro (Boston: Beacon, 1968), 103.

78. Gitlin, *The Whole World Is Watching*, 148.

79. Jacques Lacan, *Ecrits: A Selection*, trans. Alan Sheridan (London: Routledge, 1977), 303.

80. See Harris, *Pictures at a Revolution*, 237; "Behind the Lens," *Time* 99, no. 12, 1972, 102. Though Eastman does not name the movie, it is most likely *The Fortune* (Nichols, Columbia, 1975), which turned out to feature Jack Nicholson but not Jeanne Moreau.

81.  Peter Lev, *American Films of the '70s* (Austin: University of Texas Press, 2000), 21.

82.  Derek Nystrom, "Hard Hats and Movies Brats: Auteurism and the Class Politics of the New Hollywood," *Cinema Journal* 43, no. 3 (Spring 2004): 33.

83.  Susan Sontag, "One Culture and the New Sensibility," in *Against Interpretation and Other Essays* (New York: Picador, 1966), 300.

84.  Sontag, 297.

85.  Dwight Macdonald, *Masscult and Midcult* (New York: NYRB Classics, 2011), 53, 70.

86.  Fried, "Art and Objecthood," 149, 150.

87.  Fried, 154, 155; italics original.

88.  Sontag, "One Culture and the New Sensibility," 300.

89.  See Harris, *Pictures at a Revolution*.

90.  Though BBS in general cross-pollinated with the art world, such that a version of Andy Warhol's Factory appears in *Head* (Rafelson, Columbia, 1968) and Toni Basel would appear in *Easy Rider* and *Five Easy Pieces* only after appearing in Bruce Conner's *Breakaway* (1966), it is the case that these associations happened through Dennis Hopper, who had befriended Warhol and Conner in the early '60s through his association with Walter Hopps and Irving Blum at the Ferus Gallery in Los Angeles.

91.  Kirk Douglas, *The Ragman's Son*, (New York: Simon & Schuster, 1988), 323.

92.  Harris, *Pictures at a Revolution*, 247.

93.  Compare this to Colin McCabe's account in "Revenge of the Author," *Critical Quarterly* 31, no. 2 (1989): 3–13.

94.  These Robert Altman quotes are from a 1975 interview on *Nashville* (New York: Criterion, 2016).

95.  "Revolution! The Making of *Bonnie and Clyde*," on *Bonnie and Clyde* (Burbank, CA: Warner Home Video, 1997).

96.  "Revolution!"

97.  Robert Kerwin, "Pictures Are All Politics and Power," *Chicago Tribune Magazine*, October 13, 1974, 30.

98.  Fox, "Talking with Robert Altman," 13.

99.  It should be noted that Altman's gesture was more or less a repetition of Alfred Hitchcock's gesture. In a famous MGM publicity still, Hitchcock is shown "directing" Leo the Lion's roar. The image was made before Hitchcock directed his one MGM movie, *North by Northwest* (1959), at a time just following the great, final shakeup of the studio: in a span of only a few years in the midfifties, Nicholas Schenck retired and was replaced by Marcus Loew's son and longtime MGM executive, Arthur, who was then overthrown by Joseph Vogel, who in turn fired the would-be central producer Dore Schary. Hence, MGM was hollowed out of the personnel supplying its identity, such that when Hitchcock signed on for *North by Northwest*, he was as qualified as anyone to retrain Leo the Lion.

100. J. D. Connor, *The Studios After the Studios* (Stanford, CA: Stanford University Press, 2015), 22.

101. Doran William Cannon, "The Kid Wanted to Fly—So They Gave Him the Air," *New York Times*, February 7, 1971.

102. Vincent Canby, "The Screen: Innocence and Corruption," *New York Times*, December 24, 1970.

103. Linda Stein, "Altman Is Determined to Make Pix Own Way," *FILMTVDAILY*, March 3, 1970.

104. Richard Zanuck to Robert Altman, Robert Altman Collection, 1969–2007, Projects: 1970s, box 48, University of Michigan. In *Easy Riders, Raging Bulls* (New York: Simon & Schuster, 1998), Peter Biskind claims that the note from Zanuck put an end to the possibility that Altman would receive points on profit. According to Biskind, the note said, "Thank Bob Altman for this and forget about the percentage." The note, preserved in the archives, says no such thing; it only says, "Dear Bob, Thanks a lot." It is possible that Zanuck had written one note to Altman's agent, George Litto, and this is the one Biskind quotes, and then another to Altman himself, and this is the one held in the Robert Altman Collection. It is just as likely, however, that Biskind is going off the memory of his interview subject, Litto, without corroborating it against the archival record.

105. Biskind, 96. Richard Zanuck disputes Biskind's version of events.

106. Biskind, 97. Biskind uses the term "anti-s" to designate Altman's themes, which were antimilitary, -clergy, and -authoritarian.

107. Mitchell Zuckoff, *Robert Altman: The Oral Biography* (New York: Knopf, 2009), 168.

108. Zuckoff, 174.

109. Zuckoff, 172. This is a quote from Tom Skerritt, recalling Altman's advice during the production.

110. Zuckoff, 126. This comes from a quote from Reza Badiyi: "Bob loved actors, but he had an enormous disagreement—I wouldn't say hatred, but almost like the neighbor who puts up a fence—toward the management."

111. Peter Stamelman, "A Conversation with Robert Altman," *Print*, July–August 1976, 70.

112. In *Brewster McCloud* the architecture was the newly built Houston Astrodome. But in *McCabe*, the crew (which included local carpenters in Vancouver) built the houses that became the movie set, and in fact, the process of building them constitutes the movie's mise-en-scène. In *Quintet*, by contrast, the set was the ruins of Expo '67 in Montreal. The architecture, then, was not itself *pleasurable*, given that the movie was dystopian. But nonetheless, as the project manager Rita Schaffer attests, "They go to great lengths to make the set homey. Cast and crew, stars and grips, all are expected and encouraged to speak up with ideas and contributions to the film. Sumptuous lunches, including steak, lobster, and roast beef, are provided by chef Mickey Chronos, another Altman regular." See Wayne Grigsby, "Robert Altman: A Young Turk at 54," *Maclean's*, April 23, 1979, 8.

113. Stamelman, "A Conversation with Robert Altman."

114. Jan Stuart, *Nashville Chronicles* (New York: Limelight, 2003), 31–32.

115. Grigsby, "Robert Altman," 8.

116. Zuckoff, *Robert Altman*, 212.

117. Zuckoff, 183.

118. John Huddy, "The Enigma of Robert Altman," *Miami Herald*, May 15, 1977, 3.

119. Grigsby, "Robert Altman," 8. He makes this remark, it should be qualified, about the crew for *Quintet*.

120. Bruce Williamson, "Robert Altman," *Playboy*, August 1976, reprinted in *Robert Altman Interviews*, ed. David Sterritt (Jackson: University Press of Mississippi, 2000), 42.

121. Russ AuWerter, "Robert Altman," *Action: Director's Guild of America*, January–February 1971, 3.

122. Fox, "Talking with Robert Altman," 13.

123. Christopher Newfield, "Corporate Pleasures for a Corporate Planet," *Social Text* no. 44 (Autumn–Winter 1995): 33.

124. MGM Production Notes, "Brewster McCloud," Special Collections, Margaret Herrick Library.

125. "'McCloud' Preem Preps for 40,000 in the Astrodome," *Daily Variety*, June 17, 1970, 8.

126. "'McCloud' Preem."

127. "What Metro OK'd in Script, & Final 'McCloud' of Bob Altman Far Apart; 'Surrealism' Engages Likers, Dislikers," *Weekly Variety*, December 30, 1970.

128. For the Lou Adler quote, see "'McCloud' Preem," 8. For the Robert Altman quote, see Jeff Millar, "Looping the Films," *Houston Chronicle*, July 5, 1970, 18.

129. Monaco, *The Sixties*, 5.

130. Williamson, "Robert Altman," 42.

131. Robert Levine, "R. Altman & Co.," *Film Comment*, January–February 1977, 4.

132. Williamson, "Robert Altman."

133. F. Anthony Macklin, "The Artist and the Multitude Are Natural Enemies," *Film Heritage* 12, no. 2 (Winter 1976–77), reprinted in Sterrit, *Robert Altman Interviews*, 65.

134. Macklin.

135. Macklin, 78.

136. R. Milton Laird to Robert Altman, November 25, 1974, Business and Financial Records, box 645, Robert Altman Collection.

137. Letter from Allan E. Biblin of Mitchell, Silberberg & Knupp, October 17, 1975, Robert Altman Collection.

138. Letter from Allan E. Biblin.

139. "Robert Altman, Hollywood's 'Beneficent Monarchist,'" *Coast*, August 1971, 33.

140. Kerwin, "Pictures Are All Politics and Power," 30.

141. Williamson, "Robert Altman," 41–42.

## 3. TELEVISION TOTALITIES

Epigraph: Thomas Elsaesser, "The Pathos of Failure: American Films in the 1970s," in *The Last Great American Picture Show*, ed. Alexander Horwath, Thomas Elsaesser, and Noel King (Amsterdam: Amsterdam University Press, 2004), 281.

1. David Helperin, "At Sea with Steven Spielberg," in *Steven Spielberg Interviews*, ed. Lester B. Friedman and Brent Notbohm (Jackson: University Press of Mississippi, 2000), 6.

2.   Helperin, 7.

3.   Helperin, 6.

4.   Judith Crist, "Fish Story on a Grand Scale," *New York*, June 23, 1975, 69.

5.   Helperin, "At Sea with Steven Spielberg," 6.

6.   Fredric Jameson, *A Singular Modernity* (London: Verso, 2002), 170.

7.   "Leaving Warner Bros. After 17 Months to 'Make Pix of Our Own,'" *Variety*, July 10, 1972, 1, 4.

8.   Frederick Wasser, *Steven Spielberg's America* (Malden, MA: Polity, 2010), 39.

9.   Jameson, *A Singular Modernity*, 177.

10.  Marshall McLuhan, *Understanding Media* (New York: McGraw-Hill, 1964), 7.

11.  Lisa Parks, *Cultures in Orbit* (Durham, NC: Duke University Press, 2005), 25, 30.

12.  *Medium Cool* (Wexler, Paramount, 1969) is no doubt the ideal movie for understanding how this conceptual problem was being worked out.

13.  Helperin, "At Sea with Steven Spielberg," 7. Spielberg says that if he were given the chance to make *The Sugarland Express* again, he would have done a better job of matching the film's form to its theme. "I would have made it just like a documentary with the whole thing hand-held," he said. "Color, but the whole picture would have been done behind the police cars, shooting over them to the fugitives, the way we see it on television. It would have been from Ben Johnson's point of view; Ben Johnson would have been the star and you would have gotten to know these people through binoculars, monoculars, police radios, rear-view mirror glimpses on the horizon, long shots, small figures standing by the car, and I would have told the whole story from behind the police lines" (15).

14.  Stanley Cavell, *Pursuits of Happiness* (Cambridge, MA: Harvard University Press), 64.

15.  Fredric Jameson, *Postmodernism, or, The Cultural Logic of Late Capitalism* (Durham, NC: Duke University Press, 2001), 69, 71.

16.  Raymond Williams, *Television* (London: Routledge, 1990), 91.

17.  Jameson, *Postmodernism*, 79.

18.  This was an object of concern for many in the rising generation, I demonstrate in this chapter, but perhaps the finest point was put on it by James Burnham's *The Managerial Revolution* (New York: Day, 1941).

19.  Christopher Anderson, *Hollywood TV* (Austin: University of Texas Press, 1994), 6–7.

20.  Steve Chagollan, "Oscar Winning Producer Richard Zanuck Dies at 77," *Variety*, July 13, 2012, https://variety.com/2012/film/news/oscar-winning-producer-richard-zanuck-dies-at-77-1118056567/.

21.  See Peter Lev, *Twentieth Century-Fox: The Zanuck-Skouras Years* (Austin: University of Texas Press, 2013), 71–78; Rudy Behlmer, *Memo from Darryl F. Zanuck: The Golden Years at Twentieth Century Fox* (New York: Grove, 1993), 219–57.

22.  Darryl Zanuck, "Entertainment vs. Recreation," *Hollywood Reporter*, 126, no. 36, section 2.

23.  Thomas Schatz, *The Genius of the System* (Minneapolis: University of Minnesota Press, 2010), 62.

24.  Stuart Byron, "Zanuck Auditions His Gusto," *Variety*, January 31, 1968.

25. The "modernism" of New Hollywood has been defined variously, sometimes in terms of revising the generic tradition, notably John Cawelti, "*Chinatown* and Generic Transformation in Recent American Films," in *Film Genre Reader IV*, ed. Barry Keith Grant (Austin: University of Texas Press, 2012), 279–97; other times in terms of formal and narrative ambiguity, such as Todd Berliner, *Hollywood Incoherent* (Austin: University of Texas Press, 2010); other times in terms of allusion and self-consciousness, such as Noel Carroll, "The Future of Allusion," *October* 20 (Spring 1982): 51–81; and still other times in terms of the late-modernist relationship between highbrow criticism and the mass culture of the movies, such as Greg Taylor, *Artists in the Audience* (Princeton, NJ: Princeton University Press, 2001).

26. Garrett Stewart, *Between Film and Screen* (Chicago: University of Chicago Press, 1999), 63.

27. See Lionel Trilling, "On the Teaching of Modern Literature," in *Beyond Culture* (New York: Harcourt, 1978).

28. See Andrew Horton, *The Films of George Roy Hill* (Jefferson, NC: McFarland, 2010), 25–26.

29. See Ben Rogerson, "'Nobody Knows Anything': Professionalism and Publics in *The Great Waldo Pepper*," *Cinema Journal* 58, no. 2 (2019).

30. The claim that aesthetic autonomy defines modernism is commonly associated with Clement Greenberg, but the notion that such autonomy becomes an institutional credential in the late-modernist period is from Jameson, *A Singular Modernity*.

31. Lev, *Twentieth-Century Fox*, 180.

32. Lev, 250–51.

33. Behlmer, *Memo from Darryl F. Zanuck*, 260.

34. David Brown to Bertram Bloch, July 26, 1962, David Brown Papers, 1934–2010, American Heritage Center, University of Wyoming Libraries.

35. David Brown, *Let Me Entertain You* (Beverly Hills: New Millennium, 2003), 86–87.

36. Lev, *Twentieth-Century Fox*, 268.

37. Lev, 137.

38. Lev, 159–60.

39. John Gregory Dunne, *The Studio* (New York: Vintage, 1968), 112.

40. Brown, *Let Me Entertain You*, 137.

41. Brown, 213.

42. Mel Gussow, "The Last Movie Tycoon," *New York*, February 1, 1971, 39.

43. Dunne, *The Studio*, 209.

44. Stanley Cavell, "The Fact of Television," *Daedalus* 111, no. 4 (Fall 1982): 82–83.

45. Cavell, 205.

46. The final scene of confession is largely constituted by three long takes running, respectively, two minutes twenty-seven seconds, three minutes twenty-eight seconds, and two minutes forty-seven seconds. The Strangler's confession leads to a reenactment of a murder, at which point the long-take cinematography gives way to rapid, fragmentary montage.

47. See my discussion in chapter 2 of Susan Sontag's "One Culture and the New Sensibility," in *Against Interpretation and Other Essays* (New York: Picador, 1966). See,

too, David Newman and Robert Benton, "The New Sentimentality," *Esquire*, July 1964, 25–31; Jerome Christensen's discussion of their piece in his chapter, "Saving Warner Bros.: *Bonnie and Clyde*, the Movements, and the Merger," in *America's Corporate Art* (Stanford, CA: Stanford University Press, 2012). For a book-length study of the New Sensibility, see George Cotkin, *Feast of Excess: A Cultural History of the New Sensibility* (Oxford: Oxford University Press, 2015).

48. Mark Harris, *Pictures at a Revolution* (New York: Penguin, 2007), 2–3.

49. David Brown to Ernest Lehman, January 21, 1964, David Brown Papers.

50. Memo, David Brown to Richard Zanuck, April 21, 1970, David Brown Papers.

51. Memo David Brown to Richard Zanuck, October 22, 1970, David Brown Papers.

52. David Brown to Herbert Mayes, January 23, 1970, David Brown Papers.

53. David Brown to Bertram Bloch, February 15, 1962, David Brown Papers.

54. See Connie Bruck, *When Hollywood Had a King* (New York: Random House, 2003), 179–95.

55. David Brown to Bertram Bloch, February 15, 1962, David Brown Papers.

56. Brown longs for a "progressive organization" in his February 15, 1962, letter to Bertram Bloch, but he complains that Fox is "inhibited by past concepts of organization" in a quite long December 14, 1969, letter to Darryl Zanuck, David Brown Papers.

57. Chagollan, "Oscar-Winning Producer."

58. Bruck, *When Hollywood Had a King*, 338.

59. Bruck, 341–42.

60. Dunne, *The Studio*, 82.

61. Dunne, 175.

62. See Michael Ryan and Douglas Kellner, *Camera Politica* (Bloomington: Indiana University Press, 1988), for the schematic version of this criticism; Robert B. Ray, *A Certain Tendency of the Hollywood Cinema, 1930–1980* (Princeton, NJ: Princeton University Press, 1985), for the more dialectical version.

63. Harris, *Pictures at a Revolution*, 69–70.

64. Roger Ebert, "Interview with Ross Hunter and Dolores Taylor," August 13, 1967, RogerEbert.com, http://www.rogerebert.com/interviews/interview-with-ross-hunter-and-dolores-taylor.

65. See Christensen, *America's Corporate Art*, chap. 3, 77–78.

66. See Peter J. Schuyten, "How MCA Rediscovered Movieland's Golden Lode," *Fortune*, November 1976, 123.

67. Julia Phillips, *You'll Never Eat Lunch in this Town Again* (New York: Signet, 1992), 139.

68. For an account of how *The Sting* nearly shifted from Zanuck-Brown to MGM, see Phillips, 139–45. Richard Zanuck offers his side of the story in the Oral History Collection, Margaret Herrick Library.

69. Handwritten note, Richard Zanuck to George Roy Hill, George Roy Hill Collection, Margaret Herrick Library.

70. Helperin, "At Sea with Steven Spielberg," 9–10.

71. Phillips, *You'll Never Eat Lunch*, 139.

72. It was Redford's project first because he was friends with producer Julia Phillips. Once Hill was involved, he brought it to Newman, who needed persuading before

he would commit to it. See Phillips, 139; Horton, *The Films of George Roy Hill*, 99–100; "The Art of *The Sting*," featurette, *The Sting* (Universal City, CA: Universal, 2010).

73. See Jameson, *Postmodernism*, 18–21.

74. See J. D. Connor, *The Studios After the Studios* (Stanford, CA: Stanford University Press, 2015).

75. See J. Hoberman, "Nashville Contra Jaws, or 'The Imagination of Disaster' Revisited," in *The Last Great American Picture Show*, ed. Alexander Horwath, Thomas Elsaesser, and Noel King (Amsterdam: Amsterdam University Press, 2004), 195.

76. See Paul Virilio, *The Original Accident* (Cambridge, MA: Polity, 2007).

77. See Joseph McBride, *Steven Spielberg* (Jackson: University Press of Mississippi, 2011), 183–93; Molly Haskell, *Steven Spielberg* (New Haven, CT: Yale University Press, 2017), 50.

78. McBride, 157.

79. Haskell, *Steven Spielberg*, 44; McBride, *Steven Spielberg*, 157.

80. McBride, 174.

81. McBride, 186.

82. McBride, 183.

83. Michael Sragow, "A Conversation with Steven Spielberg," in Friedman and Notbohm, *Steven Spielberg Interviews*, 111.

84. Steve Poster, "The Mind Behind *Close Encounters of the Third Kind*," in Friedman and Notbohm, *Steven Spielberg Interviews*, 55.

85. Richard Combs, "Primal Scream: An Interview with Steven Spielberg," in Friedman and Notbohm, *Steven Spielberg Interviews*, 33.

86. Susan Royal, "Steven Spielberg in His Adventures on Earth," in Friedman and Notbohm, *Steven Spielberg Interviews*, 87.

87. Haskell, *Steven Spielberg*.

88. Haskell, 94. On this point, François Truffaut's quip might double as Spielberg's own: when asked of working on *Close Encounters* whether he himself believed in UFOs, Truffaut replied, "I believe in the cinema." See McBride, *Steven Spielberg*, 280.

89. Stanley Cavell, *The World Viewed: Reflections on the Ontology of Film* (Cambridge, MA: Harvard University Press, 1979), 41.

90. In *The World Viewed*, Cavell claims that the difference between "a film type and a stage type is that the individuality captured on film naturally takes precedence over the social role in which that individuality gets expressed" (34–35). But cinema inherited, Erwin Panofsky claims, a "fixed iconography" (Cavell points to Baudelaire's *The Painter of Modern Life* to help explain its source), which includes "the Vamp and the Straight Girl, . . . the Family Man, and the Villain" (33). Such "devices persist," Cavell says, "as long as there are still Westerns and gangster films and comedies and musicals and romances" (33).

91. See "The Making of *Jaws*," bonus feature on *Jaws* (Universal City, CA: Universal, 2016).

92. "The Making of *Jaws*."

93. "The Making of *Jaws*." In this account of film ontology, Cavell is not alone but joins company with André Bazin, Siegfried Kracauer, and other classical film theorists.

94.  Connor, *The Studios After the Studios*, 92. Part of Connor's argument is that this vision of studio supremacy was nostalgic, part of a past that auteurs imagined as a counterpart to their own project. In conglomerate Hollywood, Connor says, "Friedkin (and Lucas, and Coppola) had a deeper belief in the omnipotence of the studio than most studio executives and owners did" (166). The overall argument is that this could be an "implicit benefit" to studios if they could harness the auteurist imagination of their power and hence exercise it through studio freelancers.

95.  In *Steven Spielberg*, Joseph McBride says that in "adulthood" Spielberg sought out "fathers/mentors in such powerful figures as Sheinberg and Time Warner's Steve Ross" (327). And he quotes Spielberg saying that he and Zsigmond became "almost brothers" on *Sugarland Express* (215).

96.  McBride, 211–13.

97.  Joseph McBride, "Richard Zanuck and David Brown," in *Filmmakers on Filmmaking* (Los Angeles: Tarcher, 1983), 31.

98.  McBride, 29.

99.  Poster, "The Mind," 61.

100. McBride, *Steven Spielberg*, 215.

101. Helperin, "At Sea with Steven Spielberg," 10.

102. Steven Spielberg, "The Unsung Heroes, or Credit Where Credit Is Due," *American Cinematographer* 59, no. 1 (January 1978): 88.

103. McBride, *Steven Spielberg*, 233.

104. See McBride, "Richard Zanuck and David Brown," 32, for David Brown's explanation of why they did not want "an 'engineer'-type director" for *Jaws* but rather someone who could make a "film as well as a movie." And see McBride, *Steven Spielberg*, 233, for Richard Zanuck's account of Lew Wasserman's recommendation for directors.

105. See Annette Michelson, "Bodies in Space: Film as Carnal Knowledge," *Artforum*, February 1969, 54–63.

106. See "The Making of *Jaws*."

107. Anthony Haden-Guest, "The Rise, Fall, and Rise of Zanuck-Brown," *New York*, December 1, 1974, 44, 47.

108. McBride, "Richard Zanuck and David Brown," 31.

109. McBride, *Steven Spielberg*, 233.

110. McBride, "Richard Zanuck and David Brown," 32.

111. See Paul Monaco, *The Sixties: 1960–1969* (Berkeley: University of California Press, 2001), 2.

112. Julie Turnock, *Plastic Reality: Special Effects, Technology, and the Emergence of 1970s Blockbuster Aesthetics* (New York: Columbia University Press, 2015), 172. Turnock links this particular strategy for dynamizing screen space to Jordan Belson's *Allures* specifically and the work of the West Coast avant-garde film community generally.

113. Wasser, *Steven Spielberg's America*, 62.

114. Mik Cribben, "On Location with *Jaws*," *American Cinematographer*, March 1975, 331.

115. See Theodor Adorno, "Marginalia to Theory and Praxis," in *Critical Models* (New York: Columbia University Press, 1998), 259–78.

116. Cribben, "On Location with *Jaws*," 331.

117. For this account of the "cinematic," I am relying not only on so-called classical film theory, including Béla Balázs, Jean Epstein, and Siegfried Kracauer, but also on Gilles Deleuze's philosophical reformulation of it.

118. As J. Hoberman puts it, the disaster movie depicts "the total breakdown of an institution hubristically imagined to be safe, and these ocean liners, airplanes, skyscrapers, theme parks, and cities, were, of course, microcosms of America," "Nashville Contra Jaws," 198.

119. Walter Benjamin, "The Work of Art in the Age of Its Reproducibility," in *Selected Writings, 1935–1938* (Cambridge, MA: Belknap, 2002), 115.

120. In analyzing Miriam Hansen's argument, Daniel Morgan explains how this can work: "The success of American cinema, that is, had to do with how its films 'brought into optical consciousness . . . and disseminated a particular historical experience.' For Hansen, this happens in terms of the represented content—the depiction of a world undergoing changes and transformations, the focus on new configurations of gender, work, and amusement—but also at a formal level." That is to say, the content and form tended to be united in one historical moment, but the union is not a necessary condition. See Morgan, "'Play with Danger': Vernacular Modernism and the Problem of Criticism," *New German Critique* 122, 41, no. 2 (Summer 2014): 68.

121. Haden-Guest, "The Rise, Fall, and Rise of Zanuck-Brown," 54.

122. See David Harvey, *A Brief History of Neoliberalism* (Oxford: Oxford University Press, 2007), 4.

## 4. THE ETHOS OF INCORPORATION

Epigraph: Patrick McGilligan, *Jack's Life* (New York: Norton, 1994), 21. This quote refers to Bert Schneider, who was well connected because his brother and father were executives at Columbia Pictures.

1. Julia Phillips, *You'll Never Eat Lunch in This Town Again* (New York: Signet, 1992), 114.

2. Bob Rafelson makes this comment in "Afterthoughts," featurette on *The King of Marvin Gardens* (New York: Criterion, 2010).

3. Barry King, "Articulating Stardom," *Screen* 26, no. 5 (1985): 28.

4. Richard Dyer, *Stars* (London: BFI, 1979), 36.

5. Nico Baumbach, "On Robert Bresson and Filmed Animals," *Fiction International* 40 (Fall 2007), http://fictioninternational.sdsu.edu/wordpress.catalog/issue-40-animals/on-robert-bresson-and-filmed-animals/.

6. Jean Epstein, "On Certain Characteristics of *Photogénie*," in *French Film Theory and Criticism, Vol. 1, 1907–1939*, ed. Richard Abel (Princeton, NJ: Princeton University Press, 1993), 317.

7. Andy Warhol, *The Philosophy of Andy Warhol* (San Diego, CA: Harcourt, 1975), 231.

8. Jerome Christensen, *America's Corporate Art* (Stanford, CA: Stanford University Press, 2012), 177.

9. In discussing the "goodwill" at the heart of corporate personality, Christensen includes Adolph Berle's theorizing of a "transcendental margin," which would be the set of "norms of responsibility" that corporate managers would honor if they were to maintain the firm's "legitimacy," but Christensen thinks that the term "transcendental" ought to be replaced by "charismatic" and that Max Weber would then be the interpretive key for understanding corporate power (175–76).

10. Scott R. Bowman, *The Modern Corporation and American Political Thought* (University Park: Pennsylvania State University Press, 1996), 1–34. Bowman's analysis of this entwined power is multipart, but he makes this fundamental remark: "In one basic sense, corporate power is political by its nature because it is based on a reconstituted relationship between the public sphere and the private sphere" (24).

11. The television show *The Monkees*, for my purposes, works as a synecdoche for the process that Thomas Frank studies in his book, *The Conquest of Cool* (Chicago: University of Chicago Press, 1998), but as he turns to the advertising and menswear industries for his case studies, he overlooks perhaps the most obvious case studies, the film and television industries. He gestures to them at points but does not bear down on them: "And from its very beginnings down to the present, business dogged the counterculture with a fake counterculture, a commercial replica that seemed to ape its every move for the titillation of the TV-watching millions and the nation's corporate sponsors. Every rock band with a substantial following was immediately honored with a host of imitators" (7).

12. See the anthology of *New York Times* articles, *The Corporation in the American Economy*, ed. Harry M. Trebing (Chicago: Quadrangle, 1970).

13. Candice Bergen, *Knock Wood* (New York: Linden, 1984), 253.

14. See Bo Burlingham, "Politics Under the Palms," *Esquire*, February 1976.

15. The famous denunciation of "radical chic" was made by Tom Wolfe, *Radical Chic and Mau-Mauing the Flak Catchers* (New York: Picador, 2009).

16. For the canonical statement, see Ronald Coase, "The Nature of the Firm," in *The Firm, the Market, and the Law* (Chicago: University of Chicago Press, 1990).

17. In discussing Adolph Berle's *The Corporate Revolution in the 20th Century*, Jerome Christensen says that Berle understood charisma within the corporate organization "not as transcendental but as intangible, not as extrapersonal but as hyperpersonal." Christensen, *America's Corporate Art*, 176.

18. See Janet Staiger, "Seeing Stars," in *Stardom: Industry of Desire*, ed. Christine Gledhill (New York: Routledge, 1991), 3–16.

19. Lawrence Linderman, "*Gallery* Interview: Dennis Hopper," in *Dennis Hopper Interviews*, ed. Nick Dawson (Jackson: University Press of Mississippi, 2012), 66.

20. Rafelson's claim to a "fuck-all" attitude is from Peter Biskind, *Easy Riders, Raging Bulls* (New York: Simon & Schuster, 1999), 177.

21. Jay Boyer, *Bob Rafelson* (New York: Twayne, 1996).

22. Christopher Newfield, "Corporate Pleasures for a Corporate Planet," *Social Text* 44 (Autumn–Winter 1995): 33.

23. In Bo Burlingham's "Politics Under the Palms," 49, he describes the two photographs on Bert Schneider's office wall, one of him and Fidel Castro and the other of him and

Huey Newton. Peter Bogdanovich refers to Corman's "guerrilla university" in the documentary *A Decade Under the Influence* (New York: Docurama, 2003.

24.  "BBS Productions Grosses Hit $65 Million Worldwide," *Hollywood Reporter*, February 7, 1972.

25.  Dennis Hopper offers this Godard citation in *A Decade Under the Influence*.

26.  Lee Beaupre, "It Appears 'Beaver' Has 'Gone' Into Hibernation; BBS Seems to Have Dumped Pic," *Daily Variety*, November 8, 1972, 2.

27.  "Local 659 Levels Unfair Charges vs. BBS Prods," *Daily Variety*, September 20, 1972, 1, 3.

28.  The Bob Rafelson quotation comes from "Reflections of a Philosopher King," featurette on *The King of Marvin Gardens*.

29.  See McGilligan, *Jack's Life*, 204.

30.  See Eric W. Orts, "Theorizing the Firm: Organizational Ontology in the Supreme Court," *DePaul Law Review* (Winter 2016): 563. The distinction turns on whether the state creates the firm or whether its participants do.

31.  McGilligan, *Jack's Life*, 191.

32.  See Francesco Alberoni, "The Powerless 'Elite': Theory and Sociological Research on the Phenomenon of the Stars," in *The Celebrity Culture Reader*, ed. P. David Marshall (New York: Routledge, 2006), 108–23.

33.  McGilligan, *Jack's Life*, 163. McGilligan chronicles Nicholson and Monte Hellman's visit to Paris to present their films, *The Shooting* (Walter Reade Organization, 1966) and *Ride in the Whirlwind* (Walter Reade Organization, 1966), which they took to Cannes as well but were unable to present (158–63).

34.  Teresa Grimes, "BBS: Auspicious Beginnings, Open Endings," *Movie*, Winter 1986, 55.

35.  Grimes, 55.

36.  Grimes.

37.  Candice Bergen calls Schneider the "romantic lead of the company" in her memoir, *Knock Wood*, 187. But for a general account of the free-floating charisma at BBS, see McGilligan, *Jack's Life*, 201–2.

38.  Lee Beaupre, "Camera Import Nix for 'Beaver,'" *Weekly Variety*, November 8, 1972, 3, 30.

39.  "Local 659 Levels Unfair Charges vs. BBS Prods," 3.

40.  Beaupre, "Camera Import Nix for 'Beaver,'" 30. It is unclear how hard they pressed, because testimonials were given by Mike Nichols, Francis Ford Coppola, Richard Roud, Haskell Wexler, and others, which ought to have been enough, but according to dates, these might not have been filed in time. There is speculation that BBS ultimately used the case as a way to get out of their deal with McBride, as relations had gone badly throughout the process.

41.  Alex Simon, "Dennis Hopper Is Riding Easy," in Dawson, *Dennis Hopper Interviews*, 201.

42.  Howard Becker, *Art Worlds* (Berkeley: University of California Press, 2008), 16–17.

43.  Becker, 17.

44.  See Caroline Jones, *The Machine in the Studio* (Chicago: University of Chicago Press, 1996), in particular chap. 4 on Warhol's Factory. She notes that the Factory was replete with "signifiers, shifting from the proletarian to the executive to the

consumer" (189). This was also true of Frank Stella's self-presentation, Jones writes, as he moved between the image of executive and manual laborer.

45.  Helen Molesworth, *Work Ethic* (University Park: Pennsylvania State University Press, 2003), 18.

46.  Jones, *The Machine in the Studio*, 197, 196.

47.  Michael Nesmith makes this remark on the commentary track for *Head* (New York: Criterion, 2010).

48.  Mitchell S. Cohen, "The Corporate Style of BBS: Seven Intricate Pieces," *Take One* (Winter 1973): 20.

49.  See Boyer, *Bob Rafelson*, 1–2.

50.  Peter Tonguette, "Bert Schneider, 1933–2011," *Sight and Sound*, November 18, 2016, BFI, https://www.bfi.org.uk/news-opinion/sight-sound-magazine/comment/obitu aries/bert-schneider-1933-2011.

51.  David Cook, *Lost Illusions: American Cinema in the Shadow of Watergate and Vietnam, 1970–1979* (Berkeley: University of California Press, 2000), 544n99.

52.  McGilligan, *Jack's Life*, 231.

53.  Bowman, *The Modern Corporation*, 191.

54.  When I say the class of knowledge workers were emerging in a society "designed for industrial workers," I am referring to a hard-won achievement of the midcentury. "In the 1950s industrial blue-collar workers had become the largest single group in every developed country," Peter Drucker notes. "In all developed free-market countries they had economically become 'middle class.' They had extensive job security; pensions; long, paid vacations; comprehensive unemployment insurance or 'lifetime employment.' Above all, they had achieved political power." I take this from Drucker, "A Century of Social Transformation—Emergence of Knowledge Society," in *The Essential Drucker* (New York: HarperCollins, 2001), 302. Everything else I have summarized in this paragraph comes from Drucker's series of books in the immediate postwar years: *The Future of Industrial Man, Concept of the Corporation*, and *The New Society*.

55.  Peter Drucker, *The Practice of Management* (New York: Harper & Row, 1954), 46.

56.  Drucker, 37; italics original.

57.  Christensen, *America's Corporate Art*, 177.

58.  Gary M. Kramer, "Henry Jaglom," *Bomb*, April 29, 2014, http://bombmagazine.org /articles/henry-jaglom/.

59.  See Steve Denning, "The Origin of 'The World's Dumbest Idea': Milton Friedman," *Forbes*, June 26, 2013, https://www.forbes.com/sites/stevedenning/2013/06/26/the -origin-of-the-worlds-dumbest-idea-milton-friedman/#9385bc0870e8. See, too, Michael Jensen and Dean William Heckling, "Theory of the Firm: Managerial Behavior, Agency Costs, and Ownership Structure," *Journal of Financial Economics* 3 (1976): 305–60.

60.  Nils Gilman, "The Prophet of Post-Fordism: Peter Drucker," in *American Capitalism*, ed. Nelson Lichtenstein (Philadelphia: University of Pennsylvania Press, 2006), 119; italics original.

61.  Gilman, 117.

62.  Peter Drucker, *Concept of the Corporation* (New York: John Day, 1946), 28.

63.  Lawrence Webb, "New Hollywood in the Rust Belt," *Cinema Journal* 54, no. 4 (2015): 117.

64.  Gilman, "The Prophet of Post-Fordism," 119.

65.  Hank Werba, "It All Became So 'Easy' After Peter Fonda Met Bert Schneider," *Daily Variety*, November 5, 1969, 12.

66.  Drucker, *The Practice of Management*, 47.

67.  Drucker, 47–48.

68.  Karl Marx, *The Eighteenth Brumaire of Louis Bonaparte*, 1852, Marxists.org, https://www.marxists.org/archive/marx/works/1852/18th-brumaire/ch01.htm.

69.  Paul Schrader, "Easy Rider," *Los Angeles Free Press*, July 25, 1969, 26.

70.  Andrew Schroeder, "The Movement Inside: BBS Films and the Cultural Left in the New Hollywood," in *The World the Sixties Made*, ed. Van Gosse and Richard Moser (Philadelphia: Temple University Press, 2003), 121.

71.  The first is Bert Schneider to Huey Newton, August 21, 1972, and the second a memo, Bob Rafelson to Huey Newton, both located in the Dr. Huey P. Newton Foundation Inc. Collection, Stanford University.

72.  Steve Blauner to Huey Newton, November 29, 1972, box 2, folder 11, Newton Foundation Collection.

73.  Huey Newton, *To Die for the People* (San Francisco: City Lights, 2009), 93.

74.  Burlingham, "Politics Under the Palms," 118.

75.  Burlingham, 49.

76.  Biskind, *Easy Riders, Raging Bulls*, 76–77.

77.  Jacoba Atlas and Marni Butterfield, "Odd Man In—Jack Nicholson," *Show*, May 1971, 25.

78.  Hugh Pearson, *The Shadow of the Panther: Huey Newton and the Price of Black Power in America* (Cambridge, MA: Perseus, 1996), 113.

79.  Daniel Cohn-Bendit, *Obsolete Communism*, trans. Arnold Pomerans (New York: McGraw-Hill, 1968), 231.

80.  Bowman, *The Modern Corporation*, 194. The phrases I quote are Drucker's from *The New Society* (New Brunswick, NJ: Transaction, 1993).

81.  Schroeder, "The Movement Inside," 129.

82.  Notes for an interview Mitch Tuchman conducted with Bert Schneider, December 13, 1974, Mitch Tuchman Interview Transcripts, Margaret Herrick Library.

83.  "Local 659 Levels Unfair Charges," 8.

84.  "Local 659 Levels Unfair Charges."

85.  See John Cocohi, "Producers Seek Hand in Marketing Films," *Box Office* 105, no. 5 (May 13, 1974): 8. See also transcript of interview with Bert Schneider, Mitch Tuchman Papers.

86.  Thurman Arnold, *The Folklore of Capitalism* (New York: Routledge, 2017), 185.

87.  Elaine Brown, *A Taste of Power* (New York: Anchor, 1994), 244.

88.  Included in this are the project hatched with Schneider's friend, Gerd Stern, of Intermedia, which involved audio recordings but was intended to branch into film and video. It remains unrealized, but it is documented in the Newton Foundation Collection.

89.  Huey Newton, "He Won't Bleed Me," in *To Die for the People*, 113.

90.  Brown, *A Taste of Power*, 347–48.

91. Bobby Seale, *Seize the Time* (Baltimore, MD: Black Classics, 1991), 182.

92. Amy Abugo Ongiri, *Spectacular Blackness* (Charlottesville: University of Virginia Press, 2010), 54, 81.

93. Bergen, *Knock Wood*, 233.

94. For George Jackson's bequest to the Panthers, see Ongiri, *Spectacular Blackness*, 55. For documents on J. Herman Blake v. Stronghold, see the Newton Foundation Collection.

95. Brown, *A Taste of Power*, 328–30.

96. Brown, 329.

97. Pearson, *The Shadow of the Panther*, 297.

98. See Rakesh Khurana, "The Curse of the Superstar CEO," *Harvard Business Review* (September 2002).

99. John Gallagher, "Between Action and Cut: Peter Bogdanovich," in *Peter Bogdanovich Interviews*, ed. Peter Tonguette (Jackson: University Press of Mississippi, 2015), 114.

100. Stephen Farber, "The Man Who Brought Us Greetings from the Vietcong," *New York Times*, May 4, 1975, 149.

101. Biskind, *Easy Riders, Raging Bulls*, 77.

102. Farber, "The Man."

103. Bob Rafelson cites these three experimental filmmakers in the commentary to *Head*.

104. Bowman, *The Modern Corporation*, 194.

105. Burlingham, "Politics Under the Palms," 52.

106. See transcript of interview with Bert Schneider, Mitch Tuchman Papers.

107. Peter Davis, "Remembering Bert Schneider," *Huffington Post*, December 28, 2011, https://www.huffingtonpost.com/peter-davis/bert-schneider_b_1173164.html.

108. See Biskind, *Easy Riders, Raging Bulls*, 275; and Rick Perlstein, "Politics and Oscar Night," *Nation*, February 25, 2013: https://www.thenation.com/article/politics-and -oscar-night/#sthash.nk6cdziJ.dpuf.

109. Farber, "The Man."

## AFTERWORD

Epigraph: Ed Catmull, *Creativity, Inc.* (New York: Random House, 2014), 152.

1. Jon Lewis, "Money Matters: Hollywood in the Corporate Era," *New American Cinema*, ed. Jon Lewis (Durham, NC: Duke UP, 1999), 87–121.

2. See Andrew Britton, "Blissing Out: The Politics of Reaganite Entertainment," *Movie*, 31/31, 1986, 1–42, and Jennifer Holt, *Empires of Entertainment* (New Brunswick, NJ: Rutgers UP, 2011).

3. See Jeff Menne, "The Counterculture Squared: Albert Brooks' *SNL*," *The Films of Albert Brooks*, ed. Christian Long (Edinburgh: Edinburgh UP, forthcoming).

4. Yannis Tzioumakis, "'Independent,' 'Indie,' and 'Indiewood,'" *American Independent Cinema*, ed. Geoff King, Claire Molloy, and Yannis Tzioumakis (New York: Routledge, 2012).

5. Tzioumakis.

6.  Stephen Prince, *Digital Visual Effects in Cinema* (New Brunswick, NJ: Rutgers UP, 2012), 19–22.

7.  Julie Turnock, *Plastic Reality* (New York: Columbia UP, 2015), chapter 5.

8.  Ed Catmull, "How Pixar Fosters Collective Creativity," *Harvard Business Review*, Sept. 2008. https://hbr.org/2008/09/how-pixar-fosters-collective-creativity.

9.  Richard Neupert, *John Lasseter* (Urbana, IL: Univ. of Illinois Press, 2016), 46.

10. Ed Catmull, *Creativity, Inc.: Overcoming the Unseen Forces That Stand in the Way of True Inspiration* (London: Transworld, 2014), 144.

11. See Jerome Christensen, *America's Corporate Art* (Stanford: Stanford UP, 2012), chapter 7.

12. Catmull, *Creativity, Inc.*, 245.

13. Catmull, 245.

14. Catmull, 246, 245.

15. Catmull, 248–50.

16. For discussion of the "California Ideology," see Yann Moulier-Boutang, *Cognitive Capitalism*, trans. Ed Emery (Cambridge, UK: Polity, 2011).

17. Catmull, "How Pixar Fosters Collective Creativity."

18. Anthony Lane, "Fun Factory," *New Yorker*, May 16, 2011: https://www.newyorker.com/magazine/2011/05/16/the-fun-factory.

19. Lane.

20. Lane.

21. Catmull, "How Pixar Fosters Collective Creativity."

22. See *The Pixar Story* (Disney, 2007).

23. Lane, "Fun Factory."

24. Caldwell, *Production Culture*, 47.

25. Paul Flaig, "Slapstick after Fordism: *WALL-E*, Automatism and Pixar's Fun Factory," *Animation* 11, no. 1 (2016), 65.

26. Angela Allan, "*Cars 3*: A Children's Movie, and a Fable about Mentorship," *Atlantic*, July 13, 2017: https://www.theatlantic.com/business/archive/2017/07/cars-3-mentorship/533436/

27. Catmull, "How Pixar Fosters Collective Creativity."

28. Catmull, *Creativity, Inc.*, 248–50.

29. Catmull, 135.

# INDEX

Abbey, Edward, 37, 61–62
Academy Awards Ceremony, 25, 31, 206–8
Adorno, Theodor, 59
Aglietta, Michel, 26
AIP (American International Pictures), 36
*Airport*, 143–46
Almendros, Nestor, 176, 177–78, 198
*Alex in Wonderland*, 66
Allen, Irwin, 143–44
Altman, Robert, 22, 30, 79, 110–24, 125, 152, 175, 213
*Amblin'*, 152, 153, 154
Amblin Entertainment, 158, 210
American Zoetrope, 2, 13, 211
Anabasis, 36
Anderson, Christopher, 130–31
*Apartment, The*, 52
Arendt, Hannah, 42, 48
Arnold, Thurman, 172, 198
Arrighi, Giovanni, 18–19, 47, 48
Auteur theory, 6, 8, 13–15, 22–23, 25, 86, 109, 110–12, 122, 128, 131, 143, 158–59, 173, 177, 202, 213

BBS Productions, 2, 22, 31–32, 82, 86, 109–10, 169–208
*Badlands*, 31, 82, 86, 125, 126–27
Ballard, Carol, 13
Bart, Peter, 2
Baumbach, Nico, 72, 171
*Battle of Midway, The*, 39
Bazin, André, 38, 40, 42, 90, 129
Beatty, Warren, 72, 96, 98, 109, 111, 117, 140, 206
Becker, Howard, 178–79
Bell, Daniel, 4, 94
*Bend in the River*, 42
Benjamin, Walter, 167
Benton, Robert, 71, 72–73, 103
Bergen, Candice, 177, 201
Berkeley, University of California, 3, 86–89, 92–93, 196
*Big Country, The*, 40
*Billy Jack*, 33, 36, 37
Birmingham School (cultural studies), 27
Biskind, Peter, 115, 196
Black Panthers, 193–97, 199–202, 204, 208
Blauner, Steve, 174, 195, 199
*Bob & Carol & Ted & Alice*, 65

Bogdanovich, Peter, 1–2, 70, 175, 177, 190, 202
Boltanski, Luc, 26
*Bonnie and Clyde*, 16, 17–18, 24, 30, 69, 72–73, 78, 81, 83, 85, 93–94, 96–101, 111, 112, 140
Booth, Max, 52
Bordwell, David, 80
*Boston Strangler, The*, 137–40
Bowman, Scott, 172, 186, 199
Brackman, Jacob, 7, 148, 184
Braudel, Fernand, 18–19
*Brewster McCloud*, 30, 79, 82, 112–15, 117, 118–23
*Broken Arrow*, 41
Brouillette, Sarah, 26
Brown, David, 15–16, 28, 30, 31, 127–37, 140–44, 147–49, 150, 160, 163
Brown, Elaine, 199, 201
Bryna Productions, 15–16, 22, 30, 36–37, 48–73, 142, 175
*Butch Cassidy and the Sundance Kid*, 132–33
Butler, Bill, 159, 161, 164

Calahan, Sharon, 214
Caldwell, John, 27, 33, 216
Canby, Vincent, 115
Cannon, Doran William, 114–15
Capra, Frank, 39, 45
*Carrie*, 29
Carroll, Noël, 54
*Cars 3*, 217
Cassavetes, John, 28–29, 210
Castro, Fidel, 53, 57, 175
Catmull, Ed, 211–14, 218–20
Cavell, 82, 129–30, 140, 156–57
*Champion*, 51
*Cheyenne Autumn*, 40–41
Chiapello, Eve, 26
Chiaromonte, Nicola, 82
Christensen, Jerome, 93, 147, 171, 187, 213, 218

Christopherson, Susan, 21
*Citizen Kane*, 14
Cleaver, Eldridge, 200
*Close Encounters of the Third Kind*, 31, 148, 152, 155
*Cleopatra*, 16, 134, 136
Coase, Ronald, 211
Cohn-Bendit, Daniel, 196
Columbia Pictures, 36, 109–10, 141, 169, 174, 175, 181, 185–88, 190, 193, 195
Connor, J. D., 28, 113, 153, 157
*Conversation, The*, 4–6, 162
*Cool Hand Luke*, 33–36, 81, 112
Coppola, Francis Ford, 1–2, 4, 13, 70, 127, 206–7, 210–11
Corkin, Stanley, 66
Corman, Roger, 175
Corporate personhood, 21
Creative economy, 25–28, 32, 210, 216
Crowther, Bosley, 93
Curtis, Tony, 140

Davis, Peter, 205, 206
Davis, Rennie, 97
De Antonio, Emile, 197, 205
Debord, Guy, 98
Debray, Régis, 57
Deleuze, Gilles, 34
De Palma, Brian, 25, 29, 30, 148, 155
Deren, Maya, 127, 139
Dern, Bruce, 170, 198, 202
Director's Company, the, 1–2, 28
Disney (Walt Disney Company), 49, 210, 211, 212–13, 215, 219–21
Disney, Walt, 215, 219, 221
*Doctor Dolittle*, 17, 116, 137, 140
Donaldson, Ivanhoe, 3, 95, 97
Douglas, Kirk, 15, 22, 28–29, 33–37, 44, 47, 49–73, 76, 110, 142
*Drive, He Said*, 177, 183
Drucker, Peter, 2, 5, 10–12, 14, 46, 48, 85, 186–89, 191, 197, 204, 206, 215

*Duel*, 153
Dyer, Richard, 171

Eastman, Carole, 102–3
*Easy Rider*, 24, 82, 83, 86, 101, 103, 110, 112,
   141, 169, 181, 182, 183, 184, 190, 193, 202
Eisenhower, Dwight D., 61
Eisner, Michael, 215, 219–20
Elsaesser, Thomas, 23, 24, 79–80, 153, 202
Embassy Pictures, 36, 109
Epstein, Jean, 171
Evans, Walker, 96

Famous Artists, 50
Fellini, Federico, 66
*First Blood*, 33–36, 62, 68–69
*Five Easy Pieces*, 24, 31, 81, 85, 101–10, 169,
   184
Fleischer, Richard, 134, 137–40
Florida, Richard, 25
Fonda, Jane, 32, 148, 173, 195–96,
   197–98
Fonda, Peter, 70, 101, 190
Ford, John, 13, 37, 38–41, 45, 65, 76, 78
Foucault, Michel, 34
Frank, Stephanie, 16
Frank, Thomas, 12, 22
Free Speech Movement (FSM), 86–93
Fried, Michael, 85, 107–9
Friedkin, William, 1–2
Friedman, Milton, 7, 188
Frye, Northrop, 84
*Fury, The*, 29

General Motors, 14
*Get to Know Your Rabbit*, 29
Gilman, Nils, 10, 11, 189
Gitlin, Todd, 88, 93–94, 97
Godard, Jean-Luc, 72, 175, 198
Goodman, Paul, 3
Gould, Elliott, 115–116
*Graduate, The*, 7, 16, 17–18, 24, 30, 36, 69,
   78, 81, 85, 86–93, 101, 112, 140–41

*Grapes of Wrath, The*, 38
Greenberg, Clement, 131

Halberstam, David, 7
Hansen, Miriam, 72, 167
Harrington, Curtis, 70–72
Harrington, Michael, 78, 94, 97, 119
Harris, Mark, 16, 39
*Harvey*, 43
Harvey, David, 19–20
Haskell, Molly, 153, 154, 155
Hawks, Howard, 13, 78
Hayden, Tom, 4, 32, 94–96, 197
*Head*, 179–83, 184, 203
*Hearts and Minds*, 31, 172, 193, 197–98,
   204–7
*Hi, Mom!*, 25, 62, 76
*Hidden Fortress*, 160
*High Noon*, 38
Hill, George Roy, 132–34, 148–52
Hoberman, J., 153
Hoffman, Abbie, 196, 204
Hoffman, Dustin, 7, 170, 171
Hollywood Renaissance, 17, 23, 55, 66, 69
Hope, Bob, 206–7
Hopper, Dennis, 109, 173, 175, 178, 181
Hozic, Aida, 46
Hunter, Ross, 134, 143–47
Huston, John, 39, 160

Iger, Bob, 213, 220
*Indian Fighter, The*, 36
Industrial Light & Magic, 211
*Introduction to the Enemy*, 198
IPC Films, 32, 198

Jaglom, Henry, 177, 188, 190, 196, 198, 202
Jalem Productions, 24, 36, 86
Jameson, Fredric, 77, 127, 128, 130, 134, 150
*Jaws*, 17–18, 23, 30, 31, 126, 147, 152–53, 154,
   157, 158–68, 207–8
Jobs, Steve, 202, 211, 212, 213, 219
*Jules and Jim*, 103

Kael, Pauline, 8–10, 14, 93–94
Kazan, Elia, 50
Kennedy, John F. (JFK), 60, 104
Kerkorian, Kirk, 114
Kerr, Clark, 87–88, 92
Keynesianiasm, 6, 20–21, 189
King, Barry, 170
*King of Marvin Gardens, The*, 31, 169–71, 173, 183–95, 196, 202–3
Kramer, Stanley, 51
Krim, Arthur, 49, 53

Lacan, Jacques, 101
Lasseter, John, 211, 214–15
*Last Picture Show, The*, 177, 183
Laughlin, Tom, 36
*Law and Jake Wade, The*, 41–42
Leo the Lion (MGM mascot), 112–13, 121
Levine, Joseph, 36, 109
Lewis, Edward, 50, 69
Lewis, Jon, 2, 53, 209
Liberty Films, 39
Lion's Gate, 22, 30, 79, 112–24, 175
Liu, Alan, 64, 65, 66
*Lonely Are the Brave*, 29, 34, 36, 37, 52, 55–62, 69–72, 76–77
Lucas, George, 31, 127, 128, 157, 160, 211, 213, 215, 221
Lucasfilm, 210, 211, 221
*Lust for Life*, 65
Lyotard, Jean-François, 168

Macdonald, Dwight, 11, 94, 107
Mailer, Norman, 57
Malden, Karl, 40
Malick, Terrence, 125–27, 184
*Man from Snowy River, The*, 60
*Man Who Shot Liberty Valance, The*, 39, 55–56
Management theory, 6–14, 32
Mann, Anthony, 42, 43, 45
Mann, Denise, 18, 50
Maoism, 195, 196–198

Marcuse, Herbert, 82, 86, 88, 97
Margulies, Stan, 36, 49–52, 63
Marx, Karl, 18, 191
Marx, Leo, 83–84
*MASH*, 30, 112, 114, 115–16, 141
Maslow, Abraham, 12
May, Elaine, 78
Mazursky, Paul, 65–66, 68
MCA, 14, 43, 45, 50, 128, 141, 147, 158, 168
McBride, Jim, 176, 177
*McCabe & Mrs. Miller*, 116, 117–18
McGregor, Douglas, 5, 12–13, 23, 85
McLuhan, Marshall, 129
McRobbie, Angela, 25–26
Mekas, Jonas, 9, 127, 210
MGM (Metro-Goldwyn-Mayer), 66, 112–15, 119, 121, 149, 172
Michaels, Walter Benn, 77
*Midnight Cowboy*, 65, 82, 83, 101, 112, 149
Military-industrial complex, 60–61, 84, 86–87, 92
Miller, David, 62
Mills, C. Wright, 3, 22, 63–64, 67, 84, 85, 94, 95, 96, 97, 173
Monaco, Paul, 120, 160
*Moby Dick* (movie), 159–60
*Monkees, The*, 172, 179–83, 184
*Monkey Wrench Gang, The*, 61
Moreau, Jeanne, 66, 103–4
*My Darling Clementine*, 39
Myerson, Alan, 195, 204–5

*Naked Spur*, 43
New Left, 3–4, 7–8, 24, 57, 58, 76, 77, 82, 84–88, 92–97
Newfield, Christopher, 22, 118, 175
Newman, David, 71, 72–73
Newman, Paul, 149–151
Newton, Huey, 173, 195–202
Nichols, Mike, 78, 81, 89, 90, 93, 103, 109, 146
Nicholson, Jack, 70, 103, 169–71, 173, 176, 177, 179, 181, 184, 188, 192, 198, 202–3

Nico, 181–82
Norton, Sam, 50
Nystrom, Derek, 18, 25, 82, 104

Orion, 36
*Our World*, 129
*Ox-Bow Incident, The*, 38

Paramount Pictures, 1–2, 28, 46, 47–48,
 49, 53
*Patton*, 30
Peck, Gregory, 159
Penn, Arthur, 72, 78, 81, 94, 109
Peters, Tom, 10, 32, 117, 118
Phillips, Julia, 148, 170, 184, 196, 202
Phillips, Michael, 148, 149, 170, 184, 196
*Pillow Talk*, 144
Pink, Daniel, 26
Piore, Michael, 20
Pixar Animation Studios, 32, 210–21
*Poltergeist*, 152, 155
Port Huron Statement, 7–8, 84–85
Post-Fordism, 16–23, 27, 168, 175, 178, 206,
 209, 214–15
*Professionals, The*, 55

Rackmil, Milton, 45, 69
Rafelson, Bob, 101–2, 171, 174, 176, 177, 179,
 181, 182, 184, 185, 188, 195, 203
Rancière, Jacques, 41, 73
*Ratatouille*, 219
Raybert Productions, 174, 176
Reford, Robert, 149–51
Regulation School (economics), 26
*Revolutionary Suicide*, 195, 199, 201
Revue Productions, 14, 45, 128, 142
Riesman, David, 84
Robert Abel and Associates, 32
Roszak, Theodore, 82
Rovere, Richard, 95–96

Sabel, Charles, 20
*Safe Place, A*, 177, 183, 196

Sale, Kirkpatrick, 87, 96
Sarris, 3, 4, 8–10, 11, 12–14, 70, 85, 88, 210
*Saturday Night Live*, 210
Savio, Mario, 92–93
Schatz, Thomas, 15, 132
Schneider, Abraham, 110, 174
Schneider, Bert, 25, 31–32, 101, 109, 169–74,
 176, 177, 179, 182, 184, 187, 190, 193,
 195–208
Schneider, Stanley, 174, 186
Schrader, Paul, 139, 193
Schulberg, Budd, 50
Schumpeter, Joseph, 208
Scorsese, Martin, 30, 148
Scott, Allen, 21
Screen Gems, 174
SDS (Students for a Democratic Society),
 4, 7, 97
Seale, Bobby, 196, 200
*Searchers, The*, 41, 76
*Seconds*, 65, 72
*Shane*, 40
Shaw, Robert, 150
Sheinberg, Sid, 153, 157
Sinatra, Frank, 206–7
Skouras, Spyros, 15, 16, 131, 134–35
Slotkin, Richard, 54
Smith, Alvy Ray, 211
SNCC (Student Nonviolent Coordinating
 Committee), 3
Sontag, Susan, 94, 105–6, 109
*Spartacus*, 49, 52, 53–54
Spielberg, Steven, 6, 23, 30–31, 125–30, 134,
 142–43, 148, 149, 152–68, 175, 213
*Spring Reunion*, 51
*Stagecoach*, 38, 40, 72
Staiger, Janet, 15
Stark, Ray, 50
*Star Wars*, 31, 160, 209
*Steelyard Blues*, 148, 196
Stein, Jules, 14, 43
Stevens, George, 37, 39–40
Stewart, Garrett, 134

Stewart, Jimmy, 43–45
*Sting, The*, 134, 147–52
Storper, Michael, 21
*Strange Love of Martha Ivers, The*, 49
*Straw Dogs*, 82, 101
Stronghold, Inc., 198–202
*Sugarland Express, The*, 23–24, 31, 125–26, 130, 142–43, 152, 153, 157–58
Surtees, Robert, 90
Sutherland, Donald, 115, 117, 148
*Sweet Sweetback's Baadasssss Song*, 200

Taber, Robert, 52, 57
Tanen, Tad, 142, 147
Tashlin, Frank, 133, 137
*Taxi Driver*, 75–77, 148
*That Justice Be Done*, 40
*There Was a Crooked Man*, 73
*Thieves Like Us*, 31, 125
Tilly, Charles, 48
*Tora! Tora! Tora!*, 30
Towne, Robert, 111, 178
*Toy Story*, 212, 215
Transamerica, 37
Trumbo, Dalton, 37, 61
Truffaut, François, 72, 103
Turnock, Julie, 30–31, 160, 211
20th Century Fox, 15, 16, 28, 30, 46, 112, 115–16, 127, 131–44, 147

*Ulzana's Raid*, 41
United Artists, 22, 36, 49, 52, 53
Universal Studios, 14–16, 22, 23, 31, 36, 42, 43–44, 45, 49, 69, 127–28, 141–54, 158, 212
*Unmarried Woman, An*, 37, 65

Vidal, Gore, 4
*Vikings, The*, 47, 52
Virilio, Paul, 153
Virno, Paolo, 27, 46, 64, 67

*WALL-E*, 216–17
Ward, David, 148
Warhol, Andy, 171, 179, 181, 183
Warner Bros., 13, 36, 68, 109, 128, 132, 143
Wasserman, Lew, 14–15, 22, 23, 42, 43, 45, 49, 69, 72, 128, 141–43, 146–48, 159, 168, 208, 210
Wayne, John, 65
Webb, Charles, 89, 93
Webb, Lawrence, 17, 189
Weber, Max, 175
Wexler, Haskell, 32
White, Timothy, 47
Whyte, William H., 11, 85
*Wild Bunch, The*, 55, 101
Williams, John, 166, 167
Williams, Raymond, 130
*Winchester '73*, 43
*Wizard of Oz, The*, 113
Wood, Robin, 75–76, 83
Wright, Will, 54
Wyler, William, 37, 39, 40

Yablans, Frank, 1–2, 28

Zanuck, Darryl (DZ), 15–16, 128, 131–32, 134–37, 141, 142, 151
Zanuck, Richard, 15–16, 28, 30, 31, 115–16, 127–37, 152, 157, 158, 168
Zanuck-Brown Company, 16, 22, 23–24, 30–31, 127–68, 175, 208, 212
Zsigmond, Vilmos, 157, 159

# FILM AND CULTURE

## A series of Columbia University Press

*What Made Pistachio Nuts? Early Sound Comedy and the Vaudeville Aesthetic*, Henry Jenkins

*Showstoppers: Busby Berkeley and the Tradition of Spectacle*, Martin Rubin

*Projections of War: Hollywood, American Culture, and World War II*, Thomas Doherty

*Laughing Screaming: Modern Hollywood Horror and Comedy*, William Paul

*Laughing Hysterically: American Screen Comedy of the 1950s*, Ed Sikov

*Primitive Passions: Visuality, Sexuality, Ethnography, and Contemporary Chinese Cinema*, Rey Chow

*The Cinema of Max Ophuls: Magisterial Vision and the Figure of Woman*, Susan M. White

*Black Women as Cultural Readers*, Jacqueline Bobo

*Picturing Japaneseness: Monumental Style, National Identity, Japanese Film*, Darrell William Davis

*Attack of the Leading Ladies: Gender, Sexuality, and Spectatorship in Classic Horror Cinema*, Rhona J. Berenstein

*This Mad Masquerade: Stardom and Masculinity in the Jazz Age*, Gaylyn Studlar

*Sexual Politics and Narrative Film: Hollywood and Beyond*, Robin Wood

*The Sounds of Commerce: Marketing Popular Film Music*, Jeff Smith

*Orson Welles, Shakespeare, and Popular Culture*, Michael Anderegg

*Pre-Code Hollywood: Sex, Immorality, and Insurrection in American Cinema, 1930–1934*, Thomas Doherty

*Sound Technology and the American Cinema: Perception, Representation, Modernity*, James Lastra

*Melodrama and Modernity: Early Sensational Cinema and Its Contexts*, Ben Singer

*Wondrous Difference: Cinema, Anthropology, and Turn-of-the-Century Visual Culture*, Alison Griffiths

*Hearst Over Hollywood: Power, Passion, and Propaganda in the Movies*, Louis Pizzitola

*Masculine Interests: Homoerotics in Hollywood Film*, Robert Lang

*Special Effects: Still in Search of Wonder*, Michele Pierson

*Designing Women: Cinema, Art Deco, and the Female Form*, Lucy Fischer

*Cold War, Cool Medium: Television, McCarthyism, and American Culture*, Thomas Doherty

*Katharine Hepburn: Star as Feminist*, Andrew Britton

*Silent Film Sound*, Rick Altman

*Home in Hollywood: The Imaginary Geography of Cinema*, Elisabeth Bronfen

*Hollywood and the Culture Elite: How the Movies Became American*, Peter Decherney

*Taiwan Film Directors: A Treasure Island*, Emilie Yueh-yu Yeh and Darrell William Davis

*Shocking Representation: Historical Trauma, National Cinema, and the Modern Horror Film*, Adam Lowenstein

*China on Screen: Cinema and Nation*, Chris Berry and Mary Farquhar

*The New European Cinema: Redrawing the Map*, Rosalind Galt

*George Gallup in Hollywood*, Susan Ohmer

*Electric Sounds: Technological Change and the Rise of Corporate Mass Media*, Steve J. Wurtzler

*The Impossible David Lynch*, Todd McGowan

*Sentimental Fabulations, Contemporary Chinese Films: Attachment in the Age of Global Visibility*, Rey Chow

*Hitchcock's Romantic Irony*, Richard Allen

*Intelligence Work: The Politics of American Documentary*, Jonathan Kahana

*Eye of the Century: Film, Experience, Modernity*, Francesco Casetti

*Shivers Down Your Spine: Cinema, Museums, and the Immersive View*, Alison Griffiths

*Weimar Cinema: An Essential Guide to Classic Films of the Era*, edited by Noah Isenberg

*African Film and Literature: Adapting Violence to the Screen*, Lindiwe Dovey

*Film, a Sound Art*, Michel Chion

*Film Studies: An Introduction*, Ed Sikov

*Hollywood Lighting from the Silent Era to Film Noir*, Patrick Keating

*Levinas and the Cinema of Redemption: Time, Ethics, and the Feminine*, Sam B. Girgus

*Counter-Archive: Film, the Everyday, and Albert Kahn's Archives de la Planète*, Paula Amad

*Indie: An American Film Culture*, Michael Z. Newman

*Pretty: Film and the Decorative Image*, Rosalind Galt

*Film and Stereotype: A Challenge for Cinema and Theory*, Jörg Schweinitz

*Chinese Women's Cinema: Transnational Contexts*, edited by Lingzhen Wang

*Hideous Progeny: Disability, Eugenics, and Classic Horror Cinema*, Angela M. Smith

*Hollywood's Copyright Wars: From Edison to the Internet*, Peter Decherney

*Electric Dreamland: Amusement Parks, Movies, and American Modernity*, Lauren Rabinovitz

*Where Film Meets Philosophy: Godard, Resnais, and Experiments in Cinematic Thinking*, Hunter Vaughan

*The Utopia of Film: Cinema and Its Futures in Godard, Kluge, and Tahimik*, Christopher Pavsek

*Hollywood and Hitler, 1933–1939*, Thomas Doherty

*Cinematic Appeals: The Experience of New Movie Technologies*, Ariel Rogers

*Continental Strangers: German Exile Cinema, 1933–1951*, Gerd Gemünden

*Deathwatch: American Film, Technology, and the End of Life*, C. Scott Combs

*After the Silents: Hollywood Film Music in the Early Sound Era, 1926–1934*, Michael Slowik

*"It's the Pictures That Got Small": Charles Brackett on Billy Wilder and Hollywood's Golden Age*, edited by Anthony Slide

*Plastic Reality: Special Effects, Technology, and the Emergence of 1970s Blockbuster Aesthetics*, Julie A. Turnock

*Maya Deren: Incomplete Control*, Sarah Keller

*Dreaming of Cinema: Spectatorship, Surrealism, and the Age of Digital Media*, Adam Lowenstein

*Motion(less) Pictures: The Cinema of Stasis*, Justin Remes

*The Lumière Galaxy: Seven Key Words for the Cinema to Come*, Francesco Casetti

*The End of Cinema? A Medium in Crisis in the Digital Age*, André Gaudreault and Philippe Marion

*Studios Before the System: Architecture, Technology, and the Emergence of Cinematic Space*, Brian R. Jacobson

*Impersonal Enunciation, or the Place of Film*, Christian Metz

*When Movies Were Theater: Architecture, Exhibition, and the Evolution of American Film*, William Paul

*Carceral Fantasies: Cinema and Prison in Early Twentieth-Century America*, Alison Griffiths

*Unspeakable Histories: Film and the Experience of Catastrophe*, William Guynn

*Reform Cinema in Iran: Film and Political Change in the Islamic Republic*, Blake Atwood

*Exception Taken: How France Has Defied Hollywood's New World Order*, Jonathan Buchsbaum

*After Uniqueness: A History of Film and Video Art in Circulation*, Erika Balsom

*Words on Screen*, Michel Chion

*Essays on the Essay Film*, edited by Nora M. Alter and Timothy Corrigan

*The Essay Film After Fact and Fiction*, Nora Alter

*Specters of Slapstick and Silent Film Comediennes*, Maggie Hennefeld

*Melodrama Unbound: Across History, Media, and National Cultures*, edited by Christine Gledhill and Linda Williams

*Show Trial: Hollywood, HUAC, and the Birth of the Blacklist*, Thomas Doherty